SCOTLAND
·AND·HER·
TARTANS·

Designed by Philip Clucas MSIAD
Edited by David Gibbon
Featuring the Photography of Neil Sutherland

CLB 2593
© 1991 Colour Library Books Ltd, Godalming, Surrey, England.
All rights reserved.
This edition published in 1991 by Gallery Books,
an imprint of W.H. Smith Publishers, Inc.,
112 Madison Avenue, New York 10016.
Printed and bound in Hong Kong
ISBN 0 8317 7717 6

Gallery Books are available for bulk purchase for sales promotions
and premium use. For details write or telephone
the Manager of Special Sales, W.H. Smith Publishers, Inc.,
112 Madison Avenue, New York, New York 10016 (212) 532-6600.

SCOTLAND
· AND · HER ·
TARTANS

THE ROMANTIC HERITAGE OF THE
SCOTTISH CLANS AND FAMILIES

·ALEXANDER·FULTON·

GALLERY BOOKS
An imprint of W. H. Smith Publishers Inc.
112 Madison Avenue
New York City 10016

**Autumn peace belies the drama which is inseparable
from the story of the Highlands.**

Contents

**A Drum Major at the Braemar Gathering, wearing a
piper's plaid of the Royal Stewart tartan.**

Foreword

If one had to choose five people who consciously or unconsciously made the most lasting contributions to the development of the Scottish tartan tradition, they would be a queen, the son of a pretender to the thrones to which she acceded, a scholar-lawyer who also wrote poetry and novels, and a pair of literary forgers. Thus it is that Queen Victoria, Charles Edward Stuart, Sir Walter Scott, and the Sobieski Stuart brothers feature in the story which is told in the first six chapter of this book. Charles Edward, "Bonnie Prince Charlie," grandson by his second marriage of King James VII of Scotland (II of England), and the abortive rebellion against the Crown which he initiated and led in 1745, recur frequently in the historical accounts of clans and families which follow. For the '45 is the focal point of much of the romance with which the Highlands subsequently became imbued, though it is only fair to add that more Scots fought against Bonnie Prince Charlie than for him during his campaign.

The origins of ancient clans or families may be of greater significance to those who can claim an association with one of them. Here is revealed the astonishing amalgam of Celtic, Pictish, British, Scandinavian, Anglo-Saxon, and French cultures from which the Scottish people and nation have emerged. Then, beginning early in the eighteenth century and building up to a peak during the nineteenth century, Scots took the composite traditions which they had acquired to lands overseas.

The clan tartan is the most powerful worldwide symbol of kinship, and the kilt the most distinctive national dress. There are records of check patterns (the essential element of tartan) from early times, King James III, who appointed his tailor to his Secret Council, may have had tartan curtains round the royal bed in 1488. The kilt is a product of the earlier part of the eighteenth century, and the clan tartan, worn as a mark of corporate recognition, came rather later. Yet by the 1850s, for Lowland families as well as for Highland clans, tartan had become so much the fashion that even in the predominantly agricultural Hillfoots district of Clackmannanshire it is recorded that "no lady considered herself dressed without a tartan plaid or shawl."

The awesome standing stones of Callanish reflect the
beliefs of those who lived four thousand years ago.

The Clan Tradition

When the Romans finally left Britain shortly after 400 AD, they had never subdued Caledonia, as they called the region beyond Hadrian's Wall, that massive defensive structure right across northern Britain from coast to coast. It may have been the weather, or the terrain, or perhaps the northern temperament, which had for almost four hundred years prevented them from completing their conquest. Out of the Dark Age mists which followed their departure, there emerged in the Highland region of what was to become Scotland a system of social kinship which today spans the world. Where it came from or how it evolved are questions

After the Romans came the Vikings, whose descendants established in Shetland the traditional fire festival of Up-Helly-A', still celebrated today.

which have taxed modern historians, but it is probable that it was brought by the invading Scots from Ireland. It may well also have already been inherent in some form in the practices of the Picts, those mysterious people who occupied the northernmost part of Britain from about 250 AD, and then vanished, or became subsumed into the Scottish race, leaving only a few traces of their existence.

From the sons of Somerled, warrior, statesman, and progenitor of the lords of the Isles, who was killed in 1164, were descended two of the oldest and most famous clans, MacDonald, with its manifold branches, and MacDougall, but their members, like those of many other clans, liked to claim descent from much earlier noble, royal, or even mythical ancestors. Common descent, or the claim of a common descent, is accepted in legal terms as distinguishing members of a particular clan, who theoretically all bear the same name. For the meaning of 'clan' in Gaelic is 'children', or more loosely and appropriately 'family'. Branches of a clan which owe allegiance to the clan chief are known as septs.

The chief staked out his territory, or territories, which he acquired by settlement, inheritance, or conquest, and jealously guarded his lands against incursions by other clans, or by the Government. In return for ensuring the wellbeing of his people, the clansmen were bound to offer the chief part of their produce, whether crops or animals, and to take up arms for him. In time of outright war they fought for him, and for whichever side he supported, rather than for one cause or the other. The call to arms came by means of the 'fiery cross', a rough wooden construction, one end of the crosspiece of which was burning or charred, and to the other end of which was attached a piece of bloodstained cloth. Relays of runners took each of the two crosses through the clan lands, shouting the clan's war cry or slogan, whereupon all the able-bodied men gathered at once at the clan's meeting place. The last time this device was used to mobilise troops is said to have been in the winter of 1812-13 in Canada, when the men of Glengarry were summoned by their local chief to fight off a band of American raiders.

The clan had its own customs and laws, and its own methods of, often summary, justice. It offered a means of protection not only to its own people, but also to those of its associated septs and sometimes to members of smaller clans, against the oppression of stronger or more warlike clans. The clan system has not survived, but the kinship of the clan, fostered by modern methods of mass-communication and travel, gains strength year by year. Or is it perhaps that in an age in which broken marriages are commonplace, the tradition of the wider and more indestructible family unit is now coming into its own again?

Right: Eilean Donan Castle, a Mackenzie stronghold since the thirteenth century. Below: remains of a broch, a pre-Pictish circular fortress with no windows.

Above: excavating Hadrian's Wall at Housesteads, Northumberland.

James Edward Stuart, who, as the son of King James VII, might have been James VIII.

The Kinship of the Clan

Glencoe, sombre surroundings for one of the darkest deeds in Scottish history, at which the Government connived.

Successive lords of the Isles, secure in their remoteness from the centre of government, caused king and country headaches galore, until in 1493 the twenty-year-old James IV called it a day, and courageously stripped the incumbent of his title and his estates. The inter-clan conflicts inherent in the system continued largely unabated until well into the eighteenth century – Campbells against MacDonalds, Mackays against Gordons, Camerons against Mackintoshes, MacDonells of Glengarry against Mackenzies of Kintail, and almost everyone against the MacGregors.

Clan Feuds and Fights

Sometimes the cause was insignificant: the outcome was often spectacular. A dispute over lands seems to have instigated the trial by combat before King Robert III on the North Inch of Perth in 1396. It was gruesomely contested between two teams each of thirty heavily-armed warriors representing, it is now believed, the Macmillans of Lochaber and the Shaws (or Mackintoshes) of the celebrated

confederacy known as Clan Chattan. The Shaws won by the equivalent of a knockout, losing only 19 men against twenty-nine of the opposition – the thirtieth swam across the River Tay and escaped.

If that fight was about a point of corporate honour, the battle between the MacDonalds and the Frasers at Loch Lochy in 1544, of which it is said only fourteen of the eight hundred warriors survived, was ignited merely by a MacDonald chieftain's complaint that he had been insulted. The place became known as 'The Field of Shirts', the day being so hot that the contestants fought in their shirt-tails.

The last clan battle, in 1688, over another contested territorial claim, was between the MacDonells of Keppoch, who held the land by tradition, and the Mackintoshes, who had obtained a government deed naming them as owners. The MacDonells won handsomely, but the government of the day, conscious of its status, retaliated by sending a disciplinary force against them and ravaging their lands and possessions.

Archibald Campbell, 9th Earl of Argyll, who made an amazing escape from Edinburgh Castle.

The Power of the Campbells

The first Campbell chieftain of whom we know anything was nicknamed *Cailean Mór* (Big, or Great, Colin), and the head of the family has been called MacCailean Mór ever since. Colin, 2nd Lord Campbell, was created Earl of Argyll in 1457, and he and subsequent chiefs of the clan were for many years as notorious for their cruelty as for their affiliations. Archibald 'the Grim', 7th Earl, earned the undying hatred of the MacDonalds when their lands of Kintyre were transferred to him by the Government in return for his 'peace-keeping' activities in the West Highlands, which included the execution in 1604 of eight MacGregors who had surrendered to him under promise of exile in England.

The 8th Earl (and 1st Marquis of Argyll) commanded the army of the Covenanters against the forces of King Charles I in the Civil War, and was beheaded in 1661 at the Restoration of the Monarchy. His son, the 9th Earl, was due for the same fate in 1681, but escaped from Edinburgh Castle dressed as his step-daughter's footman, only to be caught again and executed in 1685 for dabbling in the rebellion of the Duke of Monmouth. The 10th Earl was instrumental in bringing William of Orange to England to be King in 1689, and was later created 1st Duke of Argyll for his services to the Crown. Subsequent dukes have held prominent positions of state and in the army.

The Marquis of Montrose

One of the 8th Earl of Argyll's lieutenants in the Covenanters' army was James Graham, Marquis of Montrose, young, dashing, gifted, and also no mean poet. Disillusioned with the cause, he set about raising an army in the Highlands to fight for King Charles I. In 1644, with a band of Scottish exiles from Ireland and ill-equipped men of the clans, notably Gordons and MacDonalds, he scored resounding wins at Tippermuir and Aberdeen, and then surprised Argyll himself at his castle at Inveraray in mid-winter. Argyll escaped, but Montrose got behind the rest of the Campbells at Inverlochy by means of forced march over mountain passes blocked by snow and ice, and killed fifteen hundred of them with the loss of only four of his own men.

After three more victories, he was in Glasgow. At this crucial point, his Highlanders melted away, more concerned, perhaps understandably, with their own

local preoccupations than with the general cause. With only six hundred men left, Montrose was set upon by six thousand troops sent from England. He was persuaded to leave the field and later escaped to Europe. After the execution of King Charles I, he returned in 1650 to try again, on behalf of Charles II. He was overwhelmed at Carbisdale, and then betrayed and handed over to Parliament by the Laird of Assynt, a Macleod. The death sentence had already been passed. He faced it, and his enemies in Edinburgh, with courage and nobility. Afterwards, his head was stuck up on a spike on the Tolbooth, where it remained for eleven years, to be replaced by that of the Marquis of Argyll!

'Bonnie Dundee'

John Graham of Claverhouse, Viscount Dundee, was a cousin of Montrose. In 1689, in the name of the exiled King James VII (James II of England), he raised and trained a Highland army to fight the forces of the government of William and Mary. The chiefs sent out the 'fiery cross' and some three thousand clansmen responded to the call – MacDonalds of Clanranald, Glencoe, Glengarry and Sleat, and MacDonells of Keppoch; Stewarts of Appin, and Camerons of Lochaber under their legendary leader, Sir Ewen Cameron. They called Dundee *Ian Dubh nan Cath*, 'Dark John of the Battles'. He ate with his men and slept on the ground as they did, and they worshipped him. His command of his troops was extraordinary. When the chief of the MacDonells of Keppoch exceeded his orders and indulged in a bit of over-enthusiastic burning and plundering, Dundee publicly reprimanded him and then formally dismissed him from his service before the man could himself threaten to remove his clan in a huff. It was a risky tactic, but it succeeded. Keppoch apologised profusely, and stayed.

The Government sent out against him their best troops, under General Mackay. Dundee drew up his men on a rise above the Pass of Killiecrankie, and somehow kept them motionless for two hours, until the sun in their faces had gone down, and Mackay's men had scrambled up the slope on to a narrow plain. Even after the order had been given to charge, and in the face of continuous fire, no Highlander fired back until he was a few feet from the enemy. Every bullet found its mark. Then out came the claymores. The battle was won within a few minutes, but the cause for which it had been fought was lost. For in the very moment of victory, Dundee had been struck by a stray

John Graham of Claverhouse, Viscount Dundee, whose efforts might have resulted in the restoration of King James VII to his throne.

bullet, as he encouraged his men. He died shortly afterwards, and with him went for ever the ability to weld together the clans into a really effective and disciplined fighting force.

The Massacre of Glencoe

Most of the clans still remained loyal to the Catholic James VII. When it came to the question, or rather the necessity, of their taking an oath of allegiance to William and Mary, it was accepted by the Government that those chiefs who felt they must first obtain James's permission might do so, provided that they met the deadline of 1 January 1692. When the day came, MacIan of Glencoe, chief of a sept of the MacDonalds, was one of only two who had not formally taken the oath. He had actually tried to register in time, and had walked to Fort

William to do so, only to be told that he should have gone to Inveraray instead. The passes were blocked by snow, and it was 6 January by the time he had arrived and the Sheriff had arrived and the formalities had been completed.

At the beginning of February a company of royal troops descended on Glencoe with their officer, a Campbell of Glenlyon who was related by marriage to MacIan. They

Captain Robert Campbell of Glenlyon, officer in charge of the troops at Glencoe.

asked for accommodation and, in accordance with the unwritten laws of Highland hospitality, were billeted in cottages in the glen. Before dawn on 13 February, about thirty men, women, and children were murdered. Others who tried to escape the soldiers died in the snow.

Bobbing John and the Rebellion of 1715

The Massacre of Glencoe and its subsequent cover-up were clearly the result of a government plot. Scottish loyalty to the Crown was further dented by English, and King William's, opposition to the proposal to found a trading company at Darien, on the isthmus of Panama, whose failure cost many Scottish lives and much Scottish cash. Disillusionment was increased at the time of the Union of the English and Scottish parliaments in 1707,

by which most Scots justifiably felt that they had been harshly treated. King George I came to the throne in 1714, as the result of the Act of Settlement of 1701, which tied England to the House of Hanover. The Scottish Parliament, however, had not acceded to the Act, and the Jacobites, as the supporters of James VII were called, felt free to revert to the old Stuart line, which had only technically been extinguished by the death of Queen Anne. For though James had died in 1701, his son, James Edward Stuart, was very much alive, and living in France.

Not the least disgruntled of the Scottish aristocracy was the Earl of Mar, Chief of Clan Erskine, who had been Secretary of State for Scotland until summarily dismissed and then publicly snubbed by the new King. He was known as Bobbing John, not, as is sometimes stated, because of his undeniable habit of changing political sides, but because of a disability which affected his gait. On 6 September 1715, at 'The Braes of Mar', he raised a brilliant new standard of blue silk, dedicated to James VIII and personally designed and embroidered by the young Lady Mar. Two months later, at Sheriffmuir, his army of some nine thousand clansmen met a government force of four thousand, under the 2nd Duke of Argyll. The result was a tedious draw, neither commander having the skill or dash to finish off the other side. James himself arrived in Scotland when the battle was over, and left after a few half-hearted attempts to rally support. The rebellion fizzled out. A few leading Jacobites were executed. Bobbing John went into exile, where he indulged in his less energetic hobbies of political intrigue and architectural and horticultural design.

The Outlawing of the MacGregors

A fairly small detachment of MacGregors under the command of the real-life folk hero, Rob Roy MacGregor, was present at the Battle of Sheriffmuir but did not actually participate. And in keeping with his heroic stature as a figure of romance, there is evidence that Rob Roy was acting also as a special agent for either Mar, or Argyll, or, it has been suggested, possibly even for both sides as a double agent.

The MacGregors themselves have gone down in history as the most unfortunate, or most put-upon, of clans, and for many generations they were known as

land, killing two men, and lifting nine hundred head of stock of various kinds, which they sold in the territory of the Campbells, who were also in a state of feud with the Colquhouns.

The Colquhouns' response was sheer Grand Guignol. In front of King James VI at Stirling, they paraded a bevy of mounted matrons, each claiming to have been widowed by the MacGregor raid and carrying on a spear-point her man's shirt, liberally steeped for the purpose in sheep's blood. James, who hated the sight of blood, readily granted the Colquhouns official permission to exact revenge. The MacGregors, justifiably nettled by this exhibition of sharp practice, challenged the Colquhouns to battle and routed them, killing eighty of their men and removing six hundred of their precious cattle. The King now gave orders to extirpate the MacGregors and to 'root out their posterity and name'. The Privy Council went even further and proscribed the very names of Gregor and MacGregor, and forbade those who had borne them to carry arms. From then until 1661, ten years before the birth of Rob Roy, it was not only unlawful to be called MacGregor, but no agreement entered into with a MacGregor was valid, and a MacGregor could be killed on sight without punishment. Charles II restored to the clan its name, but it never got back its lands.

Though the term blackmail appears first in the sixteenth century, Rob Roy was one of its most notable and successful early exponents. To lose your cattle to rustlers was an occupational hazard of Highland life. To balance the books, you went out into another clan's territory and pinched someone else's animals. Rob Roy added a refinement to the operation. In return for a consideration, he and his men would guard your cattle. If payment was refused, he lifted the cattle himself. He did not waste time on those who could not afford to pay: he simply took their cattle without formalities.

After the Rebellion of 1715 he was, as a confirmed Jacobite, called upon to surrender to justice. For years he was a hunted man, keeping a step ahead of his enemies, and twice escaped from captivity. He earned further legendary fame by brazenly helping those in trouble with the law or with their landlord. Finally, they gave up trying to catch him. He died quietly at his home in 1734, at the advanced age, for those times and in those climes, of 63, while the piper played at his request, 'I shall return no more'.

John Erskine, 6th Earl of Mar, leader of the Rebellion of 1715, portrayed with his son.

the Children of the Mist. Their troubles started, as so many people's did, with the Campbells, whose tenants they were. By a process of eviction, combined with legitimate oppression when the evicted turned to plunder to restore their livelihoods, they established the MacGregors' reputation for lawlessness. Matters came to a head in 1602, when a couple of MacGregors, having been unfairly refused Highland hospitality as they passed through land occupied by the Colquhouns, took refuge in a barn and were misguided enough to kill and eat a sheep which they found on the premises. The next morning they were arrested and summarily executed, though they had offered to pay for the animal. The MacGregors retaliated by raiding the Colquhoun

Scene beneath the Cuillin Hills, Skye, countryside for
bare legs and brogues.

Scotland and Her Tartans

Highland Dress

A Highland chief in his plaid, about 1680

Bare legs have been common form in the Highlands at least since the time of Magnus 'Barelegs', King of Norway, who with his courtiers adopted the local sartorial custom after subduing the Hebrides in 1098. In 1543, John Elder, a priest, wrote a letter to King Henry VIII of England, in which he explained that Highlanders were called Redshanks in Scotland, from their bare legs, and 'rough footed Scots' in England, from their shoes of untanned deerskin, worn fur side outside. The kilt, however, came much later.

The Plaid and Its Manufacture

The standard outer garment for men was a *leine-chroich*, a kind of shirt whose tails came down below the knee, dyed saffron-yellow, and made from as much as twenty-four ells (about nine metres) of pleated linen. This in time gave way to the *feileadh mór* (big wrap), whose name perfectly describes the plaid, the normal Highland dress for men during the seventeenth and eighteenth centuries. The plaid was a huge blanket of woven cloth, a double-width (about two metres) in breadth and between four and six metres long. To put it on, the Highlander lay down on it, with the lower of the two longer sides just about knee level, and wrapped it around himself, fastening a belt round his middle to keep the thing together. Then he stood up and draped the top half around his torso, and sometimes over his head, according to his whim or the weather.

In the moorland bogs and generally oozy terrain of the Highlands, bare legs were an essential contribution to health, for wet clothing could not be dried with any certainty or regularity in the damp and draughty conditions of even the more palatial homes. Indeed, of all the myriad Scottish inventions, discoveries, or initiatives which have transformed and enriched life, which include antiseptic surgery, brain surgery, anaesthesia, penicillin, the causes of scurvy and malaria, waterproof cloth, the bicycle, the pneumatic tyre, the telephone, television, radar, the steamship, and marmalade, the plaid was the earliest and perhaps not the least beneficial to the Scots themselves.

The plaid was particularly handy clothing to wear for herding cattle, and also for wearing when you went out raiding. So much so that when Highland dress was banned after the '45 Rebellion, those who opposed the Act argued that to be bereft of his plaid would be an unfair restriction on the cattle herder or drover, while the army, which had the job of enforcing the law, used the same argument to press that it would discourage cattle rustling.

The material from which the plaid was made was striped, or tartan, which is not a Highland word at all, but which means checked, or with stripes crossing each other at right angles. The scholar and cleric George Buchanan, in his twenty-volume history of Scotland, written in Latin and published in 1582, refers specifically to the striped clothing of the Highlanders, whose favourite colours were purple and blue, though dark brown was preferable when hiding in the heather on the moors. The close weave was midge-proof and moderately waterproof, and the plaid served as a sleeping bag out in the open at night, as well as a convenient garment to wear by day.

The raw wool was first soaked in human urine, which removed the grease and acted as a fixing agent for the colours. Then it was washed and dried. After spinning, each skein of wool was put in a pot with the dye plant or plants and other materials and simmered until it achieved the required colour. The fact that it was virtually impossible exactly to match shades from different batches or pots

Niel Gow (1727-1807), musician, in trews probably of his own design.

may explain why check patterns, for which comparatively small amounts of wool of different colours are required, were so popular so early on.

Various species of lichen were used to give the colours red, purple, yellow, and brown, though reds and purples could also be got from ladies' bedstraw, tormentil root, bramble, dandelion root, spindle, and St John's wort, and yellow from birch leaves, broom, and bog myrtle; while a particularly bright shade of yellow could be obtained from flowering heather. Yellow flag gave a grey-blue, while black came from alder bark. Blues were usually made from indigo, imported from abroad. Over-dyeing indigo on a yellow yarn produced green, though an especially soft green could be got from nettles, ling, or sorrel. A particular sett, or pattern, would be evolved by tradition, local skills, and the availability of the particular dyeing medium. The development of the clan tartan, though, was still far away.

Tartan Trews

Tartan trews, or trousers, are referred to at a comparatively early date. John, Lord of the Isles, had a pair in 1355, according to his accountants. And in the accounts of the Lord High Treasurer to James V, we find in 1538 the purchase of three ells of Highland tartan to make trousers 'to the Kingis grace', at 4s 3d an ell.

Tartan trews were tight-fitting breeches and stockings in one piece. When stockings were worn on their own, they were made of the same woven material as the plaid and tied with an elaborate garter, a metre long, wound several times round the leg and secured by a 'garter knot'. There is a contemporary description of Bonnie Prince Charlie's victorious but ragged army at Derby in 1745: 'A crew of shabby, lousy, pitiful look'd fellows; mixed up with old men and boys; dressed in Dirty Plaids, and as dirty shoes, without Breeches; and wore their stockings made of Plaid, not much above half-way up their Legs, some without Shoes, or next to none, and with their Plaids thrown over their shoulders'. To which a dry comment is appended to the effect that if they had not been carrying arms, they would have looked 'more like a Parcel of Chimney Sweeps than Soldiers'.

The Coming of the Kilt

The suggestion that the kilt – it is also known as the philabeg, or *feileadh-beag* (little kilt) – was invented by an Englishman sends shimmers of persecution mania through many Scottish traditionalists. The background to this particular version of its development is the political situation of the 1720s. In the aftermath of the Rebellion of 1715 and the abortive mini-rebellion in 1719 mounted by Thomas Keith, Earl Marischal of Scotland, with Spanish help, in which Rob Roy played a small but not insignificant part, the British Government appointed General George Wade as Commander-in-Chief, Scotland, to keep the clans in order. To help this process, he embarked in 1726 on a massive road-building programme, which by 1740 had produced 243 miles of serviceable roads and forty new bridges. This opening up of the Highlands had industrial as well as military applications. One of the first to take advantage

of the opportunity provided was Thomas Rawlinson, a Quaker ironmaster from Lancashire, who in 1727 established an iron foundry at Invergarry, near Inverness, to be worked by men of Clan MacDonell on whose territory it was.

Whatever advantages the plaid had when worn by men in their normal Highland pursuits, Rawlinson is said to have realised that it was hardly the thing in which to fell trees and stoke furnaces. He therefore commissioned the local regimental tailor at Inverness, whose name was Parkinson, to adapt the men's traditional dress to make it more suitable for manual labour. Parkinson achieved the modern kilt by separating the bottom half of the plaid and sewing the pleats so that they remained in place.

The invention caught on. By 1745, the well-dressed Highland gentleman's wardrobe comprised: a full-trimmed bonnet; tartan jacket and vest; tartan kilt; tartan belted plaid; trews; stockings with yellow garters; and two pairs of brogues. The brogue was the traditional Highland form of footwear of skin, which laced up. Very light, for ease of movement over rough and marshy ground, it had holes punched in the uppers to let water out.

Women's Dress in the Highlands

The fashion-conscious woman in about 1600 wore an ankle-length dress under a striped or check plaid, buckled but not belted. The ensemble was completed by a linen ruff and a headdress of similar material, with bracelets on her arms, and a necklace or necklaces according to her taste, or her husband's pocket. In the latter part of the seventeenth century and up to about 1745, the standard female garment was the *arisaid*, a tartan plaid of black, blue, or red stripes on a white background. This was secured at the breast by an elegant and elaborate metal buckle, silver or brass according to the wearer's status, which could be as big as a plate. Married women wore a linen headdress rather like a hood: maidens, or unmarried women, wore headbands or hair-ribbons. Their long stockings sometimes had no soles to the feet, in which case they were fastened by a loop over the toe.

Charles Edward Stuart, with Lochiel on his right, and
(facing page) Flora MacDonald, one of the many who
helped him escape.

The '45 Rebellion

Not only did James Edward Stuart lose his stomach for the fight to regain what the Jacobites, and many others, saw as his rightful inheritance, but the Jacobites themselves had been disillusioned by his melancholy demeanour when he finally, and too late, put in an appearance after the Battle of Sheriffmuir. Their last hopes seemed now to rest on James's son, Charles Edward Stuart ('Bonnie Prince Charlie'), born in 1720 in the Palazzo Muti in Rome, a mansion given to his father by the Pope, who baptised the infant and provided him with consecrated baby-linen to the value of six thousand scudi.

Charles grew up to be everything his father was not – a man of action, with a genuine heroic streak and an undeniable charm. Such qualities could make the impossible seem possible, but his great attempt was dogged, and ultimately undermined, by the atmosphere of intrigue and jealousy which had surrounded his upbringing and left him unable to distinguish between good and bad counsel. Throughout 1744 and early 1745, Charles was in Paris incognito, desperately and patiently trying to raise French support for an invasion of Britain. When it was clear that it would not be forthcoming, he hired a ship to carry himself and a

dozen trusted companions, and borrowed a frigate from the French navy to transport seven hundred men and a quantity of arms, artillery, ammunition, and stores. He set out on 16 July, delaying until the last minute a letter to his father explaining what he proposed to do. And when the frigate was badly damaged en route in an engagement with a British man-of-war and had to return home, he went it alone.

Some personalities involved in the Stewart succession (clockwise from top left): Mary, Queen of Scots; her son, James VI (James I of England); her second husband and James's father, Henry Stuart, Lord Darnley; Henry (1725-1807), Cardinal of York, younger grandson of James VII, and the last of the Stuarts; his brother, Charles Edward Stuart, as a young man, and towards the end of his life.

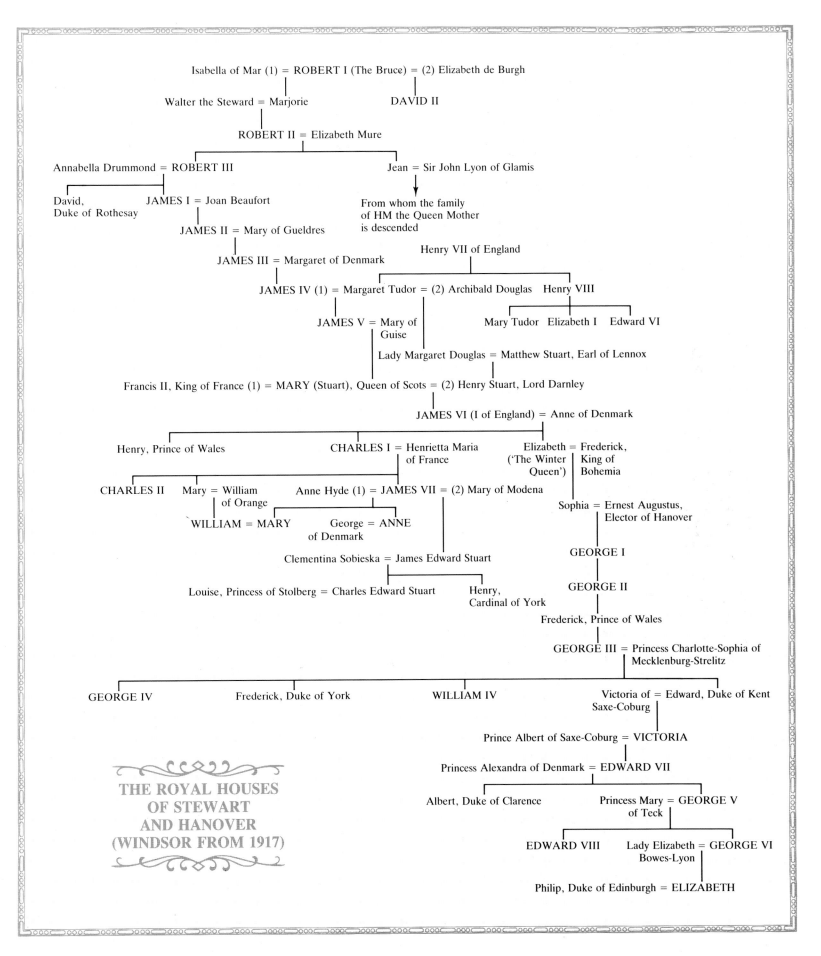

Isabella of Mar (1) = ROBERT I (The Bruce) = (2) Elizabeth de Burgh

Walter the Steward = Marjorie   DAVID II

ROBERT II = Elizabeth Mure

Annabella Drummond = ROBERT III   Jean = Sir John Lyon of Glamis

David,   JAMES I = Joan Beaufort   From whom the family
Duke of Rothesay   of HM the Queen Mother
is descended

JAMES II = Mary of Gueldres

JAMES III = Margaret of Denmark   Henry VII of England

JAMES IV (1) = Margaret Tudor = (2) Archibald Douglas   Henry VIII

JAMES V = Mary of   Mary Tudor   Elizabeth I   Edward VI
Guise

Lady Margaret Douglas = Matthew Stuart, Earl of Lennox

Francis II, King of France (1) = MARY (Stuart), Queen of Scots = (2) Henry Stuart, Lord Darnley

JAMES VI (I of England) = Anne of Denmark

Henry, Prince of Wales   CHARLES I = Henrietta Maria   Elizabeth = Frederick,
of France   ('The Winter   King of
Queen')   Bohemia

CHARLES II   Mary = William   Anne Hyde (1) = JAMES VII = (2) Mary of Modena   Sophia = Ernest Augustus,
of Orange   Elector of Hanover

WILLIAM = MARY   George = ANNE
of Denmark

Clementina Sobieska = James Edward Stuart   GEORGE I

Louise, Princess of Stolberg = Charles Edward Stuart   Henry,   GEORGE II
Cardinal of York

Frederick, Prince of Wales

GEORGE III = Princess Charlotte-Sophia of
Mecklenburg-Strelitz

GEORGE IV   Frederick, Duke of York   WILLIAM IV   Victoria of = Edward, Duke of Kent
Saxe-Coburg

Prince Albert of Saxe-Coburg = VICTORIA

Princess Alexandra of Denmark = EDWARD VII

Albert, Duke of Clarence   Princess Mary = GEORGE V
of Teck

EDWARD VIII   Lady Elizabeth = GEORGE VI
Bowes-Lyon

Philip, Duke of Edinburgh = ELIZABETH

THE ROYAL HOUSES
OF STEWART
AND HANOVER
(WINDSOR FROM 1917)

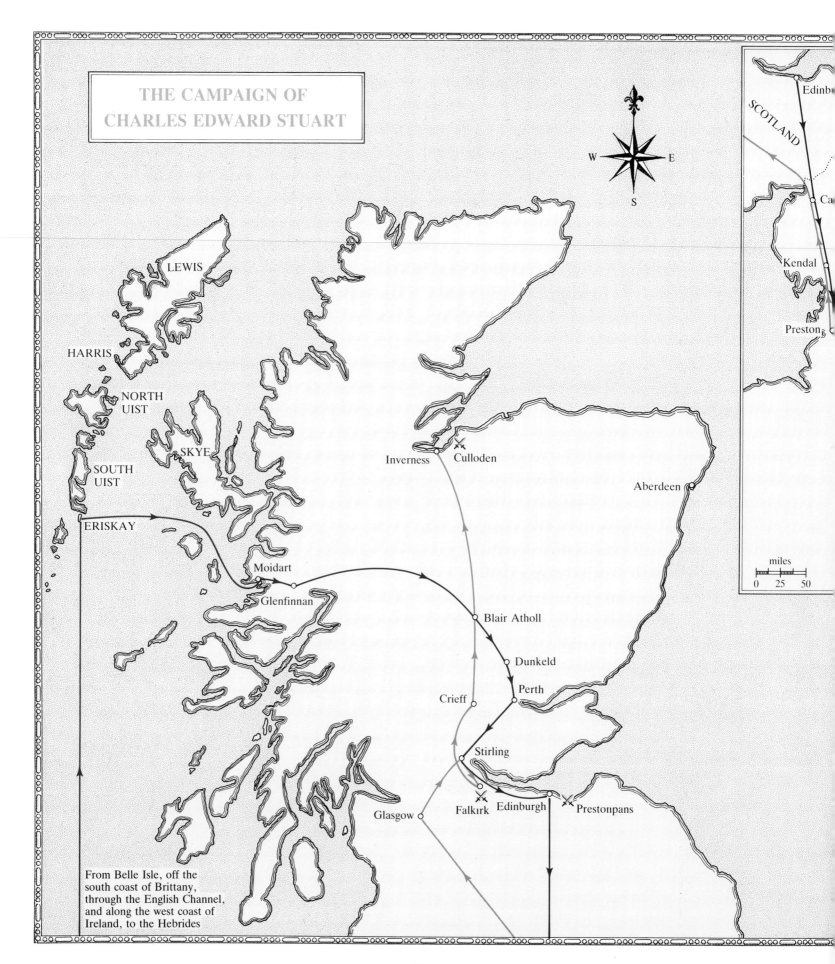

THE CAMPAIGN OF CHARLES EDWARD STUART

W E
S

LEWIS

HARRIS

NORTH
UIST

SKYE

SOUTH
UIST

ERISKAY

Moidart

Glenfinnan

Inverness Culloden

Aberdeen

Blair Atholl

Dunkeld

Crieff Perth

Stirling

Glasgow Falkirk Edinburgh Prestonpans

From Belle Isle, off the
south coast of Brittany,
through the English Channel,
and along the west coast of
Ireland, to the Hebrides

SCOTLAND

Edinb

Ca

Kendal

Preston

miles
0   25   50

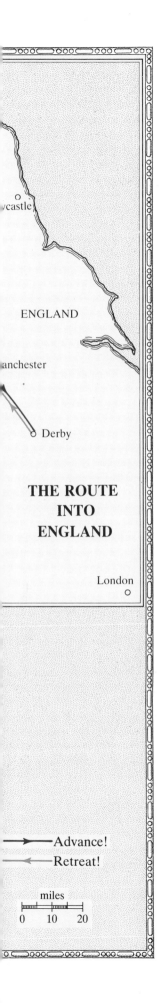

THE ROUTE
INTO
ENGLAND

Below: Princess Clementina Sobieska, wife of James Edward Stuart and mother of 'Bonnie Prince Charlie', who but for the course of history might have been Queen.

Anne, daughter of James VII by his first wife, became Queen in her own right and was the last Stewart monarch.

The Landing of Bonnie Prince Charlie

Even before he had set foot on the mainland, Highland chiefs who had met Charles off the island of Eriskay in the Outer Hebrides were advising him to return to France. He refused to do so. It was an extraordinarily brave but, on the evidence, extraordinarily foolish decision. Yet it established him once and for all as the cult figure of Highland tradition, and ensured that within a very few months Scotland would be, albeit temporarily, independent of England, that a victorious Jacobite force would be entrenched at Derby, only 125 miles from London, prepared for the final showdown with the British army, and that King George II would have ordered his royal yacht to stand by at the quay of the Tower of London for the instant evacuation of himself and his effects back to his native Hanover.

On 25 July 1745, Charles's ship anchored off the west coast of the Scottish mainland, where Loch nan Uamh joins the sea. Messages of further discouragement greeted him, and Donald Cameron of Lochiel, grandson of Sir Ewen Cameron who had fought with Viscount Dundee, came in person to advise that as there was no French support, there could be no rising. To this Charles is said to have replied that in a few days he would raise the royal standard and tell the people of Britain that Charles Stuart had come to claim the crown of his ancestors: Lochiel could stay at home and read all about it in the newspapers if he preferred. The influential Lochiel was won over, and others followed suit.

A few days later, the first skirmish of the campaign took place, when a party of MacDonells of Keppoch, on their way to join the Prince, ambushed two companies of Royal Scots and put them to flight. On 19 August, at Glenfinnan, at the head of Loch Shiel, Charles formally unfurled his royal standard, and claimed the throne of England and Scotland for his father, James VIII, with himself as Regent.

The Great Adventure

Charles now had an army of just over a thousand Highlanders, notably Camerons, MacDonells of Keppoch and MacDonalds of Clanranald, and Stewarts of Appin. By a combination of ill-judgment and ineptitude, General Cope, with a bigger, but largely untrained government army, managed to bypass them on his way north,

leaving the road clear for a triumphal Jacobite entry into Perth, with Charles riding at the head of his army, a dazzling figure in a tartan suit with gold lace edging. Realising that he had made a ghastly error, Cope embarked his men in ships at Inverness in an attempt to reach Edinburgh before the Jacobite army. Charles won the race, his men having, with a few random pistol shots, put to flight (or, as the opposition had it, encouraged the dignified withdrawal of) two regiments of dragoons who were mustered at Coltbridge, two miles from the city gates. Thanks to a piece of typical Highland cunning on the part of the Camerons, Charles was able to enter Edinburgh without a fight, and ensconced himself safely in the royal Palace of Holyroodhouse, from which he emerged a few days later to annihilate Cope's army at Prestonpans in an engagement which lasted just ten minutes.

It was now 20 September. Charles was master of Scotland, but it was the kingdom of England as well which he regarded as his family's destiny. Instead of marching south at once, he lingered in Edinburgh until 1 November, collecting and training recruits, dissuading his existing forces from looting or deserting which, as volunteer clansmen each under his own chief they felt entitled and were accustomed to do, dealing with such affairs of state as he felt were compatible with his status, and generally behaving with becoming modesty, generosity, and charm. By the time he was on his way towards London, government forces were regrouping in England and others were pouring in from the continent of Europe. He still had no more than six thousand troops, and the promised or hoped for support from Jacobite sympathisers in England did not materialise. At Derby, with General Wade with one army deployed at Newcastle, the Duke of Cumberland (son of the King) marching to meet him through the Midlands, and a third waiting for him outside London (a total of thirty thousand troops in all), Charles was persuaded that prudence was the better part of valour, and the retreat began.

Retreat to Defeat

On 20 December Charles and his troops forded the River Esk and were back in Scotland. They stopped off in Glasgow, where he milked the townspeople for waistcoats, shirts, shoes, stockings, and bonnets for all his men and held a grand parade. The newly kitted-out army scored a hollow victory at Falkirk, having induced a government force to attack across a quagmire, in pouring rain, with the wind in their faces. The inevitable was not long delayed. On the moor by Culloden, near Inverness, on 16 April 1746, in the last battle to be fought on the British mainland, the Highlanders were battered by cannon fire and raked with grapeshot, before being mown down by muskets and carved up by bayonets as they finally and forlornly advanced, while

Culloden, by David Morier, painted shortly after the '45 Rebellion. It is estimated that the seven Highlanders are between them wearing twenty-two different tartans.

Cumberland's cavalry and dragoons swept round to take them on the flanks and in the rear. Charles escaped from the carnage. The Highland fling may have ended, but the Highland legend was on its way to immortality.

Escape to Freedom

The hunt was on. For five months, until he could finally get away in the only French ship able to get through to him, Charles was pursued over land and sea in Lewis and Skye, and North and South Uist. This was the truly heroic period of his life. He remained cheerful under the most appalling and distressing conditions. He went

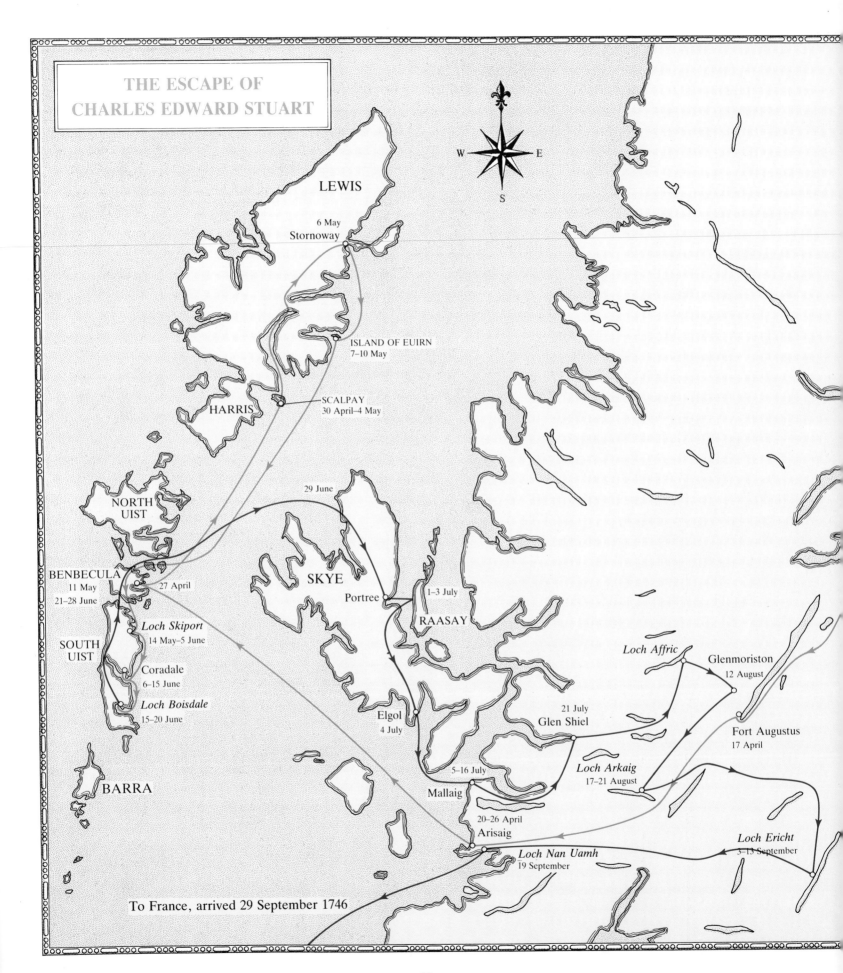

THE ESCAPE OF
CHARLES EDWARD STUART

LEWIS

6 May
Stornoway

ISLAND OF EUIRN
7–10 May

SCALPAY
30 April–4 May

HARRIS

29 June

NORTH
UIST

SKYE

BENBECULA
11 May
21–28 June

27 April

Portree

1–3 July

RAASAY

Loch Skiport
14 May–5 June

Loch Affric

Glenmoriston
12 August

SOUTH
UIST

Coradale
6–15 June

Elgol
4 July

21 July
Glen Shiel

Fort Augustus
17 April

Loch Boisdale
15–20 June

5–16 July

Loch Arkaig
17–21 August

BARRA

Mallaig

20–26 April

Loch Ericht
3–13 September

Arisaig

Loch Nan Uamh
19 September

To France, arrived 29 September 1746

30

Culloden
16 April 1746

George, Duke of Cumberland, younger son of King George II, commander of the government forces at the Battle of Culloden. The victory was made easier for him by the bad advice given to Bonnie Prince Charlie as to the choice of battleground. In addition, the Highlanders had eaten hardly anything for two days, and were suffering from the effects of a twenty-mile route march the previous night, in the course of an abortive attempt to attack Cumberland's camp.

without sleep or food, travelled on foot over the most brutal terrain, and hid in the roughest parts of the countryside. He was wet to the skin. His clothes stank, he got lice, and he suffered from intermittent dysentery. There was a reward of £30,000 on his head, but he was never betrayed. For two days at the end of June he was in and out of female clothing, acting the part of the Irish maid of twenty-three-year-old Flora Macdonald, who took him from South Uist to her native Skye. Soon after he parted from her she was arrested, and was imprisoned in the Tower of London. Otherwise he wore Highland dress, with nothing under his kilt, as we learn from someone who was with him on the mainland in July: 'He was every now and then (through the darkness of the nights) slumping into this and the other clayhole or puddle, insomuch that very often he would have been plashed up to the navel, having no breeches, but a philabeg, and when he arrived at any place to take a little rest, he would have taken a nook of his plaid and therewith have rubbed his belly and thighs to clean them the best way he could.'

The rest of his story is without heroism or romance. He wandered from place to place in Europe. In 1772, when he was fifty, he was promised a pension of 40,000 crowns a year by the French if he married someone suitable, who might also give him an heir and so embarrass the British Government. He agreed to make an arranged marriage with Louise, the twenty-year-old daughter of the widowed Princess de Stolberg, at whose insistence the wedding took place and the marriage was consummated on the day on which the pair met for the first time. Louise left him for a young Italian poet in 1780, though by this time he had become a querulous old drunkard. He finally died in the arms of his illegitimate daughter by Clementina Walkinshaw, whom he had first met in Glasgow in 1745, when he was the young Chevalier, who commandeered the finest mansion in the town, and in defiance of the townsfolk's standoffishness, for they were staunch Hanoverians, dined in public twice a day, wearing, we are told, a silk tartan jacket over crimson velvet breeches.

**Even today, much of the Highlands is bleak, and life
can be harsh.**

Scotland and Her Tartans

The Suppression
and Dispersal of the Clans

The sea offered a route to the possibility of a better way of life.

The defeat of the Jacobite forces at Culloden ensured that what had been an ideal was now reduced to mere fantasy, though its adventurous aftermath invested Charles Edward Stuart (who might have been Charles III) with the status of romantic hero. The collapse of the clan system, however, was hastened by measures taken by the Government to prevent any recurrence of rebellion from that quarter.

Proscription

The Disarming Act of 1746 not only banned the carrying of arms, but made it an offence 'within that part of Great Britain called Scotland … on any pretext whatsoever, [to] wear or put on the clothes commonly called Highland clothes (that is to say) the Plaid, Philabeg, or little Kilt, Trowse, Shoulder-belts, or any part whatsoever of what peculiarly belongs to the Highland Garb; and that no tartan or party-coloured plaid or stuff shall be used for Great Coats or upper coats'. The punishment for anyone convicted on the evidence of 'one or more

credible witness or witnesses' was six months in jail for the first offence, and transportation for seven years for the second.

Initially, the law applied equally to the clans which had supported the Jacobite cause, to those such as MacDonald of Sleat and Macleod of Dunvegan – whose chiefs had remained loyal to the Government but many of whose individual members had fought for or given personal assistance to Bonnie Prince Charlie – and to the Campbells of Argyll, four companies of whom had fought against him at Culloden. The measures were rigorously enforced, those who were merely suspected of having evaded them being required, on pain of being outlawed and possibly killed, to swear an oath of blood-curdling obedience.

That there was some relaxation of the law, or else difficulty in maintaining it in outlying parts of the land, is attested by the account of Dr Samuel Johnson, the sage, lexicographer and literary critic, who made a trip to the Western Isles in 1773, accompanied by his faithful biographer, the Scottish-born James Boswell. Johnson records that 'the fillibeg, or lower garment, is still very common', and that the 'common people' had devised an ingenious pretext for returning to the traditional overgarment, the plaid. The law against plaids, they argued, was made by Lord Hardwicke (the Lord Chancellor at the time, at whose instigation many of the measures to repress the Highlands were introduced), and since he was now dead (he died in 1764), it no longer applied.

The Act against Highland dress was repealed in 1782, but by that time the skills of dyeing and weaving the intricate tartan, if not wholly forgotten, had ceased to be a way of life. The clan system itself, and the clan spirit on which it largely depended, had in the meantime foundered as the result of further laws brought in after the Battle of Culloden, whereby the estates of many of those who had supported the Jacobite cause were forfeited to the Crown and, even more significantly, the rights of chiefs over their clansmen were abolished. The chiefs now had no authority over, or responsibility for, their people, and the people had no obligations to their chief, except as tenants.

Emigration

The measures which altered Highland society and nominally gave the Highlander his freedom, increased rather than instigated the flow of emigrants, which had begun rather earlier. Nova Scotia had briefly been a Scottish colony from 1629 to 1632, and descendants of the original 'Nova Scotia baronets' who raised money for the venture still hold their titles. It is true that during the first half of the eighteenth century many of those who crossed the Atlantic to end up in the West Indies or Maryland or South Carolina had been transported for their political or religious beliefs. Yet from the 1730s there had been a more voluntary form of emigration from the Highlands, especially of tacksmen and their sub-tenants, for whom North Carolina was a popular resort.

The tacksman was a clan middleman, who, by tradition and inheritance rather than by official appointment, acted as a landlord on behalf of his chief. As management skills developed and inflation started to bite, the tacksman tended to become redundant, and then often employed his organisational experience to persuade his tenants to join him in emigrating. Rents increased still further when the post-Culloden legislation began to take effect. Authority was not the only thing the chiefs had lost: many were financially ruined by the expenses they had incurred in supporting Bonnie Prince Charlie. Some sold their lands to speculators or succumbed to the offers of sheep-farmers from the south. Even the payment of compensation to some of the great overlords such as the Duke of Argyll to help improve the economy of their estates could not alter the living standards or financial condition of tenants who were unable, or unwilling, to move with the times. It has been suggested that between 1769 and 1774 four thousand tacksmen and tenants emigrated to North Carolina from the island of Skye alone. Among them was Flora MacDonald, who, after her release from the Tower of London, had returned to Scotland, where she was much feted, and in 1750 married Allan MacDonald of Kingsburgh, a younger son who was a farmer and tacksman. High rents and a succession of bad harvests forced him and his wife to join what had now become a flood of emigrants.

There was even a dance in Skye called 'America'. Boswell, if not Johnson, performed it in 1773: 'Each of the couples, after the common *involutions* and *evolutions*, successively whirls round in a circle, till all are in motion; and the dance seems intended to shew how emigration catches, till a whole neighbourhood is set afloat.' While emigration required courage and

fortitude, and the enduring of heartbreaks at parting, privation en route, and hardships on arrival, it could ultimately bring rewards. The minister of North Uist in the 1770s stated that islanders emigrated to North Carolina after receiving 'the most flattering accounts' of the place, and 'in their turn gave friends at home the same flattering accounts that induced themselves to go'. Another influence was the army, when its members returned from North American postings and reported the conditions there.

The first Highland regiment, the 43rd (from 1749 the 42nd) Regiment, known as the Black Watch from its dark tartan plaid, was formally constituted in 1740 from the six Highland companies which had been raised by General Wade in the late 1720s. Initially, the uniform was a belted plaid over a red jacket and waistcoat: the kilt was only worn off duty. After some eighteen months' training in Scotland, the regiment set out to march to London to be reviewed by George II. As a preview for the King, who had never seen a Highlander, three private soldiers, noted for their looks and athletic ability (one of them was nicknamed 'Gregor the Beautiful'), were sent ahead. One died on the way, but his companions performed their military exercises so skilfully before the King and assembled officers that they were each tipped a guinea (an extremely generous emolument in those days), which they gave to the porter at the palace gate as they went out!

The Black Watch was one of the regiments brought back to England at the time of the '45 Rebellion, but sensibly, for some three hundred of the men had fathers or brothers on the other side, it was not required to serve in the north. And being exempt from the Disarming Act, its members continued to wear their uniform tartan plaid. At the outset of the Seven Years War (1756-63), the regiment sailed for America and fought with distinction in the disastrous attack on Ticonderoga. Two other newer Highland regiments, the 77th (Montgomery's Highlanders) and the 78th (Fraser's

Top: traditional methods of dyeing wool were preserved in Harris even in the 1930s. Bottom: though the introduction of sheep affected the Highland economy, in the eighteenth century the birth rate had increased so much that the land could no longer support the population.

Highlanders), also took part in the campaign, at the end of which they were offered the chance of settling in the newly acquired colony of Canada. The men who did so chose Murray Bay as their home, and they and those who preferred to return helped to publicise the prospects in the new homeland – 'A day labourer can gain thrice the wages he can in this country,' ran an advertisement in 1774, 'There are no beggars in North America.'

The Frasers and Montgomeries, formed the first battalion of the Royal Highland Emigrants, raised in 1775 at the beginning of the American War of Independence. The war put a temporary stop to American immigration, but it caused existing Highland immigrants to move in their thousands to Canada, including many families that had only recently settled in the Colony of New York – among them MacDonells, Chisholms, Grants, Camerons, MacIntyres, and Fergusons.

For some years after the war Canada took the lion's share of immigrants – in 1785 the citizens of Glengarry, Canada, persuaded five hundred Glengarries to come and join them, and in 1799 a large number of Camerons of Lochiel founded a Canadian Lochiel. The hardships at home increased with the evictions of tenants in the interests of the sheep farmers, but it took the potato famine of 1846-47 to impress upon officialdom that emigration could be beneficial and that help was required. So the Highlands and Islands Emigration Society was established, as a result of whose policies and activities other lands were opened up – between 1852 and 1857 the society enabled five thousand Highlanders to settle in Australia. Nor was mass emigration confined to those from the Highlands. In 1819 a party of distressed weavers had founded New Glasgow in Nova Scotia. In 1848 two ships with 344 Scots on board arrived in New Zealand, to inaugurate the Free Church settlement of Dunedin, which was the original name for Edinburgh.

By now, the clan and family tartan tradition, from its extraordinary and somewhat misty beginnings only a few years earlier, had become firmly established. Succeeding emigrants took it with them wherever they went.

Above: Cameron.
Left: Glen Etive displays much that is typical of Scotland's mountain landscape. Foreboding crags, rigs and moors are snow-laden for much of the year.

Left: 1867 kilt and plaid of the tartan of MacDonald of
the Isles and Sleat, and (right) kilt of the MacDonald
tartan.

Scotland and Her Tartans

The Highland Romantic Revival

If Charles Edward Stuart is the focal point of so much of the romance with which the Highland tradition is imbued, James Macpherson, who was a boy on his father's farm in Inverness-shire at the time of the '45, provided the cultural impetus. In 1760 he published a series of translations of ancient Gaelic poetry 'collected in the Highlands of Scotland'. These so excited the literary establishment of the time that Macpherson was commissioned to look for lost manuscripts in the Highlands and to investigate further its oral tradition. He duly returned with what he claimed to be a lost epic by Ossian, a third-century Gaelic poet and warrior, son

The famous painting by Sir David Wilkie (1785-1841) of King George IV in full Highland dress on the occasion of his state visit to Edinburgh in 1822.

of the legendary Fingal. Macpherson's 'Ossian Poems', published between 1762 and 1765, were in fact largely if not entirely his own composition, but they appealed enormously to a public enthralled by the concept of the noble savage and avid for tales of primitive passion and heroic action in sublime settings. It was not only Scots who wanted the poems to be genuine. The poet Lord

Byron, who was by birth half Scottish, thought them splendid, and Napoleon is said to have carried a copy with him wherever he went.

Sir Walter Scott and the Royal Highland Extravaganza

No single year, apart from 1745, contributed so much to the Highland myth as 1822. It was the occasion of King George IV's visit to Scotland, the first by a reigning monarch since Charles II over 150 years earlier. The affair was stage-managed by Sir Walter Scott (he had been made a baronet in 1820), famous as a Scottish folklorist and historian, as a Romantic poet, and as the man who had cracked the 111-year-old mystery of the whereabouts of the Scottish crown jewels and royal regalia. Curiously, he was not yet known as the author of the hugely successful 'Waverley Novels', with their new, graphic, but fair appraisal of events in Scottish history, including *Rob Roy*, *The Heart of Midlothian*, and *Redgauntlet*, for they had been published anonymously. The secret of their authorship was not to be publicly revealed until 1827.

King George IV presented with the keys of the city of Edinburgh on his arrival.

Scott's assistant and technical consultant in the royal venture was Colonel David Stewart of Garth, a former officer in the Black Watch, who had founded the Celtic Society of Edinburgh, one of whose aims was 'to promote the general use of the ancient Highland dress', which its members wore at club dinners. The President was Scott himself, who commented on the horseplay and general high spirits demonstrated at one meeting by members 'liberated from the thraldom of breeches …. Such jumping, skipping, and screaming you never saw.'

In 1822 Stewart published *Sketches of the Character, Manners, and Present State of the Highlanders of Scotland*, in which he asserted: 'In dyeing and arranging the various colours of their tartans, they displayed no small art and taste, preserving at the same time the distinctive patterns (or setts, as they were called) of the different clans, tribes, families and districts. Thus a Macdonald, a Campbell, a Mackenzie, &c, was known

by his plaid.' He produced no source or evidence for this important claim, but the visit of the King the same year gave him the opportunity to make up in practical ways for the lack of proof with which to support his assertion.

Though even Scott's devoted biographer (and son-in-law), John Gibson Lockhart, could not hide his scepticism as to whether all the arrangements were 'in the most accurate taste', it was certainly the most glittering occasion, enlivened by the presence not only of the members of the Celtic Society in what they imagined to be full Highland regalia, but also of the Highland chiefs whom Scott had personally invited, with their followers. 'Do come and bring half-a-dozen or half-a-score of clansmen,' he wrote to one, '… Highlanders are what he will best like to see.'

The Royal Stewart tartan.

Not only did the King like to see Highlanders, he actually appeared as one himself at a reception in the Palace of Holyroodhouse, thus giving no little offence to many of the assembled Lowland Scots. The outfit, in what has come to be known as the Royal Stewart tartan, was devised and made for him by an army tailor, George

Hunter, and had been put on with the assistance of Colonel Stewart, who adjusted the folds of the royal plaid and pronounced the King 'a verra pretty man'. The effect, however, was bizarre. George IV was a portly personage, the kilt was rather short ('As he is to be here for so short a time, the more we see of him the better,' observed Lady Hamilton cattily), the stockings were too skimpy, and the gaps between kilt and stockings were decorously covered in flesh-coloured tights.

The proceedings were rendered even more farcical by the sudden appearance of an even fatter man, in an identical outfit! This was Sir William Curtis, a biscuit manufacturer who was chairman of the Tory party in the City of London. Curtis's pomposity had already taken a knock as he marched ponderously along one of the long corridors to the reception in the company of a sharp city councillor from Aberdeen, who suggested that the effect was not all it should be. Curtis, who had spared no expense on his appearance, demanded an explanation and, as he did so, glanced approvingly down at the splendid *sgian dubh*, whose handle protruded from the top of his tartan stocking. 'Oo ay, the knife's all right, mon,' replied the Aberdonian, 'but where's your spoon?' Even worse was to follow when a John Hamilton Dundas, mistaking one fat, kilted dignitary for the other, solemnly and reverently knelt and kissed the hand of the biscuit manufacturer instead of that of the King.

The fact that many of the genuine Highlanders were dressed in clan tartans, including, from a contemporary account, 'Clan Gregor, about fifty in number. Their tartan was red', as well as 'the Celtic Society … each in his own clan tartan', would suggest evidence for Colonel Stewart's assertion about the existence already of a clan tartan tradition. What seems to have happened, however, is that the Highlanders had been invited, nay persuaded, to come in full Highland dress. Many had to buy it for the occasion, and the suppliers were bombarded with orders. There was also the question, if tartan was going to be worn, of which pattern and colour it should be. The main supplier was William Wilson and Son of Bannockburn, who had sufficient market awareness to have established certain patterns as belonging to particular clans. Some of the patterns were of genuine antiquity, but their allocation was unscientific if not often haphazard. When the demand came, in 1822, it

predictions. One Edinburgh firm reported: 'We are like to be torn to pieces for tartan, the demand is so great we cannot supply our customers.' Wilsons could only satisfy the overwhelming demand from their customers by putting in forty extra looms.

The problem was rather more than one of just the short supply of tartan, it was also the limited availability of registered patterns. Wilsons, in particular, were not to be defeated. If they could not supply a customer 'to order', they would do so 'off the peg' – the firm liked to give heroic names to some of their designs: they even had one called Robin Hood! Duncan Macpherson of Cluny, chief of the clan to which James Macpherson had belonged, had a few years before selected as his clan tartan No 43 in Wilsons' commercial pattern-book, which was also known as 'Caledonia' and sometimes 'Kidd', a man of that name having a few years earlier bought a bulk lot in which to attire his West Indian slaves.

Sir Walter Scott, for all his genuine enthusiasm for the Highlands and its traditions, was a Lowlander whose family came from the Borders. Though in the years which followed his brilliant public relations coup in 1822 he vehemently denied that Lowlanders had ever worn plaids or had distinctive family tartans, there is some suggestion that the black and white check tartan associated with Clan Scott was designed by him for his personal use as a plaid.

The Sobieski Stuart Enigma

Some kind of authoritative and systematic record of clan tartan setts was now clearly called for. The first of its kind was by James Logan from Aberdeen, who, incidentally, as a boy had been hit on the head by the 17lb weight during a Highland games hammer-throwing event. His book, *The Scottish Gael* (1831), was not illustrated, but it contained detailed descriptions of 55 regimental and clan tartans. Next to test the market were the two brothers Allen, who were of sound English stock, though where they came to Scotland from and what their earlier life was like are questions that have never been answered. Cultured and undeniably talented, they were welcomed by members of the Scottish aristocracy, and between about 1820 and 1840 changed their name successively to the more Scottish Allan, to Hay Allan, and to Hay, finally calling themselves

respectively John Sobieski Stuart (John Sobieski had been King of Poland and was the grandfather of Bonnie Prince Charlie's mother, Clementina Sobieski) and Charles Edward Stuart.

In 1842 they published a limited edition of fifty copies of *Vestiarium Scoticum* (Scottish Costume). It had pictures of 75 tartans in full colour, most of them new even to the clans to which they were said to belong. A significant number were attributed to Lowland and Border families, and with Scott now dead, no one stood up publicly to question whether this was feasible. The Sobieski Stuarts claimed that they had compiled the book from an ancient manuscript which, however, they

declined to produce for scrutiny. The work itself was a fake, but nearly all the tartans became accepted, and are still widely worn as appropriate setts by particular clans and families.

The pair then published an even more sumptuous and erudite volume, *The Costume of the Clans* (1844), but their credibility was undermined when, shortly afterwards, they subtly spread stories suggesting that Prince Charles had had a son by his wife Louise, who in his turn had had two sons, now living in Scotland. It did not require much imagination to see that the Sobieski Stuarts were now claiming to be the legitimate great-great-grandsons of James VII. This was too much for the Establishment. The claims were duly demolished in the press, and the brothers ended their lives in dignified penury.

Facing page: one of the original copies of *Vestiarium Scoticum*. This page: the Gillies' Ball at Balmoral Castle, 1859.

Queen Victoria and the Balmoral Effect

In 1872 Queen Victoria was petitioned on behalf of the Sobieski Stuart brothers to grant them a pension. This was refused on the grounds that they had suggested not only that they were distantly related to her but that by inference they had a claim to her crown. They did have a kinship with her, however, in that she shared their genuine love of the Highlands and contributed to the promotion, if not also in some respects to the creation, of the tartan tradition.

Queen Victoria and her husband, Prince Albert, first visited Scotland in 1842, when she was 23. A few years later, on the advice of the royal doctor, who recommended the climate of the banks of the River Dee as being good for rheumatism, from which they both suffered, the royal couple bought the estate of Balmoral and knocked down the existing castle, having built the present edifice a hundred yards to the northwest. Besides personally designing much of the new Balmoral Castle and planning its interior decoration, Prince Albert also devised the Balmoral tartan, which is exclusively for the use of the royal family and with which he carpeted many of the rooms (less important parts had tartan linoleum), covered much of the furniture, and clothed a large section of the staff. After his death, the Queen was persuaded to publish *Leaves from the Journal of Our*

Left: baronial mansion at Inveran, Easter Ross. The Victorians were as obsessed with recreating medieval architecture as they were with creating a tartan image. Facing page: in this 1869 painting by Kenneth Macleay (1802-78), Donald MacBeath (left) is in the uniform of a sergeant-major in the Atholl Highlanders. On the right is a gillie. Both men are wearing the Murray of Atholl tartan.

Life in the Highlands (1867), and this and its sequel *More Leaves …* (1884), which was dedicated to the memory of her faithful but eccentric personal attendant John Brown, not only popularised the monarchy as had never been done before, but gave a permanent boost to the Scottish tourist industry.

The Development of the Clan Tartan

The Lord Lyon King of Arms, as an appointed officer of state and a member of the royal household, is the supreme authority on all Scottish armorial, heraldic, and genealogical matters, and thus also on the chieftainship of the clans. It is, however, the chief of each clan or family who arbitrates on the authenticity of a clan or family tartan or on the acceptability of a new or additional design, which may then be submitted to the Lord Lyon for registration.

The original theory behind the 'hunting tartan' was that the bright colours of many tartans made concealment difficult out of doors and especially on the moors, and a more muted version was called for, in which a green, blue, or brown might be substituted for a red or yellow in the original, or a darker background colour might replace a light one. In practice, however, many hunting tartans, like the Erskine, are modern but accepted additions to the range. A further late-nineteenth-century development was the 'dress tartan', nominally for evening wear, for which a white background is usually but not invariably substituted for the original colour.

Some tartans are described as 'ancient' or 'old'. This is a reference to the shades of the colours, not to the sett or design itself, and the practice began after World War I in an attempt to recreate with modern techniques the softer results obtained from the old vegetable dyes.

Traditionally, the right to wear a clan tartan is vested in those who have the name of the clan or family to which it belongs. Custom has decreed, however, that those who bear the name of a sept associated with a particular clan may also wear that clan's tartan – in cases where a sept name is associated with more than one clan, recourse must be had to family history or tradition to decide which tartan shall be worn.

THE ARMS OF HER MAJESTY'S LORD LYON KING OF ARMS

The Arms of Her Majesty's Lord Lyon King of Arms and
(facing page) the Royal Arms as on Her Majesty's
Great Seal for Scotland.

Clan and Family Tartans

The arms of a chief of a clan or the head of a family fulfil the same functions as those of the Sovereign, or Her Lord Lyon King of Arms, and indicate presence or authority. The chiefly crest, encircled by a strap and buckle with the appropriate motto engraved on it, may be worn by a follower of that chief. Only chiefs and their heirs wear the crest within a plain circlet, surmounted by three feathers for a chief, and by two for a chieftain: the chieftain, or lesser chief, is likely to be the head of a branch or to have some territorial authority within the clan. The chief's standard is a long, narrow flag with, next to the pole, either the cross of St Andrew or the chief's personal arms. The rest of the design will incorporate the crest and motto, and in some cases the clan's plant badge and/or other heraldic devices.

The maps in this chapter which follow the list of Sept and Family Names indicate general territorial areas of influence at about the time of King James VI, but taking the history of each region or family as a whole.

Sept and Family Names

The origins of many surnames may be grouped according to four main types:

1 **Patronymic**, e.g. MacWilliam, Wilson, both of which derive from William;
2 **Trade or calling**, e.g. Baxter, Clerk, Fletcher, Smith, Weaver;
3 **Physical description or distinctive physical feature**, e.g. Dow (black or dark), More (big or great), Cameron (crooked nose), Crookshanks;
4 **Territorial**, e.g. Comrie, Dallas, Dyce, Ross, Strachan

Many affiliations between a sept and a clan are based simply on tradition, and where one tribe of a particular name is linked with a clan, other people bearing that name, though their original descent was different, may have come to be thought to be associated with that clan. Many names, though traditionally connected with a particular clan, may also be linked with other clans, while some holders of that name may have no clan link at all. Bearers of many names which originated in the Lowlands may have no association with a particular clan or family, or with any of the great Lowland houses. In the list below, the words 'also general' indicate that the evidence for a general origin is stronger than that for a clan affiliation. It should further be noted that many names allied to Mackintosh and Macpherson are more properly associated with Clan Chattan.

*Own tartan

†Indicates the existence of a principal family or families

A

Abbot, Abbotson: *MacNab, also general*
***†Abercrombie**
Abernethy: *Leslie, MacDuff*
†Adam: *Gordon*
†Adamson: *Mackintosh*
Adie: *Gordon*
Airlie: *Ogilvy*
***†Alexander:** *MacAlister, MacDonald, MacDonell of Glengarry, also general* **Allan, Allanson:** *MacDonald of Clanranald, MacFarlane*
†Allardice: *Graham of Menteith*
***†Allison**
Alpin: *MacAlpine*
***Anderson (also MacAndrew):** *Mackintosh, Ross, also general*
Andrew: *Ross*
Angus: *MacInnes*
***†Arrol**
Arthur: *MacArthur*
***Austin:** *Keith*
Ayson: *Mackintosh*

B

***†Baillie**
†Bain: *MacBean, Mackay, MacNab*
Bannatyne: *Campbell, Stewart of Bute*
†Bannerman: *Forbes*
Bartholomew: *MacFarlane, Leslie*
***Baxter:** *Macmillan*

†Bayne: *MacBean, Mackay, MacNab*
Bean: *MacBean*
Beath, Beaten, Beathy: *Macbeth, MacDonald, Maclean*
†Beaton: *MacDonald, Maclean, Macleod*
Begg: *MacDonald, also general*
Beirton, *see Bethune*
***Bell:** *Macmillan, also general*
Berkeley: *Barclay*
†Bethune (also Leech, Leitch): *MacDonald, Maclean, Macleod*
†Beton: *MacDonald, Maclean, Macleod*
Binnie: *MacBean*
Black: *Lamont, MacGregor, Maclean, also general*
†Bontein, Bontine, Buntin: *Graham of Menteith*
***Bowie:** *MacDonald*
***Boyd:** *Boyd, Stewart*
Brebner: *Farquharson*
Brewer: *Drummond, MacGregor*
Brieve: *Morrison*
***†Brown:** *Lamont, Macmillan, also general*
***†Buchan:** *Buchan, Comyn*
Burdon: *Lamont*
Burk(e): *MacDonald, also general*
***Burnes, Burness, Burns:** *Campbell*
***†Burnett:** *Campbell*

C

Caddell: *Campbell of Cawdor*
Caird: *MacGregor, Sinclair*
†Calder: *Campbell of Cawdor*
Callum: *Macleod of Raasay, Malcolm*
Cariston: *Skene*
***†Carmichael:** *MacDougall, Stewart of Appin, Stewart of Galloway*
***†Carnegie**
Carson: *Macpherson, also general*
Cattanach: *Macpherson*
Caw: *MacFarlane*
†Chalmers: *Cameron*
Cheyne: *Sutherland*
***Christie:** *Farquharson, also general*
†Clark, Clarke, Clarkson, Clerk: *Cameron, Clan Chattan, Mackintosh, Macpherson*
Clouston: *Sinclair*
Clyne: *Sinclair*
***†Cochrane**
***†Cockburn**
Collier: *Robertson*
Colman: *Buchanan*
Colson: *MacDonald*
Colyear: *Robertson*
Combich: *Stewart of Appin*
Combie: *MacThomas, Mackintosh*
Comrie: *MacGregor*
Conacher: *MacDougall, Robertson*

***Connal:** *MacDonald*
Conochie: *Campbell*
Cook: *Stewart, also general*
Coulson: *MacDonald*
†Coutts: *Farquharson*
Cowan: *Colquhoun, MacDougall*
***†Cranston**
***Crawford:** *Lindsay*
Crerar: *Mackintosh*
Crombie: *MacDonald*
Crookshanks: *Stewart of Atholl*
†Currie (also MacBurie, MacMurrich, MacVurrich, MacVurie, and in some cases MacMordoch/ MacMurdoch): *MacDonald of Clanranald, Macpherson*

D

†Dallas, Doles: *Mackintosh*
***†Dalzell, Dalziel**
†Darroch: *MacDonald*
Davie, Davis, Davison: *Davidson*
Dawson: *Davidson, also general*
Denoon: *Campbell*
†Deuchar: *Lindsay*
Dewar: *MacNab, Menzies*
Dingwall: *Munro, Ross*
Dis, Dyce: *Skene*
Dochart: *MacGregor*
Doig: *Drummond*
Donachie: *Robertson*
Donald, Donaldson: *MacDonald*
Donleavy: *Buchanan*
Dougall: *MacDougall*
Dove: *Buchanan*
Dow: *Buchanan, Davidson, also general*
Dowall: *MacDougall*
†Drysdale: *Douglas*
Duff: *MacDuff*
Duffie, Duffy: *MacFie*
Duilach, Dullach: *Stewart*
***†Dunbar**
***†Duncan:** *Robertson*
Dunnachie: *Robertson*

E

Edie: *Gordon*
Elder: *Mackintosh*
Esson: *Mackintosh*
Ewan, Ewen, Ewing: *MacEwen, MacLachlan*

F

Fair: *Ross*
Farquhar: *Farquharson*
Federith: *Sutherland*
Fergus: *Ferguson*
Ferries: *Ferguson*
Ferson: *Macpherson*
Fife, Fyfe: *MacDuff*
Findlater: *Ogilvy*

Findlay, Findlayson, Finlay: *Farquharson*
†Fleming
†Fletcher: *Fletcher, MacGregor*
Fordyce: *Forbes*
*†Forsyth
Foulis: *Munro*
France: *Stewart*
Fresell, Frizell: *Fraser*
Frew: *Fraser*
†Fullarton, Fullerton: *Stewart*

G

*†Galbraith: *MacDonald, MacFarlane*
Gallie: *Gunn*
Garrow: *Stewart*
Garvie: *Maclean*
Gaunson: *Gunn*
Geddes: *Gordon*
Georgeson: *Gunn*
Gibb: *Buchanan*
†Gibson: *Buchanan*
Gilbert, Gilbertson: *Buchanan*
Gilbride: *MacDonald*
Gilchrist: *MacLachlan, Ogilvy*
Gilfillan: *MacNab*
Gillanders: *Ross*
Gillespie: *Macpherson*
*Gillies: *Macpherson*
Gilmore: *Morrison*
Gilroy: *Grant, MacGillivray*
Glen, Glennie: *Mackintosh*
Gorrie: *MacDonald*
*Gow: *MacDonald, Macpherson*
Gowrie: *MacDonald, also of territorial origin*
†Gray: *Stewart of Atholl, Sutherland, also general*
Gregor, Gregorson, Gregory: *MacGregor*
Greig: *MacGregor*
Greusach: *Farquharson*
Grier, Grierson: *MacGregor*

H

*†Haig
Hallyard: *Skene*
Hanna: *Hannay*
Hardie, Hardy: *Farquharson, Mackintosh*
Harper, Harperson: *Buchanan*
Harris: *Campbell, also general*
Hawes, Haws, Hawson: *Campbell*
Hawthorn: *MacDonald*
†Henderson
Hendrie, Hendry: *Henderson, MacNaughten*
Hewison: *MacDonald*
*†Home
†Houston: *MacDonald*
Howison: *MacDonald*
Hughson: *MacDonald*
*†Hunter

Huntly: *Gordon*
Hutcheson, Hutchinson, Hutchison: *MacDonald*

I

Inches: *Robertson*
*†Inglis
Innie: *Innes*
*†Irvine

J

Jameson, Jamieson: *Gunn, Stewart of Bute, also general*
*†Jardine
Johnson (see also MacIan): *Gunn, MacDonald*
*†Johnston(e)

K

Kay: *Davidson*
Kean: *MacIan, MacDonald, Gunn*
*Keith: *Macpherson, Sutherland*
Kellie, Kelly: *MacDonald, also general*
Kendrick: *Henderson, MacNaughten*
Kenneth, Kennethson: *Mackenzie*
*†Kilgour
†Kilpatrick: *Colquhoun*
King: *MacGregor*
Kinnell: *MacDonald*
*Kinnieson: *MacFarlane*
†Kirkpatrick (Galloway), Kirkpatrick: *Colquhoun*

L

Lachlan: *MacLachlan*
Lamb, Lambie, Lammie: *Lamont, also general*
Lammond: *Lamont*
Landers: *Lamont, also general*
Lang: *Leslie, MacDonald, also general*
*†Lauder
Laurence: *MacLaren*
Law: *MacLaren*
Lawrie: *MacLaren*
Lean: *Maclean*
†Leckie, Lecky: *MacGregor*
Leech, Leitch, *see Bethune*
Lees: *MacPherson, also general*
*Lennie, Lenny: *Buchanan*
*Lennox: *MacFarlane: Stewart*
Lewis: *Macleod of Lewis, also general*
Limond, Limont: *Lamont*
Lobban: *Logan*
Loudoun: *Campbell (Ayrshire)*
Love: *MacKinnon*
Low: *MacLaren*
Lucas: *Lamont*
*Lumsden: *Forbes*
†Lyall: *Sinclair*
†Lyon: *Farquharson, Lamont*

M

MacAdam: *MacGregor*
†MacAdie (Ayrshire and South West), MacAdie: *Munro (Note: Fergusons of Balmachruchie in Strathardle, Atholl, were known as MacAdie)*
MacAindra: *MacFarlane*
Macaldonich: *Buchanan*
Macalduie: *Lamont*
MacAllan: *MacDonald of Clanranald, MacFarlane*
Macandeoir: *Buchanan, MacNab, Menzies*
MacAndrew, *see Anderson*
MacAngus: *MacInnes*
Macara: *MacGregor, MacRae*
Macaree: *MacGregor*
MacAskill, *see MacCaskill*
MacAuslan, MacAusland: *Buchanan*
*MacAulay: *Macleod of Lewis*
MacAy: *Mackintosh*
MacBaxter: *Macmillan*
*Macbeath, Macbeth: *MacBean, MacDonald, Maclean*
MacBeolain: *Mackenzie (Note: O'Beolains were progenitors of the earls of Ross)*
MacBrayne: *MacNaughten*
MacBride: *MacDonald*
MacBrieve: *Morrison*
MacBurie, *see Currie*
MacCaa: *MacFarlane*
MacCaig: *Farquharson, Macleod*
*MacCainsh: *MacInnes*
MacCaishe: *MacDonald*
*MacCall: *MacColl, MacDonald*
*MacCallum: *Malcolm*
MacCalman, MacCalmont, MacCammon, MacCammond: *Buchanan*
MacCamie: *Stewart of Bute*
MacCardney: *Farquharson, Mackintosh*
MacCartair, MacCarter: *MacArthur*
MacCash: *MacDonald*
*MacCaskill: *Macleod of Lewis*
MacCaul: *MacDonald*
MacCause (sometimes also MacTavish): *MacFarlane*
MacCaw: *MacFarlane, Stewart of Bute*
MacCay: *Mackay*
MacCeallaich: *MacDonald*
MacChlerich, MacChlery: *Cameron, Clan Chattan, Macpherson*
MacChoiter: *MacGregor*
MacChruiter: *Buchanan*
MacCloy: *Stewart of Bute*
MacClure: *Macleod*

MacClymont: *Lamont*
MacCodrum: *MacDonald*
*MacColl, †MacColl (South West Scotland): *MacDonald*
MacColman: *Buchanan*
MacComas: *Gunn*
MacCombe, MacCombie: *MacThomas, Mackintosh*
MacCombich: *Stewart of Appin*
MacConacher: *MacDougall*
MacConachie: *MacGregor, Robertson*
MacConchy: *Mackintosh*
MacCondy: *MacFarlane*
MacConnach: *Mackenzie*
MacConnechy: *Campbell, Robertson*
MacConnell: *MacDonald*
MacCooish: *MacDonald*
MacCook: *MacDonald*
MacCorkill, MacCorkle: *MacCorquodale, Gunn*
MacCorkindale: *MacCorquodale, Macleod*
MacCormack, MacCormick: *Buchanan, MacLaine of Lochbuie*
*†MacCorquodale
MacCorrie, MacCorry: *Macquarrie*
MacCoull: *MacDougall*
MacCowan: *Colquhoun, MacDougall*
†MacCracken (also MacRankine): *Maclean (if originally from Mull)*
*MacCrae, MacCrea: *MacRae*
MacCrain: *MacDonald*
MacCraw: *MacRae*
MacCreath: *MacRae*
MacCrie: *Mackay, MacRae*
MacCrimmon: *Macleod*
MacCrowther: *MacGregor*
MacCuag: *MacDonald*
MacCuaig: *Farquharson, Macleod*
MacCuish: *MacDonald*
MacCuithen: *MacDonald*
†MacCulloch (Galloway and Easter Ross), MacCulloch: *MacDonald,*
MacDougall, Munro, Ross
MacCunn: *MacQueen*
MacCutcheon: *MacDonald*
Macdade, Macdaid: *Davidson*
MacDaniell: *MacDonald*
MacDavid: *Davidson*
MacDermid: *Campbell of Argyll*
*MacDiarmid: *Campbell of Argyll*
MacDonachie: *Robertson*
Macdonleavy: *Buchanan*
†MacDowall, MacDowell: *MacDougall*
Macdrain: *MacDonald*
MacDuffie: *MacFie*

MacDulothe: *MacDougall*
MacEachan: *MacDonald of Clanranald*
MacEachern: *MacDonald*
MacEaracher: *Farquharson*
MacElfrish: *MacDonald*
MacElheran: *MacDonald*
MacEoin: *MacFarlane*
Maceol: *MacNaughten*
MacErracher: *Farquharson, MacFarlane*
***MacEwan, MacEwen:** *MacLachlan*
***MacFadyen, MacFadzean:** *MacLaine of Lochbuie*
MacFall: *Clan Chattan, Mackintosh*
MacFarquhar: *Farquharson*
MacFater: *MacLaren*
MacFeat: *MacLaren*
MacFergus: *Ferguson*
MacGaw: *MacFarlane*
MacGeachie, MacGeachin: *MacDonald of Clanranald*
MacGeoch: *MacFarlane*
†Macghee, Macghie: *Mackay*
MacGibbon: *Buchanan, Campbell of Argyll, Graham of Menteith*
MacGilbert: *Buchanan*
MacGilchrist: *MacLachlan, Ogilvy*
***†MacGill**
MacGilledow: *Lamont*
MacGillegowie: *Lamont*
MacGillivantic: *MacDonell of Keppoch*
MacGillonie: *Cameron*
MacGilp: *MacDonell of Keppoch*
MacGilroy: *Grant, MacGillivray*
MacGilvernock: *Graham of Menteith*
Macglashan: *Stewart of Atholl, Mackintosh*
Macglasrich: *MacIver, MacDonell of Keppoch*
MacGorrie, MacGorry: *MacDonald, MacQuarrie*
***MacGowan:** *MacDonald, Macpherson*
MacGreusich: *Buchanan, MacFarlane*
Macgrewar: *Drummond, MacGregor*
Macgrime: *Graham of Menteith*
MacGrory: *MacLaren*
MacGrowther, MacGruther: *Drummond, MacGregor*
MacGruder: *MacGregor*
MacGruer: *Fraser*
MacGuaran: *MacQuarrie*
MacGuffie: *MacPhie*
MacGugan: *MacDougall, MacNeill*
MacGuire: *MacQuarrie, also general*

MacHaffie: *MacPhie*
***MacHardy:** *Farquharson, Mackintosh*
MacHarold: *Macleod*
MacHay: *Mackintosh*
MacHendrie, MacHendry: *Henderson, MacNaughten*
MacHenry: *MacDonald*
MacHowell: *Macdougal*
MacHugh: *MacDonald*
MacHutchen, MacHutcheon: *MacDonald*
***MacIan:** *MacDonald, Gunn*
Macildowie: *Cameron, also general*
Macilleriach, Macilreach, Macilriach: *MacDonald*
Macilrevie: *MacDonald*
Macilroy: *Grant, MacGillivray*
Macilvain: *MacBean*
Macilvora: *MacLaine of Lochbuie*
Macilvride: *MacDonald*
Macilwham, Macilwhom: *Lamont*
Macilwraith: *MacDonald*
Macilzegowie: *Lamont*
Macimmey: *Fraser*
Macinally: *Buchanan*
Macindeor: *Buchanan, MacNab, Menzie*
Macindoe: *Buchanan*
***†MacInroy**
Macinstalker: *MacFarlane*
MacIsaac: *Campbell, MacDonald of Clanranald*
MacJames: *MacFarlane*
MacKail: *Cameron*
MacKames: *Gunn*
MacKeachan: *MacDonald of Clanranald*
MacKeamish: *Gunn*
MacKechnie: *MacDonald of Clanranald*
***MacKean:** *MacDonald (MacIan of Ardnamurchan and Glencoe), Gunn*
Mackee: *Mackay, Mackie (Galloway)*
Mackeggie: *Mackintosh*
MacKeith: *Keith, Macpherson*
MacKellachie, MacKellaig: *MacDonald*
***MacKellar:** *Campbell*
MacKelloch: *MacDonald*
MacKemmie: *Fraser*
***MacKendrick, MacKenrick:** *MacNaughten*
MacKeochan: *MacDonald of Clanranald*
MacKerchar, MacKerracher: *Farquharson*
MacKerlich: *Mackenzie, Campbell*
MacKerras: *Ferguson*

***†MacKerrell of Hillhouse**
MacKersey: *Ferguson*
Mackessock: *Campbell, MacDonald of Clanranald*
MacKichan: *MacDonald of Clanranald, MacDougall*
†Mackie: *Mackay*
MacKillican: *Mackintosh*
***MacKillop:** *MacDonell of Keppoch*
MacKim, MacKimmie: *Fraser*
Mackindlay (see also Mackinlay): *Farquharson*
***†Mackinlay:** *Buchanan, Farquharson, MacFarlane, Stewart*
MacKinnell: *MacDonald*
Mackinney, Mackinning: *Mackinnon*
***†MacKirdy:** *Stewart of Bute*
MacKissock: *Campbell, MacDonald of Clanranald*
Macknight: *MacNaughten*
Maclae: *Stewart of Appin*
***Maclagan:** *Robertson*
MacLairish: *MacDonald*
MacLamond: *Lamont*
MacLardie, MacLardy: *MacDonald*
MacLarty: *MacDonald*
MacLaverty: *MacDonald*
Maclay, Macleay: *Buchanan, Stewart of Appin, also (in Appin) Livingstone*
Maclehose: *Campbell of Argyll*
***Macleish:** *Macpherson*
MacLeister: *MacGregor, Fletcher*
***†MacLellan:** *MacDonald*
MacLergain: *Maclean*
Maclerie: *Cameron, Mackintosh, Macpherson*
MacLeverty: *MacDonald*
MacLewis: *Macleod, Stewart of Bute*
***†MacLintock**
MacLise: *Macpherson*
MacLiver: *MacGregor*
MacLucas: *Lamont, MacDougall*
MacLugash: *MacDougall*
MacLulich: *MacDougall, Munro, Ross*
Maclure: *Macleod*
MacLymont: *Lamont*
MacMartin: *Cameron*
MacMaster: *Buchanan, MacInnes*
MacMath: *Matheson*
MacMaurice: *Buchanan*
MacMenzies: *Menzies*
MacMichael: *Stewart*
MacMinn: *Menzies*
MacMonies: *Menzies*
MacMordoch (see also Currie): *MacDonald, Macpherson*
MacMorran: *Mackinnon*

MacMunn: *Stewart of Bute*
MacMurchie: *Buchanan, MacDonald, Mackenzie*
MacMurdo: *MacDonald, Macpherson*
MacMurray: *Murray*
MacMurrich (see also Currie): *MacDonald of Clanranald, Macpherson*
MacMutrie: *Stewart of Bute*
MacNair, MacNayer: *MacFarlane, MacNaughten*
MacNamell: *MacDougall*
MacNee: *MacGregor*
MacNeilage: *MacNeill*
†MacNeish: *MacGregor*
MacNelly: *MacNeill*
MacNeur: *MacFarlane*
***MacNicol:** *Macleod of Lewis*
MacNider: *MacFarlane*
MacNie: *MacGregor*
†MacNish: *MacGregor*
MacNiter: *MacFarlane*
MacNiven: *Comyn, Mackintosh, MacNaughten*
MacNuir: *MacNaughten*
MacNuyer: *Buchanan, MacFarlane, MacNaughten*
MacOmie: *Mackintosh*
MacOmish: *Gunn*
MacOnie: *Cameron*
Macoul, Macowl: *MacDougall*
MacOurlic: *Kennedy (Highland line)*
MacOwen: *Campbell of Argyll*
MacPatrick: *Lamont, Maclaren*
MacPeter, MacPetrie: *MacGregor*
MacPhadden (see also MacFadyen): *MacLaine of Lochbuie*
***MacPhail:** *Cameron, Clan Chattan, Mackintosh, Mackay*
†MacPhater: *Maclaren*
MacPhedran: *Campbell, MacAulay*
MacPhilip: *MacDonell of Keppoch*
MacPhorich: *Lamont*
MacPhun: *Campbell, Matheson*
Macquaire: *MacQuarrie*
Macquey: *Mackay*
Macquhirr: *MacQuarrie*
MacQuistan: *MacDonald*
Macquoid: *Mackay*
Macra: *MacRae*
Macraild: *Macleod*
MacRaith: *MacDonald, MacRae*
MacRankin(e) (see also MacCracken): *Maclean*
MacRath: *MacRae*
MacRitchie: *Mackintosh*
MacRob, MacRobb: *Gunn, Innes, MacFarlane, Robertson*
MacRobbie: *Drummond, Robertson*

MacRobert: *Robertson*
*MacRorie, MacRurie: *MacDonald*
MacRuer: *MacDonald*
MacShannachan: *MacDonald*
MacShimes, MacShimmie: *Fraser of Lovat*
MacSimon: *Fraser of Lovat*
MacSorley: *Cameron, Lamont, Macdonald*
*MacSporran: *MacDonald*
MacSuain, MacSween: *MacQueen*
MacSwan: *MacDonald, MacQueen*
MacSymon: *Fraser of Lovat*
*MacTaggart: *Ross*
MacTary: *Innes*
MacTause: *MacTavish, Campbell of Argyll*
*†MacTavish (see also MacCause): *Campbell of Argyll*
MacTear: *MacIntyre; Ross*
*†MacThomas: *Campbell of Argyll, Mackintosh*
MacTier, MacTire: *MacIntyre, Ross*
MacUlric: *Kennedy (Highland line)*
MacUre: *MacIver, Campbell of Argyll*
Macvail: *Cameron, Mackay, Mackintosh, Macpherson*
MacVanish: *Mackenzie*
MacVarish: *MacDonald of Clanranald*
MacVeagh (see also Macbeth): *MacDonald, Maclean*
MacVean: *MacBean*
MacVey (see also Macbeth): *MacDonald, Maclean*
MacVicar: *Campbell, MacNaughten*
MacVinish: *Mackenzie*
MacVurie (see also Currie): *MacDonald of Clanranald*
MacVurrich (see also Currie): *MacDonald of Clanranald, Macpherson*
MacWalrick: *Kennedy (Highland line)*
MacWalter: *MacFarlane*
MacWattie: *Buchanan*
MacWhannell: *MacDonald*
MacWhirr: *MacQuarrie*
*†MacWhirter: *Buchanan*
*†MacWilliam: *Gunn, MacFarlane*
Malcolmson: *MacCallum, Macleod, Malcolm*
Malloch: *MacGregor*
Mann: *Gunn*
Manson: *Gunn, also general*
Marnoch: *Innes*

Marr: *Gordon, Mar*
†Marshall: *Keith*
Martin: *Cameron, MacDonald*
Masterton: *Buchanan*
Mathie: *Matheson*
*†Maxwell
May: *MacDonald*
Means: *Menzies*
Meikleham: *Lamont*
Mein, Meine: *Menzies*
*†Melville
Melvin: *Macbeth*
Mengues: *Menzies*
Mennie: *Menzies*
Menteith: *Graham of Menteith, Stewart*
Meyners: *Menzies*
Michie: *Forbes*
*Middleton: *Innes*
Miller: *MacFarlane, also general*
*Milne: *Innes, Ogilvy*
Minn, Minnus: *Menzies*
*†Mitchell: *Innes, also general*
*†Moffat
†Moir: *Gordon, also general*
Monach: *MacFarlane*
Monzie: *Menzies*
Moray: *Murray*
More: *Leslie, also general*
Morgan: *Mackay, also general*
*Mowat: *Sutherland*
*†Muir
Munn: *Stewart of Bute*
Murchie, Murchison: *Buchanan. MacDonald, Mackenzie*
Murdoch, Murdochson: *MacDonald, Macpherson*

N

*Napier: *MacFarlane*
Neal, Neil, Neill: *MacNeill*
Neilson: *Mackay, MacNeill*
Nelson: *Gunn, also general*
*Nicholson, Nicoll, Nicolson: *MacNicol (Note: Lowland Nicholsons follow Nicolson of Lasswade)*
*†Nisbet
Nish: *MacGregor (see also MacNeish)*
Niven: *Comyn, Mackintosh, MacNaughten*
Noble: *Mackintosh*
Norie: *MacDonald*
Norman: *Macleod, Sutherland, also general*

O

*†Oliphant: *Skene, Sutherland*
*†Oliver: *Fraser (in Borders)*

P

Parlane: *MacFarlane*
Paterson: *Maclaren, also general*
Patrick: *Lamont*

Paul: *Cameron, Mackay, Mackintosh*
Peter: *MacGregor*
Philipson: *MacDonell of Keppoch*
†Pitullich: *MacDonald (Note: Patillo in Angus has no connection with MacDonald)*
Polson: *Mackay*
Purcell: *MacDonald*

R

Rae: *MacRae*
*†Raeburn
*Rankin, Rankine: *Maclean*
*Rattray: *Murray*
Reid: *Robertson*
Reidfurd: *Innes*
Reoch, Riach: *Farquharson, MacDonald*
Revie: *MacDonald*
Risk: *Buchanan*
Ritchie: *Mackintosh*
Robb: *MacFarlane*
Robinson, Robison, Robson: *Gunn, also general*
*†Rollo
Ronald, Ronaldson: *MacDonell of Keppoch*
Rorison: *MacDonald*
Roy: *Robertson, also general*
Ruskin: *Buchanan, also general*
*†Russell
*†Ruthven

S

†Sanderson: *MacDonell of Glengarry*
Sandison: *Gunn*
Scobie: *Mackay*
*†Seaton, Seton
Shannon: *MacDonald*
Sim, Sime, Simon: *Fraser of Lovat*
Simpson, Simson: *Fraser of Lovat, also general*
Small: *Murray, also general*
*†Smith: *Clan Chattan, also general*
Sorley: *Cameron, Lamont, MacDonald*
†Spalding:
*†Spence, Spens: *MacDuff*
Spittal, Spittel: *Buchanan*
Sporran: *MacDonald*
Stalker: *MacFarlane*
Stark: *Robertson*
Strachan: *Mar*
*†Sturrock
Swan: *MacQueen*
Swanson: *Gunn*
Syme, Symon: *Fraser of Lovat*

T

Taggart: *Ross*
Tarrill: *Mackintosh*

Tawesson: *MacTavish, Campbell of Argyll*
Tawse: *MacTavish, Farquharson*
*Taylor: *Cameron, also general*
Thomas: *MacTavish, Campbell of Argyll, also general*
Thomason: *Campbell of Argyll, MacFarlane*
*Thomson: *MacTavish, also general*
*Thompson: *MacTavish, Campbell of Argyll, also general*
Todd: *Gordon, MacTavish*
Tonnochy: *Robertson*
Tosh, Toshach: *Mackintosh*
Tough: *Mar*
Toward, Towart: *Lamont*
Train: *MacDonald*
Turner: *Lamont, also general*
Tweedie: *Fraser (in the Borders)*
Tyre: *MacIntyre*

U

Ure: *MacIver, Campbell of Argyll*

V

†Vass (Galloway), Vass, Wass: *Munro, Ross*

W

Wallis: *Wallace*
Walters: *Forbes, also general*
*Watson: *Buchanan, also general*
Watt: *Buchanan*
Weaver: *MacFarlane*
*†Weir: *Buchanan, MacFarlane, MacNaughten*
*†Wemyss: *MacDuff*
Whannell: *MacDonald*
White, Whyte: *Lamont, MacGregor, also general*
Wilkinson: *MacDonald, also general*
Will: *Gunn*
Williamson: *Gunn, Mackay*
*†Wilson: *Gunn, also general*
*†Wotherspoon
Wright: *MacIntyre, also general*
Wylie: *Gunn, MacFarlane*

Y

Yuill, Yuille, Yule: *Buchanan*

**LORDSHIP OF
THE ISLES**

**EARLDOM OF
SUTHERLAND**

Habost
Morrison

M A C L E O D

Stornoway

LEWES

MACLEOD

M A C L E O D
Assynt
Ardreck

Macaulay

S U T H E

Loch
105
Seaforth

Coigach

Harris

MACLEOD

Ullapool

MACLEOD

Rodel

MACDONELL
Dun Donell

R O

Bernera

Loch
Maree

MacCodrum

Gairloch
MACLEOD

Strath Bran

Duntulm

M A C K E N Z

U I S T

MacCrimmon

Mac
Queen

M
A
C
D
O
N
A
L
D

Trotternish

CH

Glen Carron

Nicolson

MACLEOD

Dunvegan

F R A

CHISHOLM

Erchless

G R A

M
A
C
D
O
N
A
L
D

C
L
A
N
R
A
N
A
L
D

MACLEOD

Applecross
Applecross
Abbey

MACLEOD

Portree

Brochel Cas.

Murchison

Kintail

Comar

Glen Affric

MACLEOD
MACLEOD

Raasay

Lochalsh
MACDONELL

Matheson
Strome
Cas.
Eilean Donan
Maclennan

Glenelg

Glen Moriston

Ft. Augustus

ISLE
OF
SKYE

M
A
C
K
I
N
N
O
N

Scalpay
Donakin Cas.

MacRae

Strath

Strathairdd

M
A
C
D
O
N
A
L
D

MacAskill

Glenelg
MACLEOD

55

M A C D O N E L L

Invergarry
Castle

Glenga

Dunscaith

Garmoran

Blar-na-Leine
1544

Boisdale

Armadale

S
l
e
a
t

MacMartin

C
L
A
N

R
A
N
A
L
D

Kisimul

Rum

Mallaig

C
L
A
N

L. Arkaig
Aohnacarry

RANALD

Glenfinnan

C
A
M
E
R
O
N

Loch

Keppoch
MACDON

MacEachan

R A N A L D

Loch Eil

Torcastle

28

Ardgour

Ellean Tigram
Castle

Inverlochy Cas.
Ft. William
Ben Nevis

Ardnamurchan
Wingarry

M A C I A I N

Ardgour Ho.

Cape Wrath

S U T H

Reay Forest

St A
Strath

EARLDOM OF
CAITHNESS

EARLDOM OF
FIFE

PROVINCE OF
MORAY

EARLDOM OF
BUCHAN

EARLDOM OF
MAR

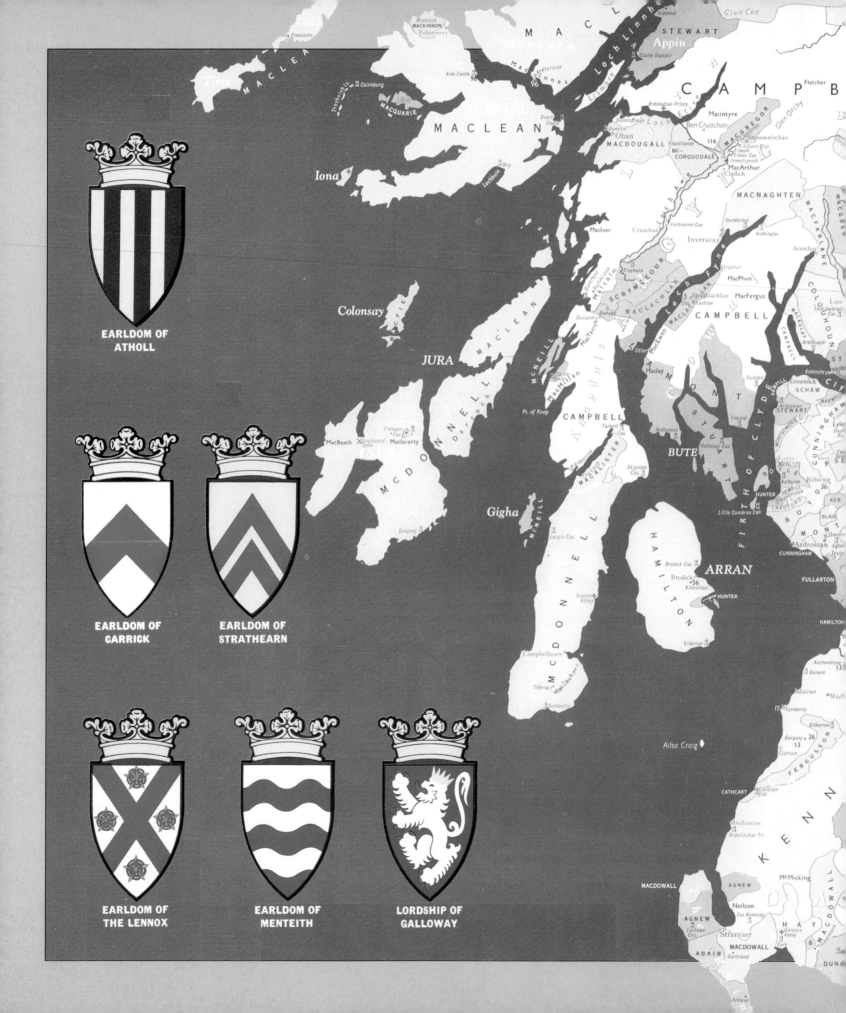

EARLDOM OF
ATHOLL

EARLDOM OF
CARRICK

EARLDOM OF
STRATHEARN

EARLDOM OF
THE LENNOX

EARLDOM OF
MENTEITH

LORDSHIP OF
GALLOWAY

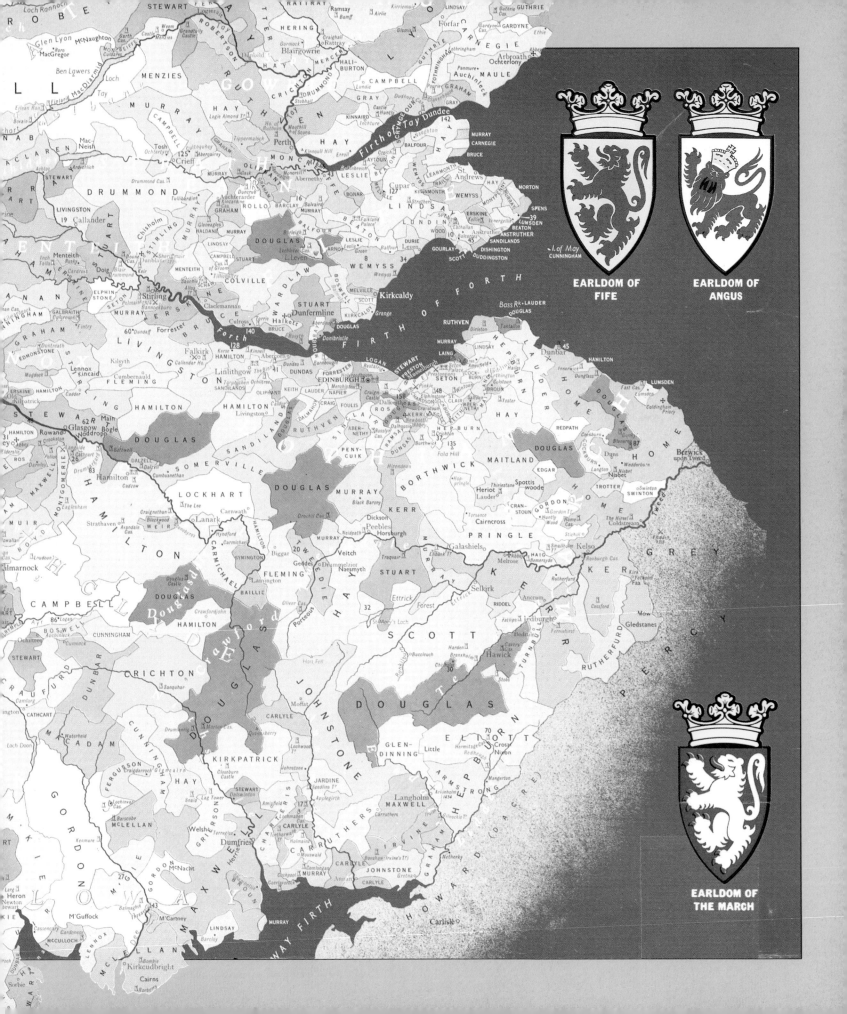

EARLDOM OF FIFE

EARLDOM OF ANGUS

EARLDOM OF THE MARCH

ABERCROMBY

Branches: *Abercromby of Birkenbog, Abercromby of Menstrie*

Tartan: *Abercromby*

Mottos: *Petit alta (Latin: He seeks the heights); Mercie is my desire*

William of Abercromby in Fife did homage to King Edward I of England in 1296. His line became extinct in the middle of the seventeenth century, its place being taken by that of Abercromby of Birkenbog, Banffshire.

Alexander Abercromby was grand falconer in Scotland to King Charles I. His eldest son, Alexander, was created 1st Baronet of Birkenbog by Charles I in 1636, but he was so active a Covenanter that, after the Battle of Auldearn in 1645, the Marquis of Montrose retaliated by billeting himself and some of his troops at Birkenbog.

Lieut-General Sir Ralph Abercromby (1734-1801), a descendant of the Birkenbog line, was born in Menstrie, near Tullibody. He took his troops to the Middle East, landing with them at Aboukir, and died of wounds received while personally leading them in an attack on the French forces at Alexandria. As a reward for her husband's bravery, his wife was created Baroness Abercromby of Aboukir and Tullibody.

ABERCROMBY

AGNEW OF LOCHNAW

AGNEW

Branch: *Agnew of Lochnaw*

Tartan: *Agnew*

Motto: *Consilio non impetu (Latin: By thought not violence)*

The name comes from the Barony d'Agneaux in Normandy, and in 1363 King David II appointed the Agnews of Lochnaw hereditary sheriffs of Galloway.

AGNEW

Andrew Agnew was appointed Constable of Lochnaw Castle in 1426 and Sheriff of Wigtown in 1451. Patrick Agnew (1616-1661), Member of Parliament for Wigtownshire for ten years, was created a baronet in 1629. Lieut-General Sir Andrew Agnew (1687-1771), 5th Baronet of Lochnaw and 12th and last hereditary Sheriff, was the eldest of 21 children. He eloped with the daughter of a fellow officer who was also his cousin, and they had eighteen children, his wife surviving him to die at the age of 87. As commander of a brigade of Scots fusiliers in 1746, he held Blair Castle against the Jacobite forces.

ALLISON

AL(L)ISON

Tartan: *Allison*

Patrick Alisonne of Berwick did homage to King Edward I of England in 1296. The name, and the family, may derive from the MacAlisters of Loup, some of whom escaped to Avondale, Lanarkshire, during the Scottish War of Independence in the fourteenth century, and may later have changed their name to Alison.

ANDERSON (also MACANDREW)

Branches: *Anderson of Candacraig (Strathdon), Anderson of Dowhill, Anderson of Wester Ardbreck*

Tartan: *Anderson (MacAndrew)*

Motto: *Stand sure*

The name means both 'son of Andrew' and 'servant of St Andrew', patron saint of Scotland. The Andersons of Dowhill go back at least to 1540. 'Little' John MacAndrew was a noted bowman, who in 1670 was on the receiving end of a cattle-rustling expedition in Badenoch on the part of men of Lochaber. The Lochaber men were pursued, hunted down, and killed, bar one man who got home to tell the tale.

ANDERSON (MACANDREW)

Professor John Anderson (1726-96) invented a field gun which he offered to the British Government, who refused it, so he presented the design to the French. He left instructions in his will for a university for working men and for women to be founded in Glasgow. Though he left no money, his wish was followed, and the original Anderson's Institution is now Strathclyde University.

'Professor' John Henry Anderson (1815-74) was not a professor at all, but a stage magician, one of whose tricks misfired in 1856, causing the complete destruction by fire of Covent Garden Theatre in London.

John Anderson (1882-1958), 1st Viscount Waverley, civil servant, politician, and statesman, was Governor of Bengal 1932-7, Home Secretary 1939-40, and Chancellor of the Exchequer 1943-5.

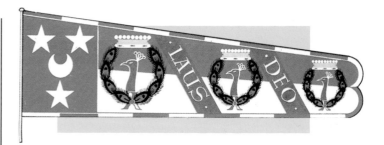

VISCOUNT OF   ARBUTHNOTT

ARBUTHNOTT

Tartan: *Arbuthnott*

Motto: *Laus deo (Latin: Praise to God)*

In about 1200 Hugo de Swinton received from Walter Olifard the Barony of Aberbothenoth in Kincardine-shire, which he had inherited from the crusader, Osbert Olifard, who had died abroad.

Robert Arbuthnott of Arbuthnott (*d.* 1655) was made Viscount Arbuthnott when he was in his early twenties, and appointed a Privy Councillor in 1649.

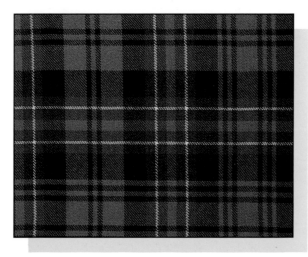

ARBUTHNOTT

Dr John Arbuthnot (1667-1735), physician to Queen Anne and friend of the greatest writers of the time, Jonathan Swift and Alexander Pope, was born in the parish, son of an episcopal clergyman.

ARMSTRONG OF   MANGERTON

ARMSTRONG

Branch: *Armstrong of Gilnockie*

Tartan: *Armstrong*

Motto: *Invictus maneo (Latin: I remain unconquered)*

The original Scottish Armstrongs came from Cumberland, and in 1376 settled in Mangerton, Liddesdale, where they multiplied and extended their power, being able in 1528, it is said, to put three thousand horsemen into the field.

John Armstrong of Gilnockie (brother of the Laird of Mangerton) was a notorious trouble-maker who, in about 1529, was summoned, persuaded, or took it arrogantly upon his own head, to parade before King James V near Hawick, with 36 of his horsemen. They were all seized and hanged on trees nearby, as the ballad *Johnnie Armstrong* relates. Another ballad hero is 'Kinmont Willie', William Armstrong of Kinmont, Dumfriesshire, a Border reiver (gangster) who was unfairly captured by the English while a truce was in force, and imprisoned in Carlisle Castle. After diplomatic

ARMSTRONG

BAILLIE

BAILLIE OF POLKEMMET

negotiations for his release broke down, he was rescued by force by Sir Walter Scott of Buccleuch (1565-1611), much to the fury of Queen Elizabeth, who, according to a contemporary historian, 'stormed not a little'.

Archie Armstrong (*d.* 1672) was court jester to both King James VI (and I) and Charles I, but was dismissed in 1637 for calling Archbishop Laud a fool in public. He had, however, amassed so much money that he was able to lend it out, on extortionate terms, and became even richer.

Neil Armstrong (*b.* 1930), an American of Scottish descent, was the first man to walk on the moon. He is reported to have carried with him a piece of Armstrong tartan.

BAILLIE OF LAMINGTON

BAILLIE

Branches: *Baillie of Dochfour, Baillie of Dunain, Baillie of Jerviswood, Baillie of Lamington, Baillie of Polkemmet*

Tartans: *Baillie, Baillie of Polkemmet (red), Baillie of Polkemmet (hunting)*

Mottos: *Quid clarius astris (Latin: What is brighter than the stars); (Polkemmet) In caligine lucet (Latin: It shines in the darkness); (Jerviswood and Mellerstain) Major virtus quam splendor (Latin: Virtue is greater than splendour)*

William de Baliol acquired by marriage the property of Lamington in Lanarkshire at the beginning of the fourteenth century, his son, Sir William Baillie, being granted a charter confirming the ownership in 1358. William Baillie's eldest grandson, Alexander, had to flee the country after he and his two next brothers had beaten their tutor, who died of his injuries, but Alexander then served in the army and was rewarded with the lands of Dunain and Dochfour, and was appointed Constable of Inverness. The fourth brother, William, married in 1492 a daughter of Sir Patrick Hume of Polwarth, and from their fourth son descended the Baillies of Jerviswood.

George Baillie of St John's Kirk (a branch of the Lamington Baillies) purchased the lands of Jerviswood, Lanarkshire, in 1636, and the estate of Mellerstain, Berwickshire, in 1643. His son, Robert Baillie of Jerviswood (1632-84), was the civil and religious reformer executed in horrific manner for his outspokenness. Robert's son, George Baillie of Jerviswood and Mellerstain (1664-1738), married his childhood sweetheart Lady Grisell Hume (1665-1746) in 1691. They began the building of Mellerstain House and are the ancestors of the present earls of Haddington.

The Baillies of Polkemmet are descended from the Jerviswood branch. William Baillie of Polkemmet (d. 1816) was appointed a judge of the Court of Session in 1793 with the title of Lord Polkemmet. Col. James Baillie of Dochfour (d. 1931) married Nellie Lisa (1878-1962), Baroness Burton, in 1894, the title of Lord Burton coming into the Baillie family through their descendants.

BAIRD

Branch:	*Baird of Auchmeddan*
Tartan:	*Baird*
Motto:	*Dominus fecit (Latin: The Lord made)*

King William I (the Lion) granted lands to a Baird at the end of the twelfth century for saving him from the attentions of a wild boar, and King Robert I (the Bruce), at the beginning of the fourteenth century, awarded the Barony of Cambusnethan to Robert Baird, descendants of whose family came to Auchmeddan in Aberdeenshire.

There was an ancient prophecy that when the eagles should stop nesting on the crags of Auchmeddan, the

BAIRD

estate would pass out of the family. This happened when the lands were bought by the 3rd Earl of Aberdeen, but the eagles returned when his son married the sister of General Sir David Baird (1757-1829). Baird was a captain in India in the recently raised 73rd Regiment when in 1780 his company was destroyed by Hyder Ali, who kept Baird and the only two other survivors in chains for four years before they were released. He commanded the Black Watch and the Cameron Highlanders at Corunna in 1809, where he lost an arm.

John Logie Baird (1888-1946), the first person successfully to demonstrate television, of which he is rightly claimed to be the inventor, was born in Helensburgh, son of a minister.

BARCLAY

Branches:	*Barclay of Ardrossan, Barclay of Collairnie, Barclay of Mathers, Barclay of Pierston, Barclay of Tolly, Barclay of Towie, Barclay of Urie*
Tartans:	*Barclay (dress), Barclay (hunting)*
Motto:	*Aut agere aut mori (Latin: To do or die)*

The original Berkeleys came to England with William the Conqueror. One of them is said to have come to Scotland in 1069 and to have had three sons, founders of the branches of Ardrossan, Gartly, and Towie-Barclay.

In 1165 Sir Walter Barclay of Gartly became Chamberlain of Scotland under King William I (the

BARCLAY OF   TOWIE

Lion), but the male Gartly line terminated in 1456. William Barclay (1547-1608), the lawyer and political philosopher, was most likely of the Collairnie branch.

Robert Barclay (1648-90), of the Urie branch, was a prominent and eloquent Quaker, who was several times imprisoned for his beliefs, and in 1672 felt moved to parade through the streets of Aberdeen clothed in sackcloth. Captain Robert Barclay-Allardyce of Urie (1779-1854) was a soldier and sportsman who, at Newmarket in 1809, walked 1,000 miles in 1,000 consecutive hours. Prince Barclay de Tolly (1761-1818), a descendant of the Tolly branch, was the Russian Minister of War and commander-in-chief during Napoleon's campaign of 1812.

BARCLAY

BAXTER

Tartan: *Baxter*

Motto: *Vincit veritas (Latin: Truth prevails)*

Baxter is 'bakester' or baker, and the first Baxters in Angus may have been bakers at the royal castle at Forfar in the thirteenth century.

William Baxter of Ellengowan (Dundee) and Balgavies (Forfarshire) had several children, including Edward Baxter of Kincaldrum (1790-1830), father of Rt Hon. William Baxter of Kincaldrum and Kilmaron (1825-1890), who was made a Privy Councillor in 1873, and Sir David Baxter (1793-1872), patron of Dundee. Baxters outside Angus are frequently regarded as a sept of Macmillan.

BAXTER

BELL

Tartan: *Bell*

There were Bells in St Andrews, Dunkeld, and Berwickshire in the thirteenth century, and Bells were noted for their unruly behaviour in the Borders in the sixteenth century. The Bells of Annandale claim descent from Gilbert Fitz Bell, who was deprived of his lands by

BELL

King Edward I of England at the beginning of the fourteenth century. Benjamin Bell (1749-1806), the notable surgeon, came of a long line of Dumfriesshire Bells. Henry Bell (1767-1830), the pioneer of commercial steam ships, was born near Linlithgow.

BIRRELL

BIRRELL

Tartan: *Birrell*

Birrells are recorded in Berwick in 1449, and in Kirkcaldy and Glasgow between 1540 and 1579. Robert Birrel, an Edinburgh burgess, wrote a diary of events from 1532 to 1605.

BIRSE

Tartan: *Birse*

The name is that of Birse in Aberdeenshire, a Duncan de Byrse being a burgess of Aberdeen during the 1460s. It is also recorded in Edinburgh in the sixteenth century.

BLAIR

BLAIR

Branches: *Blair of Blair, Blair of Balthayock, Hunter Blair*

Tartan: *Blair*

Blair means 'moor' or 'field (of battle)', and the name derives from any or some of the places of that name.

Stephen de Blare witnessed a document to do with the monastery of Arbroath between 1204 and 1211, and Sir William de Blar was Seneschal of Fife in 1235.

John Blair was chaplain to Sir William Wallace (1274-1305), and wrote an account of the travels and adventures of that famous patriot and warrior, from which the poet known as Blind Harry claims to have taken material for his long, dramatic, and often violent biographical romance in verse, *Schir William Wallace*, written at the end of the fifteenth century. The Blairs of Blair are an old Renfrewshire family, and an ancient lineage is also claimed for the Blairs of Balthayock, Perthshire. In 1770 James Hunter (1741-87), an Edinburgh banker, married Jean Blair (*d.* 1817), daughter and heiress of John Blair of Dunksey. Hunter assumed the name of Hunter Blair in 1777, and was created a baronet in 1786.

BORTHWICK, LORD   BORTHWICK

BORTHWICK

Tartans: *Borthwick, Borthwick (dress)*

Motto: *Qui conducit (Latin: Who serves)*

Borthwick Water lies between Selkirk and Roxburgh, and between 1357 and 1367 Thomas de Borthwick received a grant of lands near Lauder in Berwickshire.

Sir William Borthwick, who died in about 1448, was Captain of Edinburgh Castle in 1420, and his son, William, was made Lord Borthwick in about 1450. William, 4th Lord Borthwick, died in the Battle of Flodden in 1513, after which his son, yet another William (*d.* 1543), took charge of the infant King James V in Stirling Castle.

William (*d.* 1582), 7th Lord, was a fervent admirer and supporter of Mary, Queen of Scots, and lent her, and her new husband, the Earl of Bothwell (*d.* 1624),

Borthwick Castle (built in about 1430 and still surviving intact) for part of their scandalous honeymoon. In 1578 his pregnant wife, by whom he already had seven children, accused him in a written complaint of unreasonable behaviour and battery. He died in Edinburgh of 'the French disease'.

John (*d.* 1675), 10th Lord Borthwick, opposed Cromwell's invasion of Scotland in 1650, until he was presented with a written, personal ultimatum from Cromwell to the effect that if he did not leave Borthwick Castle quietly, with his family, men, and chattels, 'you necessitate me to bend my cannon against you, [and] you must expect what I doubt you will not be pleased with'. He left. After his death the title passed through several branches of the family, being officially confirmed by the Lyon Court in 1986 on John Henry Stuart Borthwick (*b.* 1905) as 23rd Lord Borthwick.

BELOW: BORTHWICK

BOWIE

BOWIE

Tartan: *Bowie*

A John Bowey held Dumbarton Castle against the forces of the new King, James IV in 1489, but was pardoned for doing so. Jerome Bowie was master of the royal wine cellar for King James VI from 1585 to 1589. The name frequently occurs in records of Stirling and Dunblane in the seventeenth and eighteenth centuries.

BOYD, EARL OF KILMARNOCK

BOYD

Branches: *Boyd of Merton, Boyd of Penkill, Boyd of Pitcon, Boyd of Trochrig*

Tartan: *Boyd*

Mottos: *Confide (Latin: Be trustful); (Merton) Confidas (Latin: May you be trustful)*

The first recorded Boyd is Sir Robert Boyd, so called because his hair was fair or yellow (Gaelic *buidhe*). A

Robert Boyd took the oath of allegiance to King Edward I of England in 1296, but still joined Sir William Wallace (1274-1305) in his attempt to restore Scotland to the Scots. Sir Robert Boyd was one of the commanders of King Robert I (the Bruce) at the Battle of Bannockburn in 1314, for he was afterwards granted numerous parcels of land, including Kilmarnock, Bondington, Hertschaw, and Kilbride.

Robert Boyd of Kilmarnock (*d.* 1482) was made Lord Boyd by King James II, and in 1468 he negotiated the treaty of marriage between the young King James III and the daughter of the King of Norway and Denmark, whereby Orkney and the Shetland Isles were ceded to Scotland (in fact, they were pawned, the Scandinavians being unable at the time to meet the whole dowry, and were never redeemed). His eldest son, Thomas, who died in about 1474, married Lady Mary (*d.* 1488), sister of James III, in 1467, and was created Earl of Arran. He, too, was a party to the King's marriage treaty, but in 1469 both he and his father were charged with kidnapping the King several years before and lost their titles, Thomas's marriage being annulled at the same time.

BOYD

BRODIE HUNTING

William Boyd (*d.* 1692) was made Earl of Kilmarnock in 1661 at the Restoration of Charles II.

The Boyds of Penkill, Pitcon, and Trochrig are descended from sons of Alexander Boyd, Chamberlain of Kilmarnock 1488-1504. Alan Tindale Lennox-Boyd (*b.* 1904) of Merton-in-Penninghame, Wigtownshire, was created Viscount Boyd of Merton in 1960, his descent being from Rev. William Boyd (1658-1741), Minister of Dalry, Kircudbrightshire.

BRODIE OF   BRODIE

BRODIE

Branches: *Brodie of Brodie, Brodie of Idvies, Brodie of Lethen*

Tartans: *Brodie, Brodie (hunting)*

There was a Malcolm, Thane of Brodie, at the time of King Alexander III in the thirteenth century, and his son Michael was granted lands by King Robert I (the Bruce) in 1311. The family goes back much farther than this, however, and is believed to be of ancient Pictish stock.

Alexander Brodie of Brodie (1617-80) was a Covenanter of considerable zeal, who in 1640 led the assault on Elgin Cathedral which destroyed two valuable paintings and mutilated the interior carvings, as being inappropriate for a place of worship. In the wars that followed, Brodie House was razed and the family records destroyed. Brodie himself was appointed a judge of the Court of Session in 1649, but at the Restoration of the Monarchy in 1660 he was replaced and fined £4,000 Scots, despite having done his best to avoid carrying out any orders of Cromwell, Lord Protector of England.

The present Brodie Castle, near Forres, was rebuilt to the original sixteenth-century Z-plan of Brodie House, with seventeenth-century additions, and was further enlarged in the nineteenth century.

BRODIE

BRUCE, EARL OF ELGIN

BROWN

Branch: *Broun of Colstoun*

Tartan: *Brown*

Motto: *(Colstoun) Floreat majestas (Latin: Let majesty flourish)*

Brun is Old English for brown or dark red, and also appears as a French surname, Le Brun, a family of which name owned estates in Cumberland after the Norman Conquest of England in 1066. The first recorded Scottish Brun witnessed a document between 1194 and 1214, since when Browns or Brouns have been common throughout the land.

The Brouns of Colstoun, Haddington, have held the lands since the fourteenth century and, as the three *fleurs-de-lys* on their arms would suggest, claim descent from the royal house of France.

Patrick Broun of Colstoun (*d.* 1603) was created a baronet in 1686. His second son, Robert, was drowned with his two sons in a stream on the estate in 1703, leaving four daughters, the son of the eldest of whom became Lord Colstoun as a judge of the Court of Session.

BRUCE

Branches: *Bruce of Airth, Bruce of Clackmannan, Bruce of Kennet, Bruce of Kinnaird*

Tartans: *Bruce, Bruce of Kinnaird*

Motto: *Fuimus (Latin: We have been)*

Robert de Brus came to England with William the Conqueror in 1066. His son, Robert, was granted the lands of Annandale by King David I in 1124. The fifth Robert de Brus (or Bruce) married Isabella, great-granddaughter of David I, and their son, Robert de Bruce (1210-95), known as the 'Competitor', claimed the throne of Scotland on the death of Alexander III's little granddaughter, Margaret, 'Maid of Norway'.

King Edward I of England, to whom the dispute had been referred, ruled in favour of John Balliol, on whose abdication in 1306 the eighth Robert de Bruce, Robert I (the Bruce), seized the throne, and in a glorious but desperately-fought reign defeated the English at Bannockburn in 1314. When he died in 1329 he had secured immortality for himself and, for a time, independence for Scotland. The male royal line of Bruce ended with the death of his son, King David II, in 1371, but the family succession continued with the accession of King Robert II, son of the Bruce's daughter Marjorie, who married Walter the Steward, thus inaugurating the House of Stewart.

James Bruce of Kinnaird (1730-94), known as the 'Abyssinian', was celebrated for his African explorations. He endured enormous hardships during his expedition along the Nile to Abyssinia and back between 1768 and 1772, only to die finally when he fell downstairs at Kinnaird House as he rushed to help a lady into her carriage.

Thomas Bruce (1766-1841), 7th Earl of Elgin and 11th Earl of Kincardine, descended from the Bruces of

BROWN

JAMES BRUCE OF KINNAIRD

BRUCE

Clackmannan, was the much-maligned peer who rescued from destruction the marble sculptures of the Parthenon in Athens, shipped them back to Britain, and passed them on to the nation for considerably less than he had spent in saving them.

BUCHAN

Branch: *Buchan of Auchmacoy*

Tartan: *Buchan, also known as Comyn (hunting)*

Motto: *(Auchmacoy) Non inferiora secutus (Latin: Not having followed inferior things)*

The Buchans who took their name from the district of Buchan in Aberdeenshire were not necessarily connected with the families of the various earls of Buchan who were ennobled from the thirteenth century onwards. Andrew of Buchan, who died in about 1309, was Bishop of Caithness. The Buchans of Auchmacoy were granted their lands in 1318, and Thomas Buchan of Auchmacoy (*d.* 1720) was commander of the Jacobite forces in Scotland after the death of Viscount Dundee in 1689, until his defeat the following year.

John Buchan (1875-1940), writer of adventure stories, biographer, poet, critic, and statesman, was born in Perth, son of a Free Church minister. He was made Lord Tweedsmuir of Elfield on his appointment in 1935 as Governor-General of Canada.

BUCHANAN

Branches: *Buchanan of Arnprior, Buchanan of Auchmar, Buchanan of Carbeth, Buchanan of Leny, Buchanan of Spital*

Tartans: *Buchanan, Buchanan (hunting), Buchanan (old)*

Mottos: *Audaces juvo (Latin: I help the brave); Clarior hinc honos (Latin: Brighter the honour hence)*

Slogan: *Clar Innis (Clairinch, the name of an island in Loch Lomond)*

The island of Clairinch was granted in 1225 by the Earl of Lennox to his steward, Absalon of Buchanan, the name of Buchanan deriving from the Gaelic *both-chanain*, 'canon's seat'.

BUCHANAN OF   THAT ILK

George Buchanan (1506-82), born near Killearn, just to the east of Loch Lomond, was one of the greatest scholars of his time. He was tutor to Mary, Queen of Scots, but fell out with her after the murder of her husband, Lord Darnley, in 1567, whereupon he wrote, in exquisite Latin prose, a scurrilous pamphlet about her. Much to her chagrin, he was tutor also to her son, King James VI, from 1570 to 1578.

James Buchanan (1791-1868), fifteenth President of the USA, was born in Pennsylvania of Scottish descent.

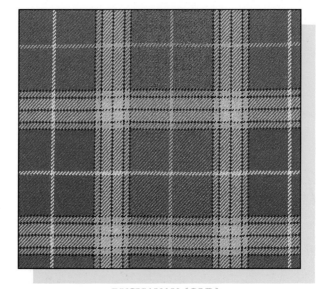

BUCHANAN

BUCHANAN

BUCHANAN (OLD)

BURNETT OF LEYS

BURNS

BURNS CHECK

BURNETT

Tartans: *Burnett, Burnett of Leys*

Motto: *Virescit vulnere virtus (Latin: Courage gains strength from a wound)*

Burnett is the Old English name, Beornhard, and Patrick Burnard held lands in Berwickshire in about 1250. The Burnetts of Leys claim descent from Alexander Burnard, who in 1324 was granted lands in Aberdeenshire by King Robert I (the Bruce), receiving from the King as a mark of his ownership the jewelled and ivory hunting horn which is still preserved. John Burnet was designated 'of Leys' in 1446.

Thomas Burnet of Leys was made a baronet in 1626, the second 't' being added in the time of his son Alexander (*d.* 1663), 2nd Baronet. Crathes Castle, the family seat, with its double square tower dating from 1553, contains three extraordinary painted ceilings, executed at the end of the sixteenth century.

ROBERT BURNS

BURNS, BURNES, BURNESS

Tartans: *Burns, Robert Burns (check)*

The name probably derives from one or more of the places in Scotland with a similar spelling or sound. Robert Burnes, a farmer in Kincardineshire, had three sons, of whom the youngest, William (1721-84), left home to find work during the uncertain times that followed the collapse of the '45 Rebellion. He became head gardener on an Ayrshire estate, marrying a local farmer's daughter when he was 36, and subsequently became a tenant farmer, only to die bankrupt because of the difficulties and conditions of the times. His elder son, Robert (1759-96), dropped the 'e' from his name, and overcame the handicap of an indigent upbringing (at the age of 15 he was the farm's chief labourer) to become the most famous, and in many respects the finest, of all Scottish poets. He wrote equally well in English and in Scots, and within a comparatively short period of a short life composed numerous technically brilliant love songs, satires, nature poems, and depictions of rustic life, as well as *Tam o' Shanter*, his version of a scary folk tale which is today recited all over the world on his birthday.

The talents of the family did not stop with him. William Burnes's eldest brother, James, was great-grandfather of James Burnes (1801-62), writer and Physician-General of Bombay, and Sir Alexander Burnes (1805-41), explorer and diplomat, who was the first westerner to follow the course of the River Indus, and was assassinated in Kabul, having done his best to avert interference in Afghanistan by both India and Russia. The Burneses of Kincardineshire were originally Campbells who were immigrants from Loch Aweside.

CAMERON OF   LOCHIEL

CAMERON

Branches: *Cameron of Lochiel, Cameron of Erracht*

Tartans: *Cameron, Cameron (hunting), Cameron of Lochiel, Cameron of Lochiel (hunting), Cameron of Erracht*

Mottos: *Aonaibh ri cheile (Gaelic: Unite) and Mo righ's mo dhuchaich (Gaelic version) or Pro Rege et Patria (Latin: For King and Country)*

SIR EWEN CAMERON OF LOCHIEL

Slogan: *Chlanna nan con thigibh a so's gheib sibh feail (Gaelic: Sons of the hounds come here and get flesh)*

The Camerons' name is supposed to come from the Gaelic *cam-shron* (crooked nose), said to have been a feature of an early chief. The first chief whose name is recorded, Donald Dubh, fought with his men on the same side as the Mackintoshes for the Lord of the Isles in the inconclusive Battle of Harlaw in 1411. By 1430 the Camerons and the Mackintoshes were at each others' throats over a territorial dispute, and remained so for two centuries.

The 13th Chief took the suffix 'Lochiel', and his family has held the chiefship of Clan Cameron ever since. Sir Ewen Cameron of Lochiel (1629-1719), who fought with Viscount Dundee, was the 17th Chief. He is attributed, during his long and active life, with killing the last wolf in Scotland, and with biting out the throat of one of General Monck's officers in an attack on a government fortress.

In 1793 Major Allan Cameron of Erracht (1753-1828) raised the Camerons' own regiment, the 79th Highlanders, which became the Queen's Own Cameron Highlanders in 1873, and since 1961, when it was merged with the Seaforths, has been the Queen's Own Highlanders. A separate family took its name from the Barony of Cameron in Fife. There is a Clan Cameron Museum at Achnacarra and much material related to the clan in the West Highland Museum, Fort William.

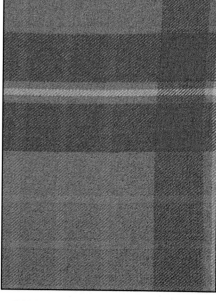

CAMERON OF LOCHIEL   CAMERON OF LOCHIEL HUNTING   CAMERON OF ERRACHT

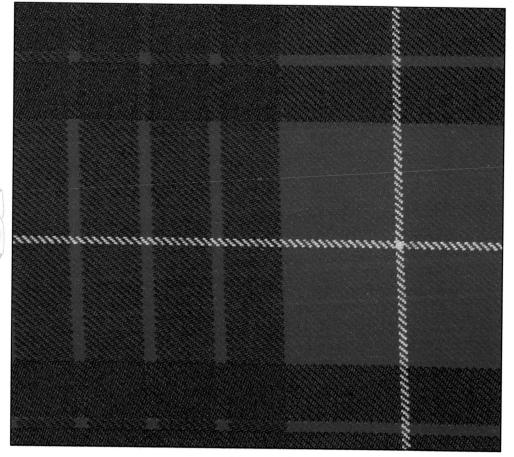

CAMERON

CAMPBELL

Branches: *Campbell of Argyll, Campbell of Breadalbane, Campbell of Cawdor, Campbell of Loudoun*

Tartans: *Campbell, Campbell of Argyll, Campbell of Argyll (dress), Campbell of Breadalbane, Campbell of Cawdor, Campbell of Loudoun, Lorne, Louise*

Mottos: *(Argyll) Ne obliviscaris (Latin: Lest you forget) and Vix ea nostro voco (Latin: I scarcely call these things our own); (Breadalbane) Follow me; (Cawdor) Be mindful; (Loudoun) I byde my time*

Slogan: *Cruachan (name of a mountain by Loch Awe)*

CAMPBELL OF CAWDOR

The surname Campbell, most probably derived from the Gaelic *cam-beul* (twisted mouth), is one of the oldest in the Highlands, and a crown charter of 1368 acknowledges Duncan MacDuihbne as founder of the Campbells, who were established as lords of Loch Awe. The founder of the Argyll line was *Cailean Mór* (*d.* 1294), whose descendant, Colin Campbell (*d.* 1493), 1st Earl of Argyll, married Isabel Stewart of Lorne. To this day the eldest son of the family has borne the title of Marquis of Lorne, and the marriage in 1871 of the Marquis, later 9th

JOHN CAMPBELL, 1st EARL OF BREADALBANE

Duke of Argyll, to HRH Princess Louise, fourth daughter of Queen Victoria, is recalled by the two tartans bearing their names.

Sir John Campbell (1635-1716), 11th Laird of Glenorchy, was created Earl of Breadalbane in 1681. Described as being 'cunning as a fox, wise as a serpent, and supple as an eel … [who] knew neither honour nor religion but where they are mixed with interest', he was involved in the scheming which resulted in the Massacre of Glencoe, but no evidence of his guilt could be produced. His line was founded by the colourful crusader 'Black' Colin Campbell (*d.* 1498), who received

CAMBPELL OF BREADALBANE

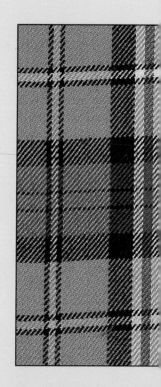

CAMPBELL OF ARGYLL DRESS

CAMPBELL

CAMPBELL OF CAWDOR

CAMPBELL OF BREADALBANE

Glenorchy in 1432 from his father, Sir Duncan Campbell, who had ejected the MacGregors from the lands.

The founder of the Cawdor branch, another Sir John Campbell (*d.* 1546), obtained his lands through his wife Muriel (1495-1573). An orphan who had inherited her father's title of Thane of Cawdor, she was kidnapped in 1499 by Campbell's father, Archibald (*d.* 1513), 2nd Earl of Argyll, and married to his son in 1510. The Campbells of Loudoun are descended from Sir Duncan Campbell, second son of the first *MacCailean Mór*, who married a Crauford of Loudoun. The Earldom of Loudoun, created for John Campbell (1598-1663), politician, has since the eighteenth century descended through the female line.

Arguably the most famous Campbell of them all, Sir Colin Campbell (1792-1863), commander of the Highland Brigade at Balaclava, Commander-in-Chief during the Indian Mutiny, the hero of Lucknow and Cawnpore, was not strictly a Campbell at all, being born Colin MacLiver, son of a Glasgow carpenter. His mother was a Campbell, though, and when her brother, Colonel John Campbell, took the fifteen-year-old boy to be interviewed for the Army by the Duke of York, the Duke wrote his name down as Campbell. And Campbell it remained.

CARMICHAEL

CARMICHAEL

Tartan: *Carmichael*

Motto: *Toujours prest (French: Always ready)*

Robert de Caramicely is mentioned in 1226, the name probably deriving from lands in Lanarkshire which were

CARMICHAEL OF CARMICHAEL

granted to Sir James Douglas in 1321, and by his nephew to Sir John Carmichael between 1374 and 1384.

Sir James Carmichael (1579-1672) was created Lord Carmichael by King Charles I in 1647, and his grandson, John (1672-1710), who was Secretary of State for Scotland 1696-1707 and Chancellor of Glasgow University, was made Earl of Hyndford in 1701. Richard Carmichael of Carmichael (*b.* 1948), the present chief, has done a great deal to revitalise the Carmichael heritage.

CARNEGIE, EARL OF SOUTHESK

CARNEGIE

Branches: *Carnegie of Ethie (Earls of Northesk),*
  Carnegie of Kinnaird, Carnegie of Southesk

Tartan: *Carnegie*

Motto: *(Southesk) Dred God*

In 1358 King David II confirmed by charter that the owner of the lands of Carnegie was John of Carnegie, direct descendant of Jocelyn de Ballinhard, who first held them in 1203. The main Carnegie line was extinct by 1563, but it was revived by the Carnegies of Kinnaird later that century.

Sir David Carnegie of Kinnaird (1575-1628), having been created Lord Carnegie of Kinnaird in 1616 for political services to Scotland, was made Earl of Southesk

CARNEGIE

CLAN CHATTAN

in 1633, when King Charles I came north for his belated Scottish coronation, eight years after his accession. The youngest of his six daughters, Magdalen (*d.* 1648), married the illustrious Marquis of Montrose when he was only seventeen. Southesk's brother, John Carnegie of Ethie(1579-1667), was made Earl of Ethie in 1647, the title being changed to Northesk in 1666. Magdalene, his eighth child, married William Graham of Claverhouse (*d.* 1652) and was thus the mother of Viscount Dundee, who was born in 1648. William, 7th Earl of Northesk (1758-1831), was third in command under Nelson of the British fleet at the Battle of Trafalgar in 1805.

The philanthropist Andrew Carnegie (1835-1918) was the son of a Dunfermline weaver, who emigrated with his family to the USA in 1848. He retired to Skibo Castle in Sutherland in 1901, and spent the rest of his life distributing the vast fortune he had made.

CLAN CHATTAN

Tartans:	*Clan Chattan, Clan Chattan (Chief's sett)*
Motto:	*Touch not the cat but [without] a glove*

The historical origin of this great federation of clans goes back to 1291, when Eva, only child of Dougall Dall, 6th Chief of Clan Chattan and son of Gilliechattan-

Patrick, married Angus Mackintosh, 6th Chief of Clan Mackintosh, who became, through his wife, 7th Chief of Clan Chattan. Traditionally, the federation comprised 17 clans, among whom were the Macphersons, the MacPhails and the Cattanachs, together with the Mackintoshes and their offshoots (Farquharsons, Shaws,

and Toshachs), and smaller clans which joined for protection, such as the Clerks, Davidsons, MacLeans, MacQueens and Smiths. Attempts were made to sabotage this formidable fighting force from within by persuading the Macphersons to challenge for the leadership. These attempts were neatly scuppered when, in 1672, the Lyon Court confirmed that the chief of Mackintosh was also chief of Clan Chattan, a ruling which held until 1938, when on the death of the Mackintosh chief with no male heir, the two chiefships were separated.

CHEAPE

CHEAPE

Tartan: *Cheape*

Cheape appears in the sixteenth century, and families of this name have long been settled in central Scotland. John Cheape of Rossie, Fife, had two sons, General Sir John Cheape (1792-1875), who served in Burma, and Douglas Cheape (1797-1861), Professor of Civil Law at Edinburgh University. There is also a Gray-Cheape line in Angus.

THE CHISHOLM

CHISHOLM

Branch: *Chisholm of Chisholm (formerly Comer and Strathglass)*

Tartans: *Chisholm, Chisholm (hunting)*

Mottos: *Feros ferio (Latin: I put fear into the fearsome) and Vi aut virtute (Latin: By strength or courage)*

The Chisholms began in the Borders, where they were

CHISHOLM

known in 1249, but they are also a Highland clan, whose chief is called The Chisholm. In the fourteenth century Robert de Chisholme succeeded to his grandfather's title and lands as Constable of Urquhart Castle on Loch Ness. His son married a local heiress, and their son founded the line of Chisholm of Comer and Strathglass. Descendants of Robert's younger son returned to Roxburghshire, and members of that family later settled in Cromlix, Perthshire, producing a remarkable episcopal succession of William Chisholms. William I (*d.* 1564) was Bishop of Dunblane; his nephew, William II (*d.* 1593), was

Bishop of Dunblane and later of Vaison, near Avignon; and William III (*d.* 1629), nephew of II, was also Bishop of Vaison.

The clan fought for Bonnie Prince Charlie at Culloden under the chief's youngest son, Roderick, who was killed by cannon fire before the final charge. After the battle his body was found, and protected, by his two

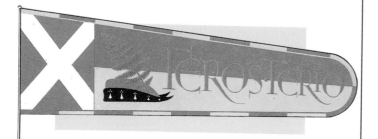

elder brothers, officers of the Royal Scots, who were on the government side. Jacobite honour was more than satisfied afterwards, however, for three of the eight legendary men of Glenmoriston, who sheltered the Prince and guided his escape in July and August 1746, were Chisholms.

CHRISTIE

Tartan: *Christie*

The name, which is a diminutive of Christian and possibly also of Christopher, is old-established in Fife and Stirlingshire. William Christie (1748-1823), son of a provost of Montrose, was the first Unitarian minister in Scotland. Thomas Christie (1773-1829), born in Carnwath, Lanarkshire, successfully introduced vaccination against smallpox in Ceylon, and was latterly a physician extraordinary to the Prince Regent.

CLERKE OF ULVA

Tartan: *Clerke of Ulva*

The name first meant a man of a religious order, and then a scholar, before becoming a family name. Clan *Clerich,* or Clark, was one of the old seventeen tribes of Clan Chattan. Ulva was the original home of Clan MacQuarrie. In about 1850 Francis William Clark, an Argyll landowner, built an impressive modern seat on the island, near the abandoned house of the 16th Chief.

CHISHOLM

CHISHOLM HUNTING

CHRISTIE

COCHRANE, EARL OF DUNDONALD

COCHRANE

Tartan: *Cochrane*

Motto: *Virtute et labore (Latin: By virtue and hard work)*

The earliest record of the name, which comes from the lands of Cochrane, near Paisley, Renfrewshire, dates from 1262. William Blair (*d.* 1686) assumed the name of Cochrane when he married into the main line of the family. He was made Lord Cochrane of Dundonald (in Ayrshire) in 1647, for services to King Charles I, and Earl of Dundonald in 1669.

Archibald Cochrane (1749-1831), 9th Earl, exhausted his energies and his savings on scientific discoveries and new industrial techniques. The exploits of his son, Thomas (1775-1860), 10th Earl, Rear Admiral, are the stuff of romance. In 1800, in command of a brig, he outgunned and captured a Spanish frigate three times the size of his ship and with six times as many crew. He was elected to Parliament in 1807, and in 1808-9 carried out a series of brilliant naval coups against the French. In 1814 he was arrested on a charge of fraudulently profiting from a rumour of the death of Napoleon. He was almost certainly innocent, but he was sentenced to a fine, to a year's imprisonment, and to an hour in the pillory, which last was remitted when a fellow Member of Parliament insisted on standing with him. He was expelled from Parliament, only to be promptly re-elected by his constituents. After nine months of his sentence, he escaped and reappeared in the House of Commons, from which he had to be forcibly returned to jail. Between 1818 and 1825 he successfully commanded the navies of Brazil, Chile, and Peru in their fights for independence from Spain and Portugal. He advocated the use of steam-powered screw propellers for naval ships, and also the employment of sulphur fumes to overwhelm ships and land bases, though this proposal was kept secret from the public until 1908.

Thomas Cochrane (1857-1951), of Crawford Priory, Fife, was made Lord Cochrane of Cults in 1919.

COCHRANE

COCKBURN OF LANGTON

COCKBURN

Tartan: *Cockburn*

Motto: *Accendit cantu (Latin: He is aroused by cockcrow)*

The lands of Cockburn were in Berwickshire, and the name is quite widely recorded in the thirteenth century.

Sir Alexander Cockburn fell at the Battle of Bannockburn in 1314, and his grandson, Alexander Cockburn, was Keeper of the Great Seal 1389-96. In 1595 Sir William Cockburn was granted the Barony of Langton, Berwickshire, and his descendant, Sir Alexander

Cockburn (1802-80), was Lord Chief Justice of England. Adam Cockburn of Ormiston (1656-1735), Lord Justice Clerk and one of the members of the commission which enquired into the Massacre of Glencoe, was created Lord Ormiston. Henry Cockburn (1779-1854), son of a sheriff of Midlothian, judge and man of letters, was made Lord Cockburn in 1834.

COLQUHOUN   OF LUSS

COLQUHOUN

Tartan: *Colquhoun*

Motto: *Si je puis (French: If I can)*

Slogan: *Cnoc Ealachain (name of a mountain by Loch Lomond, where the clan territories were)*

The name derives from the barony of Colquhoun, Dumbartonshire, and is first recorded in 1259. Towards the end of the fourteenth century, Sir Robert Colquhoun married the 'Fair Maid of Luss', heiress to the lands of Luss. The Colquhouns were fully involved in the machinations which led to the proscription of the MacGregors in 1603, having two months before that suffered at Glen Fruin a crippling defeat at the hands of an inferior force of MacGregors in a fair fight. The chief of the Colquhoun clan at the time was Sir Alexander

TOP: JOHN COCKBURN OF ORMISTON (*d.* 1578)
ABOVE: COCKBURN

COLQUHOUN

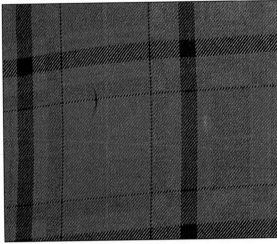

Colquhoun of Luss, whose descendant, Sir Humphrey Colquhoun (d. 1715), 17th Laird of Luss, was a member of the last Scottish Parliament and strongly opposed the Act of Union of 1707. Having only a daughter to succeed him, he made a deal with the Crown whereby he surrendered his baronetcy in return for an assurance that his daughter and son-in-law, James Grant, would inherit the lands and the chieftainship of the clan, provided that the clan name would never be under control of the Grant family.

COOPER

COMYN, CUMMING

Branches: *Cumming of Altyre, Cumming of Inverallochy*

Tartans: *Comyn, Comyn (hunting, also known as Buchan)*

Motto: *Courage*

COMYN

Robert de Comyn came to England with William the Conqueror in 1066, and was made Earl of Northumberland in 1069. His grandson, Richard Comyn, came to Scotland at the invitation of King David I. He married the daughter of King Donald III (reigned 1093-7) – 'Donalbain' of Shakespeare's tragedy *Macbeth* – and their son William (d. 1233) became Earl of Buchan through his second wife, Marjory. His eldest son by his first wife was Richard (d. 1244), whose son John (d. 1273) was Lord of Badenoch, and chief of a clan whose members included not only the Earl of Buchan, but the earls also of Atholl and Menteith.

So it came about that when Scotland was without a monarch after the abdication of King John I (Balliol) in 1296, the Lord of Badenoch's grandson John, known as the Red Comyn, had a considerable claim to the throne by reason both of his descent from King Donald III and the fact that John Balliol was his mother's brother. This added up to at least as legitimate a claim as that of Robert the Bruce, who invited the Red Comyn to meet him in the Church of the Greyfriars in Dumfries in 1306. Here an argument took place and Comyn received a stab wound, whereupon Bruce's followers charged in and finished him off.

The Cummings of Altyre are descended from the Red Comyn's uncle Robert, and the Cummings of Inverallochy from Alexander, Earl of Buchan (d. 1289), son of William and Marjory, who was Constable of Scotland 1275-89.

CONNAL

Tartan: *Connal*

The name was originally Congal, a saint from whom derives Dercongal in Dumfriesshire. There were also three sixth-century kings of the Scots in Dalriada called Congallus or Conall.

COOPER

Tartan: *Cooper*

The name has a double significance in Scotland, being both a maker of casks and a native of Cupar, Fife, where it is recorded from the thirteenth century onwards. It is commonly spelt Coupar.

CRAIG

Tartan: *Craig*

Motto: *Vive deo et vives (Latin: Live with God and you live)*

William Craig of Craigfintray, Aberdeenshire, had two sons, the younger of whom was killed at the Battle of Flodden in 1513. His other son, William (1501-90), became minister of Holyrood and assisted in the drawing up of the National Covenant in 1580. Sir Thomas Craig (1538-1608), a direct descendant of the elder son of William, acquired the estate of Riccarton, Edinburgh.

CRAIG

CRANSTOUN OF   THAT ILK

CRANSTOUN

Tartan: *Cranstoun*

Motto: *Thou shalt want ere I want*

Cranston is in Midlothian, and Thomas de Cranstoun received lands in Roxburgh at the end of the fourteenth century. William Cranstoun of Morrieston, who married Sarah, daughter of Sir John Cranstoun of Cranstoun, was charged by King James VI with keeping order in the Borders, and was made Lord Cranstoun in 1609. The title became extinct in 1869.

CRANSTOUN

CRAWFORD

Branches: *Crawfurd of Auchinames, Craufurd of Craufurdsland, Craufurd of Kilbirnie*

Tartan: *Crawford*

Motto: *Tutum te robore reddam (Latin: I will make you safe with strength)*

The Crawfords, Crawfurds, or Craufurds get their name from the Barony of Crawford in Lanarkshire. Sir John

Crawfurd (*d.* 1248) had two daughters. From the younger, who married David Lindsay, are descended the earls of Crawford. Sir Archibald Crawford, Sheriff of Ayr, was treacherously murdered by the English at a banquet in his home town in 1297. His sister Margaret married Sir Malcolm Wallace of Elderslie, and their son Sir William Wallace (1274-1305) was the famous Scottish patriot and warrior.

The Crawfurds of Auchinames are descended from a brother of Sir Archibald, and got their estate from King Robert I (the Bruce) in 1320. A third branch of the family acquired Kilbirnie in 1499.

In 1781 a baronetcy was conferred on Alexander Craufurd of Kilbirnie, who had three distinguished sons: Sir James Craufurd, British Ambassador in Hamburg 1798-1803; Lieut-General Sir Charles Gregan-Craufurd (1761-1821), who served with great courage and daring in the Netherlands in 1794; and Major-General Robert Craufurd (1764-1812), commander of the Light Brigade in the Peninsular War.

CUNNINGHAM, EARL   OF GLENCAIRN

CUNNINGHAM

Branches: *Cunningham of Auchinharvie, Cunningham of Corsehill, Cunningham of Craigends, Cunningham of Kilmaurs, Cunningham of Robertland*

Tartans: *Cunningham*

Motto: *Over fork over*

Wernibald of Cunningham, Ayrshire, is said to have been granted the property of Kilmaurs in about 1140, and a Harvey Cunningham of Kilmaurs was among the stalwarts who helped King Alexander III repel a huge Norse sea-force at the Battle of Largs in 1263.

Sir Alexander Cunningham of Kilmaurs (*d.* 1488) was made Lord Kilmaurs in about 1450, and Earl of Glencairn

CRAWFORD

CUNNINGHAM

DALRYMPLE

in 1488, for his part in opposing the lords who rebelled against King James III, but he was killed a fortnight later in the Battle of Sauchiburn, which ended the reign and life of James III and put the young James IV on the throne. The branches of Auchinharvie, Craigends, and Robertland derive from his second son.

Alexander Cunningham (d. 1574), 5th Earl of Glencairn, was a Protestant zealot who did his utmost to upset the order of things during the reign of Mary, Queen of Scots. He was personally instrumental in the desecration of the royal chapel at Holyroodhouse after her capture, and carried the sword at the coronation of her baby son, King James VI, in 1567. His son, the 6th Earl, fomented the century-old feud with the Montgomeries of Eglinton, which culminated in the murder of Lord Eglinton in 1586, and the death of numerous Cunninghams in reprisal. James Cunningham (1749-91), 14th Earl, was the friend and patron of Robert Burns, and after his death and that of his brother, the earldom became dormant. The chiefship resides with the Cunninghams of Corsehill, descended from the second son of the 3rd Earl of Glencairn.

DALRYMPLE, EARL OF STAIR

DALRYMPLE OF CASTLETON

Tartan: *Dalrymple of Castleton*

Motto: *Firm*

The name derives from the Barony of Dalrymple, Ayrshire. James Dalrymple of Stair (1619-1695) was created Viscount of Stair by King William in 1690. His third son, Hew Dalrymple (1652-1737), Lord North Berwick, was created a baronet of Nova Scotia in 1698. His second son, Sir Robert Dalrymple of Castleton (d. 1734) was a member of the Faculty of Advocates.

The baronetcy has descended through Hew, eldest son of Sir Robert by his first wife, daughter of the Master of Bargany. Their daughter Marion (1708-40) caused a stir in 1732 by turning down, against her family's advice, a proposal of marriage from the infamous, and then elderly, 11th Lord Fraser of Lovat (1667-1747). She married Donald Mackay, 4th Lord Reay, the same year. A daughter of Sir Robert's second marriage, Anne (1727-1820), married the 5th Earl of Balcarres.

DALZELL, EARL OF CARNWATH

DALZELL, DALZIEL, DALYELL

Branches: *Dalzell of Glenae, Dalyell of the Binns*

Tartan: *Dalzell*

Motto: *I dar[e]*

Dail ghil is Gaelic for 'white meadow', from which comes the name of the lands of Dalzell, and of Hugh de Dalzell, Sheriff of Lanark in 1288. Since 1259, over two hundred different forms of the name have been recorded, including the abbreviation 'D. L.', which approximates to its proper pronunciation.

Sir Robert Dalzell (d. 1639) was created Lord Dalzell in 1633, and Earl of Carnwath in 1639. Robert (d. 1654), 2nd Earl, was a lukewarm but active supporter of the Marquis of Montrose, during whose campaign in 1644 a Mrs Pierson, passing as Carnwath's daughter but with orders made out to her in the name of Captain Francis Dalzell, rode at the head of a troop of horse, with a junior officer in attendance bearing a black banner on which was embroidered a naked man hanging from a gibbet, and the family motto. On the death of the 5th Earl, the title went to Sir Robert Dalzell of Glenae (d. 1737), a descendant of the second son of the 1st Earl who, with his brother, fought for the cause of James Edward

Stewart in 1715, as a result of which he forfeited his title and estates. The branch of Binns was founded by General Thomas Dalyell (1599-1685), a distant cousin of the main stem, who escaped after the Battle of Worcester in 1651, served the Tsar of Russia for ten years, returned to Scotland, established the regiment of the Scots Greys, and was commander-in-chief of the army which defeated the Covenanters at Rullion Green in 1666. He is reported by a contemporary never to have shaved after the execution of King Charles I, his 'white and bushy beard … reaching almost to his girdle'. The baronetcy conferred on his son in 1685 can descend through the female line.

DAVIDSON OF TULLOCH

DAVIDSON

Branches: *Davidson of Cantray, Davidson of Tulloch*

Tartans: *Davidson, Davidson of Tulloch, Davidson 'Double'*

Motto: *Sapienter si sincere (Latin: Wisely if sincerely)*

The clan was known as *Clan Dhài* from the name of its first chief, David Dubh, fourth son of the chief of Clan Chattan, of which the Davidsons became a part. Their long-running feud with the Macphersons surfaced at Invernahavon in 1370, when the Macphersons refused to fight on the same side as the Davidsons, resulting in the defeat of Clan Chattan by the Camerons. The seat of the Inverness-shire Davidsons wars at Cantray. The Clan Chief was also hereditary Keeper of Dingwall Castle. The Davidsons of Tulloch took their name when Alexander Davidson married a Miss Bayne of Tulloch in about 1700, and bought the estate from her father.

DEAS

Tartan: *Deas*

The name first occurs in Dundee in 1611. A Thomas Deas was cook to the household of the Dowager Countess of Southesk, at whose funeral in 1730 the hospitality was so lavish that catering for it caused his death, too.

Francis Deas of Falkland had two sons, Lord Deas (1804-1887), a judge of the Court of Session, and Sir David Deas (1807-76), Inspector-General of military hospitals and fleets of the Royal Navy.

DAVIDSON

DALZELL

DAVIDSON

DAVIDSON OF TULLOCH

DEAS

DOUGLAS, DUKE OF DOUGLAS

DOUGLAS

Branches: *Earls of Angus, Douglas of Drumlanrig (Marquises of Queensberry)*

Tartans: *Douglas, Douglas (grey)*

Motto: *Jamais arrière (French: Never behind)*

Slogan: *A Douglas! A Douglas!*

No single family, apart from the Stewarts, has contributed so much to the course of Scottish history as that of Douglas. William de Douglas lived at the end of the twelfth century. His younger son Andrew was ancestor of the earls of Morton, of whom James Douglas (1525-81), 4th Earl by virtue of his marriage to his predecessor's daughter, was the famous, and infamous, Regent Morton during the boyhood of King James VI, who finally had him beheaded for his part in the murder of Lord Darnley fourteen years earlier.

The elder son of William, Sir William Douglas, was father of 'Good Sir James' (1286-1330), who was the right hand man of King Robert I (the Bruce) at the Battle of Bannockburn in 1314 and after it. He was called the Black Douglas from his complexion, a nickname which became attached to his line. Sir James's nephew William

DOUGLAS GREY

DOUGLAS

became 1st Earl of Douglas in 1358, the title, on the death of William's son James in 1388 without issue, reverting to Sir James's bastard son, Archibald 'the Grim' (1328-1400). In the meantime, the 1st Earl had had an affair with Margaret, Countess of Angus and Mar, widow of his wife's brother, and the outcome was George (1380-1403), who in 1389 was granted the title of Earl of Angus and became known as the Red Douglas.

The Black Douglases went through some harrowing times. The young but powerful 6th Earl (1423-40) was lured to Edinburgh Castle, seized and tried in the presence of the boy King James II, and then taken out into the yard with his brother and beheaded. James II himself stabbed to death the 8th Earl (1425-50) in Stirling Castle. The earldom was forfeited by the 9th Earl (1426-88) and passed to the Red Douglases in the person of George Douglas, 4th Earl of Angus (1412-62), whose influential son Archibald (1449-1514), 5th Earl, was known as Bell-the-Cat, from his opposition to King James III's favourites. Archibald (1489-1557), 6th Earl, married Margaret Tudor (1489-1541), widow of King James IV, and was thus the grandfather of Lord Darnley and great-grandfather of King James VI.

The Red and Black Douglases were not the only Douglas lines to descend from the wrong side of the blanket. James, 2nd Earl of Douglas, had an illegitimate son, Sir William Douglas, whose descendants became

viscounts of Drumlanrig in 1628, earls of Queensberry in 1633, marquises of Queensberry in 1681, and dukes of Queensberry in 1683. James Douglas (1662-1711), 2nd Duke of Queensberry, was the architect of the Act of Union in 1707, whereby the Scottish and English parliaments were merged, despite violent public opposition. While he and his household were out celebrating the successful conclusion of the momentous business, his eldest son, Viscount Drumlanrig, who suffered from a severe mental condition, wandered into the kitchen of the big house in Edinburgh, seized the boy who was turning a joint on the spit, and ate him.

In 1810 the title of Marquis of Queensberry went to the family of Sir Charles Douglas of Kelhead. John Sholto Douglas (1844-1900), 8th Marquis, was the celebrated formulator of the Queensberry rules of boxing, and the not so celebrated father of Lord Alfred Douglas (1870-1945), whose friendship with the Irish-born author and dramatist Oscar Wilde (1854-1900) led to Wilde's downfall, imprisonment, and ultimate death.

By no means all the famous Douglases were peers or warriors. Gavin Douglas (1474-1522), third son of Bell-the-Cat, though he shared the family penchant for political intrigue, was also Bishop of Dunkeld and a poet whose translation into Scots verse of the *Aeneid* of Virgil places him among the finest English and Scottish poets of the Renaissance. David Douglas (1798-1834), son of a Perthshire stonemason, was a distinguished naturalist, who is remembered for the species of plants, birds, and mammals which he discovered in North America, and for the manner of his demise. He fell into one of the pits he had dug in the Sandwich Islands to catch wild bulls. Unfortunately there was a bull already in it, and he was gored to death.

DRUMMOND

DRUMMOND OF PERTH

DRUMMOND

Branches: *Drummond of Perth, Drummond of Strathallan*

Tartans: *Drummond (similar to Grant), Drummond of Perth, Drummond of Strathallan*

Mottos: *Virtutem coronat honos (Latin: Honour is the crown of virtue); Gang warily (Go carefully)*

Drummond, or Drymen, is in Stirlingshire, and the first person known to have been of that name is Sir Malcolm de Drummond, who disabled the English cavalry at the Battle of Bannockburn in 1314 by spreading caltrops, ingenious spiked objects, in their way. For this King Robert I (the Bruce) rewarded him with lands in Perthshire. His son, Malcolm, had two children, Sir John and Margaret. Margaret married Sir John Logie, and when he died in about 1356, or before he died, she became the mistress of King David II, who married her on the death of Queen Joanna in 1362.

Sir John Drummond's daughter Annabella (*d.* 1401) was the wife of King Robert III and mother of King James I. Sir John Drummond (*d.* 1519) was made Lord Drummond in 1488. His eldest daughter Margaret (*b.* 1472) was engaged to King James IV and bore him a daughter in 1497, but she, and two of her sisters who were having breakfast with her, were poisoned in 1501, shortly before James announced his intention to marry the twelve-year-old Margaret Tudor, daughter of King Henry VII of England.

The 4th Lord Drummond was created Earl of Perth in 1605, and in 1609 his uncle was made Lord Maderty, the 4th Lord Maderty becoming Viscount Strathallan in 1686. The Perth and the Strathallan Drummonds were confirmed and active Jacobites, the 3rd Duke being wounded and the 4th Viscount killed at the Battle of Culloden in 1746, after which both families had their estates forfeited. The chiefship of the clan passed into French hands during the nineteenth century through a cousin of the earls of Perth, but was restored to Scotland in 1902, when it was vested in William (1871-1937), 11th Viscount Strathallan.

DUNBAR

Branches: *Dunbar of Mochrum, Dunbar of Westfield*

Tartan: *Dunbar*

Mottos: *In promptu (Latin: At the ready); Candoris praemium honos (Latin: Honour is the reward of integrity)*

The stark remains of Dunbar Castle, off the coast of East Lothian, tell many stories. The 1st Earl of Dunbar, nephew of King Duncan I (who appears in an unhistorical guise in Shakespeare's *Macbeth*), was granted the lands by King Malcolm III in 1072. Patrick (1285-1368), 9th Earl, married Agnes (1312-69), known as 'Black Agnes'. She was the daughter of the 1st Earl of Moray and is celebrated for her defence of the castle (in her husband's

absence) against the English for five months in 1338. After every round of catapult fire from the opposition, her maids went round wiping the battlements with dusters, while she shouted rude remarks down at the Earl of Salisbury and his men. On the death of her brother she inherited the earldom of Moray, that and the earldom of Dunbar ultimately devolving on the two sons of her sister Isobel. This connection between Dunbar and Moray resulted in the Dunbar family being officially recognised as a Highland clan in 1579. James Dunbar (*d.* 1430), 4th and last Earl of Moray of that line, had a son, Sir Alexander Dunbar of Westfield (*d.* 1498), born before the dispensation for his parents' marriage could arrive from Rome. Towards the beginning of the fifteenth century he was appointed the first hereditary Sheriff of Moray, and from him are descended the Dunbars of Mochrum, who were created baronets in 1694 and hold the chiefship of the clan.

DUNBAR

Gavin Dunbar of Mochrum (1445-1532) was Archbishop of Glasgow and Lord Chancellor of Scotland in the reign of King James V. William Dunbar (1460-1520), born in East Lothian of humbler descent, was a disagreeable cleric at the court of King James IV, who nevertheless wrote some of the finest of all Scottish poetry, in an astonishing variety of forms and metres.

DUNCAN

Branches: *Duncan of Camperdown, Duncan of Lundie*

Tartan: *Duncan*

Motto: *Disce pati (Latin: Learn to suffer)*

The Duncans, like the Robertsons, are descended from the ancient earls of Atholl, and took their name from the chief, *Donnachadh Reamar* (Duncan the Fat), who led them at the Battle of Bannockburn in 1314.

Adam Duncan of Lundie (1731-1804) was the second son of a royalist provost of Dundee, and at six feet four inches was of enormous height for his time. He joined the Royal Navy in 1746, and in 1795 was appointed to command the North Sea fleet. He successfully blockaded the Dutch coastline for two years, in spite of his ships being reduced by mutiny, and in 1779 scored a brilliant tactical victory at Camperdown. He was created Baron Duncan of Lundie and Viscount Duncan of Camperdown in 1800.

DUNDAS

Branches: *Dundas of Arniston, Dundas of Fingask, Dundas of Inchgarvie*

Tartan: *Dundas*

Motto: *Essayez (French: Try)*

Serle de Dundas was a subject of King William I (the Lion) in the twelfth century. Sir Hugh and Sir George Dundas fought against the English at the beginning of

DUNCAN

DUNDAS

the fourteenth century, and Sir George's grandson, John, acquired Fingask in 1364.

King James IV presented the island of Inchgarvie in the Firth of Forth to the family, together with the right to build a castle there. Sir James Dundas (*d.* 1679) was created Lord Arniston in 1662. Though he had no formal legal training he served as a judge, and he sired a notable line of legal dignitaries. Robert (1685-1753), 4th Lord, was Lord President of the Court of Session. His first wife and four of his numerous children died of smallpox in January 1734, but Robert (1713-87), 5th Lord, survived and also became Lord President. The 4th Lord Arniston married again in June 1734, and had six more children, of whom the fourth son, Henry (1742-1811), created Viscount Melville in 1802, was Lord

DUNDAS OF   THAT ILK

Advocate and a successful parliamentarian, who in 1784 introduced the bill to restore estates forfeited after the '45 Rebellion, and as chairman of the Board of Control of the East India Company exercised his influence in favour of Scottish applicants for posts in the Indian civil service. Sir Walter Scott described the Board in 1821 as 'the corn chest for Scotland, where we poor gentry must send our younger sons, as we send our black cattle to the south'.

DUNLOP

DUNLOP

Tartans: *Dunlop (dress), Dunlop (hunting)*

Motto: *Merito (Latin: By merit)*

The lands of Dunlop are in Ayrshire, and the name is first recorded in 1260. James Dunlop possessed the estate at the beginning of the fifteenth century, but his

descendant, John Dunlop, for his support of the Covenanters, was forced to hand over a large part of it to Lord Dundonald, though it was returned to his grandson later. Francis Dunlop (*d.* 1748) fought as a colonel against the Jacobites in 1715, his son marrying Frances Anne Wallace (1730-1815), the friend and patron of Robert Burns (1759-96). Their son, General James Dunlop (*d.* 1832), fought in the Duke of Wellington's army in 1811. John Boyd Dunlop (1840-1921), inventor of the pneumatic tyre, was born in Dreghorn, Ayrshire. Thomas Dunlop (1855-1938), Glasgow ship owner and merchant, was made a baronet in 1916.

ELLIOT OF   REDHEUGH

ELLIOT(T)

Branches: *Elliot of Arkleton, Elliot of Minto, Elliot of Redheugh, Eliot of Stobs*

Tartan: *Elliot*

Mottos: *Fortiter et recte (Latin: Bravely and righteously); Soyez sage (French: Be wise)*

The Elliots, with the Armstrongs, were the most troublesome of the great Border families in the Middle Ages, the Redheugh branch being regarded as the most influential of them. Robert Elwold (or Elliot) of Redheugh fell at the Battle of Flodden in 1513, and from his third son came the Elliots of Arkleton. The Stobs branch stems from 1584, and to it descended the Redheugh lands. Gilbert Elliot of Stobs (1651-1718), known as 'Gibbie with the Golden Garters', was convicted of high treason in 1685 for plotting against the Catholic Duke of York, but was pardoned, and after the accession of William of Orange in 1689 he was knighted, appointed Clerk to the Privy Council, made a judge, and created Lord Minto. His son Gilbert (1693-1766), Lord Justice

ELLIOT

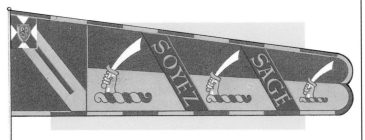

Erskine (*d.* 1385), Great Chamberlain of Scotland 1350-7, whose prompt action in 1371 against the claim of the Douglas family saved the throne for King Robert II, was granted a charter for the Barony of Dun in 1376. His son Thomas married the heiress to the earldom of Mar, and their younger son founded the branch of Dun.

The elder son, Robert, assumed the title of Earl of Mar, but was stripped of it on a technicality in 1457, and created Lord Erskine in 1467. Robert, 4th Lord Erskine, and many Erskines of Dun, fell at the Battle of Flodden in 1513. His grandson John (*d.* 1572), 6th Lord, Regent of Scotland during the sojourn in France of Mary, Queen of Scots (he later carried her son, the baby King James VI, at his coronation in 1567), was restored by her to the earldom of Mar in 1565, and also, in case her decision was ever revoked, given a new earldom of Mar, making him 18th and 1st Earl. The confusion was compounded by the actions of 'Bobbing John' (1675-1732), 23rd and 6th Earl of Mar, who forfeited both titles after his unsuccessful rebellion in 1715. Protracted lawsuits culminated in 1875 in the House of Lords with the 13th Earl of Kellie being granted also the earldom of Mar of 1565. The present 13th Earl of Mar and 15th Earl of Kellie (*b.* 1921) is chief of the family of Erskine.

Clerk of Scotland, was the father of the talented Jean Elliot of Minto (1727-1805), author of the best version of all of the traditional song *The Flowers of the Forest*, commemorating the Battle of Flodden in 1513. This line also produced Gilbert (1751-1814), 1st Earl of Minto, Governor-General of India 1806-13, and Gilbert (1847-1914), 4th Earl, Governor-General of Canada 1898-1904 and Viceroy of India 1905-10. The headship of the family resides with descendants of the 1st Baronet of Stobs, grandson of 'Gibbie' by his fourth son.

ERSKINE

Branches: *Erskine of Alva, Erskine of Cambo, Erskine of Dun, Erskine of Restormell*

Tartans: *Erskine, Erskine (hunting)*

Mottos: *Je pense plus (French: I think more); Decori decus addit avito (Latin: He adds honour to his ancestral honour)*

Henry of Erskine held the Barony of Erskine, Renfrewshire, in the reign of King Alexander II in the earlier part of the thirteenth century. Sir Robert of

ERSKINE

FARQUHARSON OF INVERCAULD

FARQUHARSON

Branches: *Farquharson of Allargue, Farquharson of Braemar, Farquharson of Finzean, Farquharson of Invercauld, Farquharson of Inverey, Farquharson of Monaltrie*

Tartan: *Farquharson*

Mottos: *Fide et fortitudine (Latin: With faith and fortitude); I force nae freen [friend], I fear nae foe*

Slogan: *Càrn na cuimhne (Gaelic: Cairn of remembrance)*

The clan began with Farquhar, son of Alexander Shaw, who lived at the beginning of the fifteenth century. His Aberdeenshire descendants called themselves Farquharson, and were prominent members of Clan Chattan. Farquhar's son Donald married Isobel Stewart of Invercauld, from whom the Farquharsons of Invercauld stemmed, as well as a number of other branches of the name.

The Farquharsons of Braemar, Invercauld, and Inverey supported the rising in 1715, and Francis Farquharson of Monaltrie commanded the three hundred Farquharsons who were in the centre of the Jacobite front line at the Battle of Culloden in 1746, though the most notable Farquharson supporter of the '45 Rebellion was a woman. Anne Farquharson of Invercauld, 20 years old and known as 'Colonel Anne' or 'La Belle Rebelle', was the wife of the chief of Clan

ABOVE AND TOP: FARQUHARSON

FERGUSSON   FERGUSSON OF KILKERRAN   FERGUSSON OF BALQUHIDDER

Mackintosh, who was away supporting the Government. She raised and personally inspected a contingent of the clan to fight on the other side, and in February 1746 entertained Bonnie Prince Charlie and organised a blacksmith and four of her servants to oppose and divert an attack on her house designed to capture him.

FERGUSSON

FERGUS(S)ON

Branches: *Fergusson of Atholl, Fergusson of Balemund, Fergusson of Balquhidder, Fergusson of Craigdarroch, Fergusson of Dunfallandy, Fergusson of Kilkerran*

Tartans: *Fergusson, Fergusson of Balquhidder*

Motto: *Dulcius ex asperis (Latin: Softer for having been through rough times)*

Slogan: *Clann Fhearghuis gu bràth (Gaelic: Clan Fergus for ever)*

The Fergussons (the spelling of the name with a single 's' is not known before the eighteenth century) are a widely spread clan, major families of which were established in various parts of Scotland before the sixteenth century. The Fergussons of Craigdarroch in the southwest probably came from Fergus, Prince of Galloway, who was a prominent figure at the beginning of the twelfth century and founded the Abbey of Dundrennan. The Fergussons of Kilkerran, Ayrshire, may be descended from 'John, son of Fergus', who witnessed a document shortly after the Battle of Bannockburn in 1314. During the eighteenth century the head of the Kilkerran branch came to be regarded as chief of the clan.

The Fergussons of Atholl have a forebear in 'Adam, son of Fergus', who held lands in Perthshire in the second half of the thirteenth century.

An earlier ancestor is claimed for all of them, however, Fergus *Mór mac Erc*, a very early, and shadowy, king of the Scots in Argyll.

Adam Ferguson (1724-1816) was a notable philosopher and historian. Sir Bernard Fergusson (1911-80), Lord Ballantrae, was one of the finest soldiers of World War II and Governor-General of New Zealand 1962-7. Robert Fergusson (1750-74) died in a madhouse, but still wrote some remarkable poetry in Scots, which strongly influenced Robert Burns (1759-96).

It was William Douglas of Fingland who wrote the original song *Annie Laurie*, about the lass with the 'rolling eye'. This seems to have been a dominant feature, for Annie, who died in 1764, married instead Alexander Fergusson of Craigdarroch.

FLETCHER OF DUNANS

FLETCHER OF SALTOUN

FORBES

FORBES DRESS

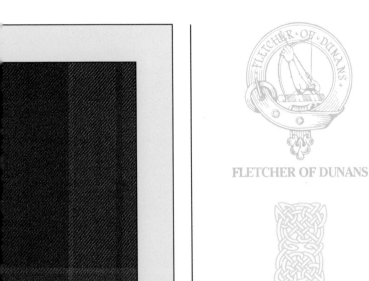

FLETCHER OF DUNANS

FORBES

FLETCHER OF DUNANS

Tartan: *Fletcher of Dunans*

A fletcher is a 'maker of arrows', and the medieval fletchers followed, and settled alongside, the clan whose needs they served. The Fletchers of Glenlyon made arrows for the MacGregors. A family of Fletchers moved to Dunans from Achallader at the head of Glenorchy, where they were replaced by Campbells. Archibald Fletcher (1746-1828), born in Glenlyon, was the eldest son of a younger brother of Archibald Fletcher of Bennice and Dunans. A lawyer and reformer (he is known as 'the father of burgh reform'), he was also an abolitionist, and favoured the cause of American independence.

FLETCHER OF SALTOUN

Tartan: *Fletcher of Saltoun*

Saltoun is in East Lothian, the estate being bought by the Fletchers of Innerpeffer, Angus, in 1643. Andrew Fletcher (*d.* 1650) was made Lord Innerpeffer in 1623. His son, Sir Robert Fletcher of Saltoun and Innerpeffer (*d.* 1665), married Catherine Bruce, daughter of Sir Henry Bruce of Clackmannan, who claimed descent from the grandfather of King Robert I (the Bruce). Their son, Andrew Fletcher of Saltoun (1653-1716), was the celebrated politician and political philosopher who strongly opposed the Act of Union of the Scottish and English parliaments in 1707.

FORBES

Branches: *Forbes of Craigievar, Forbes of Culloden, Forbes of Foveran, Forbes of Newe (Strathdon), Forbes of Pitsligo, Forbes of Tolquhoun, Forbes of Waterton*

Tartans: *Forbes, Forbes (dress)*

Motto: *Grace me guide*

Slogan: *Lónach (name of a mountain in Strathdon)*

Forbes is an ancient Aberdeenshire parish. The founder of the clan, one Oconochar, slew a bear, or a clan of bears, which was occupying the Braes o' Forbes, and took up occupation there. The tenure was confirmed by a charter of 1271. Sir John Forbes (*d.* 1406), 'John of the

Black Lip', had four sons from whom branches of the clan are descended, notably that of Tolquhoun, which dates from 1420 and from which came the lairds of Culloden.

Sir Alexander Forbes (*d.* 1448) was a famous jouster, who in 1407 was one of four knights who travelled to England for a match against four English knights. In 1424 he convoyed James I and his new queen back into Scotland after the King's imprisonment, and was later made Lord Forbes. He married a granddaughter of King Robert II, and it is from one of his grandsons that the baronets of Craigievar descended.

DUNCAN FORBES OF CULLODEN

Duncan Forbes of Culloden (1685-1747) was Lord President of the Court of Session in 1745. As a servant of the Crown he played a considerable part in dissuading sections of the Highlands from joining Bonnie Prince Charlie, and in persuading then to form Highland regiments under their own officers, though afterwards he was equally assiduous in recommending mercy for the rebels.

The Forbeses were great builders of castles, of which there are many remains, notably Corse Castle,

built in 1581 by William Forbes, who was so frustrated by vandals and burglars that he vowed, 'I will build me such a house as thieves will need to knock at ere they enter'. The result, a tower-house, was later the home of his eldest son, Patrick (1564-1635), Bishop of Aberdeen. Only a few miles away, still standing, inside and out, much as it did when it was built, is romantic Craigievar Castle, completed in 1626 by the Bishop's wealthy brother, William, known as 'Danzig Willie', for his activities as a merchant and entrepreneur in the Baltic.

FORSYTH

Tartan: *Forsyth*

The name may represent a place, possibly in the Edinburgh district, or be the Gaelic *Fearsithe*, 'man of peace'. Members of the family had connections with the royal household at Falkland Palace. In 1980 Alastair Forsyth (*b.* 1929), of Ethie Castle, Arbroath, successfully petitioned for official recognition as Clan Chief.

FORSYTH

FRAME

Tartan: *Frame*

The name is first recorded in north Lanarkshire in the fifteenth century.

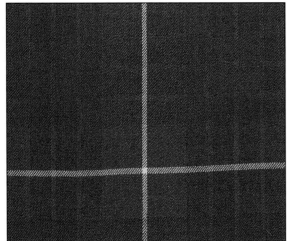

FRASER

FRASER OLD

FRASER OF LOVAT

FRASER OF LOVAT

FRASER

Branch: *Fraser of Lovat*

Tartans: *Fraser, Fraser (hunting), Fraser (old), Fraser of Lovat*

Mottos: *(Fraser) All my hope is in God; (Lovat) Je suis prest (French: I am ready)*

Slogans: *A Mhór-fhaiche (Gaelic: The Great Field); Caisteal Dhùni (Gaelic: Castle Downie)*

The first known Fraser in Scotland was Simon Fraser, who in about 1160 donated the church of Keith to Kelso Abbey. The name came from the lordship of La Fraselière in Anjou, and a descendant of Simon Fraser, Sir Gilbert Fraser, established the main line of the family in about 1250 at Touch-Fraser, Stirlingshire. His direct descendant, Alexander Fraser (*d.* 1332), was knighted by King Robert I (the Bruce) before the Battle of Bannockburn in 1314. After the battle he married the Bruce's sister, Lady Mary – who had been strung up in a cage for four years by King Edward I of England in reprisal for the Bruce's coronation – and he was later Chamberlain of Scotland. Their grandson gained the lands of Philorth in Buchan by his marriage in 1375.

Sir Alexander Fraser (1537-1623), 8th Laird of Philorth, founded Fraserburgh, and would have founded Fraserburgh University, too, if the project had not run into difficulties. He also built Fraserburgh Castle, which his family found too draughty to live in. The 9th Laird married the daughter and heiress of Lord Saltoun, their son succeeding to the Saltoun title, in which is now also vested the chiefship of Clan Fraser.

The Frasers of Lovat are descended from Sir Alexander Fraser's younger brother, Simon, who also fought at Bannockburn, and each chief of Clan Fraser of Lovat is known as *MacShimi* (son of Simon). Simon Fraser (1667-1747), 11th Lord Lovat, was one of the more colourful characters in the history of the Highlands. After his father had inherited the title of 10th Lord on the death of his great-nephew, Simon tried to abduct the 9th Lord's nine-year-old daughter and heiress. Foiled in this, he married her mother by force. In the early 1700s he regularly switched his allegiance between the Government in Britain and the Jacobites in France, playing one side off against the other. During the Rebellion of 1715, he appeared actively to support the Government. In 1745, he waited to see which way things were going, and then compromised by ordering his son to bring out the Frasers for Bonnie Prince Charlie. After the Battle of Culloden in 1746 he tried to escape, was captured, and (at the ripe age of 80) beheaded.

GAYRE

GAIR, GAYRE

Tartans: *Gayre, Gayre (hunting)*

The name may derive from Gaelic *geàrr* (short), but the ancient family which bears it is said to have originated in Cornwall, and to have come via Yorkshire to Nigg, in the northeast of Scotland. The headquarters of the clan is now at Minard Castle, Argyll.

GALBRAITH OF CULCREUCH

GALBRAITH

Tartan: *Galbraith (also Mitchell, Russell)*

Motto: *Ab obice suavior (Latin: Sweeter for there having been difficulties)*

The Galbraiths are known in Gaelic as *Clann o'Bhreatannaich*, 'the British clan', and its earliest members were Britons from north Wales who settled in Strathclyde, which was a separate kingdom until 1018. The first known chief is Gilchrist *Bretnach*, who married a daughter of the Earl of Lennox.

GALBRAITH

JOHN GILLIES, HISTORIAN

GILLIES

James, 19th Chief, is the last of the direct line of whom there is any trace. He was the grandson of Robert Galbraith of Culcreuch, 17th Chief, who died in Ireland in about 1640, a fugitive from justice, having given up all his lands to settle his debts. In 1592 Robert was one of those given a commission to harry the unfortunate MacGregors, but instead used his powers of 'fire and sword' to make life thoroughly uncomfortable for Sir Aulay Macaulay (*d.* 1617), chief of the Macaulays, who had married his widowed mother against his wishes.

Thomas Galbraith (1891-1985), created 1st Lord Strathclyde in 1955, was descended from William Galbraith of Blackhouse (1678-1757), in Stirlingshire.

GILLIES

Tartan: *Gillies*

The name means 'servant of Jesus' in Gaelic, and Uhtred, son of Gilise, held lands in Lothian in about 1160. People of this name lived in Badenoch, and it is a common surname in the Hebrides.

GORDON

Branches: *Gordon of Haddo, Gordon of Lochinvar, Gordon of Strathbogie*

Tartans: *Gordon, Gordon (red), Gordon (dress), Gordon (old, triple stripe)*

Mottos: *Bydand (Abiding); Animo non astutia (Latin: By courage not cunning)*

Slogan: *A Gordon! A Gordon!*

The name comes from the parish of Gordon in Berwickshire, and Sir Adam of Gordon (*d.* 1333) was granted Strathbogie in Aberdeenshire by King Robert I (the Bruce), in recognition of his services in reconciling the Bruce with the Pope and towards securing peace with England. His great-great-granddaughter, heiress to the family estates, married Alexander Seton of Seton, who took the name of Gordon, and their son Alexander was created Earl of Huntly in 1449.

The Gordons wielded enormous power during the sixteenth and early seventeenth centuries, to the extent that their chief was known as 'Cock of the North'. The 6th Earl was made Marquis in 1599, but the 2nd Marquis

was beheaded in 1649 by the Scottish Parliament for his loyalty to King Charles I, going to the block with the words, 'You may take my head from my shoulders, but not my heart from my king.'

The 4th Marquis became Duke of Gordon in 1684, and Alexander Gordon (1743-1827), 4th Duke, with the support of his energetic first duchess, Jane Maxwell (1749-1812), raised at their own expense in 1793 the regiment which was later resuscitated as the Gordon Highlanders, for whom a yellow stripe was introduced into the Black Watch tartan.

Patrick Gordon of Methlic was killed in 1445 in the Battle of Arbroath, which took place between two factions each wanting power during the boyhood of King James II. The family acquired the lands of Haddo in 1533. John Gordon of Haddo (*d.* 1644) was created a baronet of Nova Scotia for *his* loyalty to King Charles I, and his second son, George (1637-1720), became Lord High Chancellor of Scotland in 1682 (having survived a shipwreck on his way back from London for his formal appointment), and was made Earl of Aberdeen. John Gordon (1847-1934), 7th Earl of Aberdeen, was Governor-General of Canada 1893-8.

The Gordons of Lochinvar descended from the second son of Sir Adam of Gordon, acquiring the lands of Lochinvar and Kenmure in the fourteenth century.

The mother of the poet Lord Byron (1788-1824) was Catherine Gordon of Gight, who inherited Gight Castle and its lands, only to have to sell them in 1787 to pay off the gambling debts of her profligate husband.

GOW, MACGOWAN

Tartan: *Gow*

Motto: *Touch not the cat bot [without] a glove*

Gow is Gaelic *gobhan*, smith or blacksmith, such as every clan would have needed to make weapons and

GORDON, MARQUIS OF HUNTLY

ALEXANDER, 4TH DUKE OF GORDON

GOW

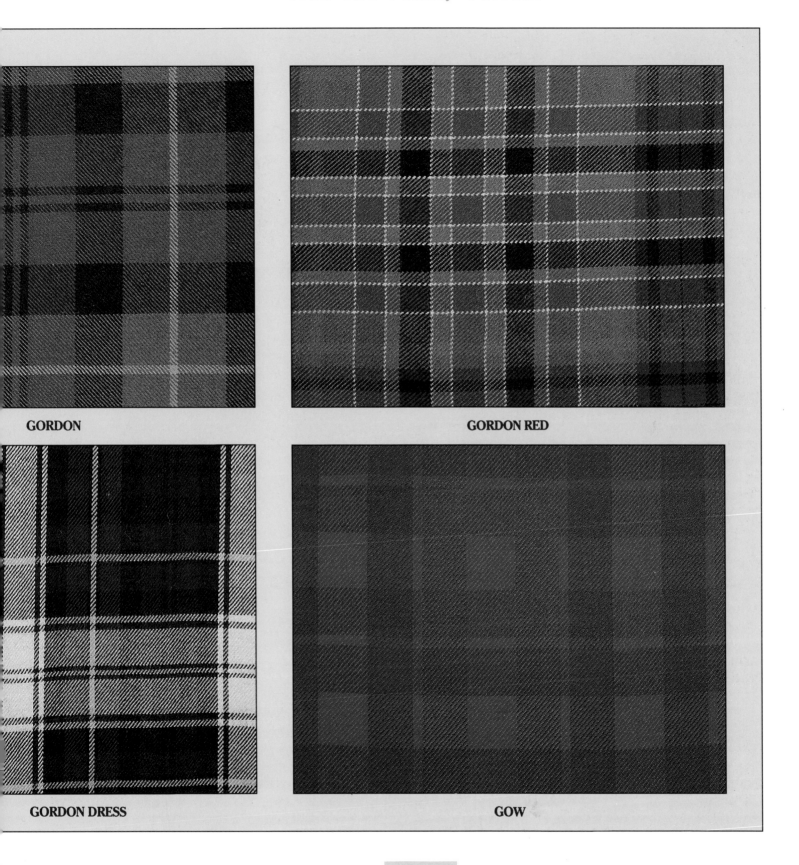

GORDON

GORDON RED

GORDON DRESS

GOW

shoes for its horses. Several ancient families are recorded, notably in Stirlingshire and Dumfriesshire, but the principal one appears to have been closely connected with Clan Macpherson.

Niel Gow (1727-1807) and his son Nathaniel (1766-1831), both born in Inver, near Dunkeld, Perthshire, were pre-eminent among composers and players of fiddle music, and it well may be that Niel, or his father (who was a plaid weaver), designed the trews he is wearing in four portraits by Sir Henry Raeburn (1756-1823), the pattern of which has become the sett of the Gow tartan.

GRAHAM OF MENTEITH

GRAHAM OF MENTEITH

Branches: *Graham of Dundaff, Graham of Esk,*
Graham of Netherby, Graham of Norton-Conyers

Tartan: *Graham of Menteith*

Motto: *Right and reason*

William de Graham witnessed the charter of the Abbey of Holyrood in 1128, and obtained from King David I the lands of Dalkeith. Towards the end of the twelfth century his descendant acquired the lands of Dundaff. Towards the end of the fourteenth century Sir Patrick Graham of Dundaff, second son of a chief of the Grahams, married Euphemia, heiress of Prince David, Earl of Stratherne, son of King Robert II. Their son, Malise Graham, had the earldom of Stratherne removed from him by King James I and given to his uncle, Robert Graham, on the grounds

that his mother should not have inherited a title whose descent was strictly through the male line, but received the earldom of Menteith instead.

The Grahams of Esk, Netherby, and Norton-Conyers are descended from Malise Graham's second son.

JAMES GRAHAM, MARQUIS OF MONTROSE

GRAHAM OF MONTROSE

Branches: *Graham of Balgowan, Graham of*
Claverhouse

Tartan: *Graham of Montrose*

Motto: *Ne oublie (French: Do not forget)*

The house of Graham of Montrose stems from the younger son of William de Graham, a descendant of whom acquired Old Montrose and lands around from Robert I (the Bruce) in 1325.

Sir William Graham of Kincardine married in about 1410 as his second wife Mary Stewart, second daughter of King Robert III and widow of George Douglas (*d.* 1403), 1st Earl of Angus, and of Sir James Kennedy, by whom she had James Kennedy (1408-65), Bishop of St Andrews and Lord Chancellor of Scotland (after Graham's death

GRAHAM, DUKE OF MONTROSE

GRANT

she acquired a fourth husband). One of their sons, Patrick Graham (*d.* 1478), succeeded Kennedy at St Andrews and persuaded Pope Paul II to promote the see to an archbishopric.

The eldest son was 1st Laird of Fintry and ancestor of the branch of Claverhouse, and from a third son descended the Grahams of Balgowan. Patrick Graham, a grandson of Sir William, was made Lord Graham in 1445, and William Graham, 3rd Lord, was advanced to Earl of Montrose in 1504.

James Graham (1612-50), 5th Earl and from 1644 1st Marquis of Montrose, was the gallant and magnetic hero of the campaigns in Scotland for King Charles I and then for King Charles II. His cousin, John Graham of Claverhouse (1648-89), Viscount Dundee, but for his unlucky death at the Battle of Killiecrankie, might have achieved what they both, and Bonnie Prince Charlie after them, so gloriously failed to do. James Graham (*d.* 1747), 4th Marquis of Montrose, was created Duke of Montrose in 1707. Between 1712 and 1724, when he gave up in desperation, he prosecuted a running feud against Rob Roy MacGregor (1671-1734).

GRAHAM OF MONTROSE

GRANT

Branches: *Grant of Ballindalloch, Grant of Corriemony, Grant of Glenmoriston, Grant of Monymusk, Grant of Rothiemurcus, Grant of Tullochgorm*

Tartans: *Grant (red), Grant (hunting), Grant of Monymusk*

Motto: *Stand fast*

Slogan: *Stand fast Craigellachie [the clan meeting place]*

The most likely of several acounts of the beginnings of the clan is that it is of Norman-Scottish origin. The earliest occurrence of the name is that of Sir Laurence de Grant, Sheriff of Inverness 1263-4. There is a tradition that some Grants, having holed up in a church the Laird of Glencharnie and his followers, and not wanting to commit sacrilege by going in and killing them, burned it and the men inside instead. Then their chief, John Grant, Sheriff of Inverness in 1434, married Glencharnie's daughter and heiress, and through her obtained the

GRANT   GRANT, LORD STRATHSPEY   GRANT HUNTING

Barony of Freuchie, of which their son, Sir Duncan Grant, is styled 1st Laird. This is the main stem of the family, Ludovic Grant, 8th Laird of Freuchie, having his name officially changed to Grant of Grant (or Grant of that Ilk) in 1694.

The oldest branch is Grant of Ballindalloch, descending from Sir Duncan's eldest son. From sons of the 2nd Laird come the Grants of Corriemony, Glenmoriston, and Tullochgorm; from a son of the 3rd Laird, the Grants of Ballintomb, who in time became the Grants of Monymusk in Aberdeenshire; and from the younger son of the 4th Laird, the Grants of Rothiemurcus.

Elizabeth Grant of Rothiemurcus (1797-1885) wrote a highly entertaining and richly detailed account of her life, *Memoirs of a Highland Lady* (1898).

In 1820 the Earl of Seafield became the last Highland chief to call out his clan by means of the 'fiery cross'. An invalid, he was barricaded inside his house in Elgin by supporters of his brother's opponent in the election for Parliament. A message was got out, the clan assembled and marched to Elgin, singing psalms (it was Sunday). At their approach the besiegers melted away.

John Charles Grant (1815-81) was created Lord Strathspey in 1858. He left as his memorial the 14 million fir trees which he planted in the Duthil district. In 1915 the chiefship of Clan Grant was inherited by the successor to the Strathspey title.

GUNN OF   KILEARNAN

GUNN

Branches: *Gunn of Banniskirk, Gunn of Kilearnan*

Tartan: *Gunn*

Motto: *Aut pax aut bellum (Latin: Either peace or war)*

The Gunns, who originally inhabited Caithness and Sutherland, claim descent from Guinn, son of the Norseman, Olaf the Black (*d.* 1237), King of Man and the Isles

A long-running feud with the Keiths began when a Keith of Ackergill brought a band of followers and abducted the beautiful daughter of a Gunn, who had

rejected his advances and become betrothed to a cousin. Many Gunns were killed in the attack on the house, and the girl herself committed suicide by jumping off the tower of Ackergill. George Gunn, a later chief of the clan, known as 'Crowner Gunn' from his office as Coroner of Caithness, proposed in 1464 that to end the feud the Gunns and the Keiths should fight on horseback, twelve horses a side. The Keiths turned up with two men on each horse, and duly slaughtered their opponents, including the chief, whose grandson responded by ambushing and killing Keith of Ackergill, his son, and ten others.

There was further trouble, this time between the Gunns and the Mackays, at the end of the sixteenth century, which was resolved when in about 1660 the daughter of Alexander Gunn of Kilearnan married the brother of the chief of Clan Mackay.

Neil M. Gunn (1891-1973) wrote some excellent novels about the emotional conflicts and clashes of culture inherent in the Highlands. There is a Clan Gunn Centre at Latheron, Caithness.

GUTHRIE

GUTHRIE

Tartan: *Guthrie*

Motto: *Sto pro veritate (Latin: I stand for truth)*

The family held the Barony of Guthrie, Forfar, in the fourteenth century, but earlier than this, in 1299, Squire Guthrie was sent to France by the northern lords to bring back Sir William Wallace (1274-1305) to help his country against the English.

Sir David Guthrie, armour-bearer to King James III and Lord Treasurer of Scotland 1461-7, had a charter in

GUTHRIE

1468 to build a tower and castle on the Guthrie lands.

An old rhyme, printed in 1841 in *Popular Rhymes of Scotland*, lists the branches of this 'respectable old Forfarshire family': 'Guthrie o' Guthrie/Guthrie o' Gaiggie/Guthrie o' Taybank/An' Guthrie o' Craigie.'

GUNN

EARL HAIG OF BEMERSYDE

HAIG

Tartan: *Haig (also known as Buccleuch and Gladstone check)*

Motto: *Tyde what may*

Peter de Haga, 1st Laird of Bemersyde, Roxburghshire, witnessed several charters made to the monks of Melrose in the twelfth century. The 27th Laird, Sophia Haig, died unmarried in 1878, and Bemersyde passed to Lieut-Colonel Arthur Haig (1840-1925), descended from a younger son of the 17th Laird. He sold it in 1921 so that it could be presented by the nation, for his services during World War I, to Field-Marshal Sir Douglas, 1st Earl Haig (1861-1928), another descendant of the 17th Laird, who thus became 29th Laird.

HAIG

JAMES, 1st DUKE OF HAMILTON

HAMILTON

Branches: *Dukes of Abercorn, Earls of Haddington, Hamilton of Airdrie, Hamilton of Dalserf, Hamilton of Preston, Hamilton of Raploch, Hamilton of Silvertonhill*

Tartans: *Hamilton, Hamilton (hunting)*

Motto: *Through*

Walter FitzGilbert, son of Gilbert of Hamilton, was given the Barony of Cadzow by King Robert I (the Bruce), his descendant, James Hamilton (*d.* 1479), 6th Laird, being made Lord Hamilton in 1445. One of his illegitimate sons was father of Patrick Hamilton (1504-28), the first martyr for the Scottish Reformation, who was burned at the stake in St Andrews. Lord Hamilton's son by his second wife, Mary, was created Earl of Arran in 1503, and from him descended the marquises of Hamilton (Dukes from 1643) and the earls of Abercorn.

HAMILTON, DUKE OF HAMILTON

HANNAY

Mary was a daughter of King James II and through that marriage the Hamiltons were for much of the sixteenth century heirs presumptive to the throne, and were also prominent in offices of state.

Anne (1636-1717), Duchess of Hamilton, married William Douglas (1635-94), Earl of Selkirk, who became 3rd Duke of Hamilton in 1663. Sir Thomas Hamilton (1563-1637), descended from a minor branch of the family, was Lord President of the Court of Session and Keeper of the Privy Seal. He was created Lord Binning in 1613, and in 1619 Earl of Melrose, which he successfully petitioned to be changed to Haddington in 1626. Lord Binning (1697-1732), elder son of the 6th Earl of Haddington, married Rachel Baillie (1696-1779), daughter of George Baillie of Jerviswood and Mellerstain (1664-1738) and Lady Grisell Baillie (1665-1746), child heroine of the Covenanting wars and poet, through whom the magnificent Mellerstain House in Berwickshire, built between 1725 and 1778, came into the family.

HANNAY

Tartan: *Hannay*

Motto: *Per ardua ad alta (Latin: Through difficulties to the heights)*

Gilbert de Hannette, in Wigtownshire, rendered homage to King Edward I of England in 1296, at about the time when the Hannays of Torbie owned lands in the same district. John of Hanna was master of one of the ships of King James I in 1424.

The Hannays were a fairly lively family, the Sorbie branch of which conducted a feud against the Murrays, as a result of which it was outlawed in 1601. The present chiefship is vested in the Kirkdale branch.

HARKNESS

Tartan: *Harkness*

The name, whose origin is obscure, is recorded in Dumfriesshire in the sixteenth century. James Harkness of Locherben led the rescue in 1684 of a group of Covenanters who were being taken for trial in Edinburgh, an act for which his brother was hanged the following year.

HAMILTON

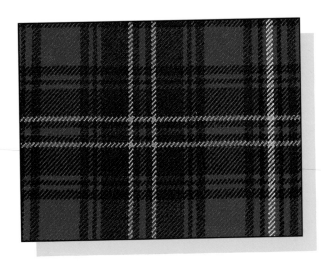

HAY

HAY

Branches: *Hay of Delgaty, Hay of Megginch and Kinfauns, Hay of Yester*

Tartans: *Hay, Hay and Leith*

Motto: *Serva jugum (Latin: Preserve the yoke)*

Slogan: *A Hay, A Hay, A Hay!*

William de Hay, of Norman descent, was joint hereditary cupbearer both to King Malcolm IV and King William I (the Lion). Between 1178 and 1182 he received from King William the Barony of Erroll, though legend (and a fifteenth-century historian) has it that it came to the family because that was the direction a falcon flew to mark out the family's reward for turning the course of a battle against the Norsemen by the vigorous use of ox-yokes. Sir Gilbert Hay, 5th Laird and Clan Chief, was made hereditary Constable of Scotland by King Robert I (the Bruce) and given Slains Castle, Buchan, which was destroyed by King James VI in 1595. The 4th High Constable married a daughter of King Robert II, and the Hays of Delgaty are descended from their second son. The elder son was grandfather of William, made Earl of Erroll in 1452. William, 4th Earl, was killed at the Battle of Flodden in 1513, along with 87 other Hays. The family also engendered the marquises of Tweeddale (through the Yester branch) and the earls of Kinnoull (through the Megginch and Kinfauns branch), but the office of chief constable and, presently, the chiefship of the clan, are vested in the earls of Erroll, and may descend through the female line.

HENDERSON (or MACKENDRICK)

Tartan: *Henderson*

Motto: *Sola virtus nobilitat (Latin: Only virtue ennobles)*

The Highland Hendersons claim to be descended from Eanruig Mór (Big Henry), son of Nechtan, King of the Picts in 710. A further tradition has it that the chiefship of the Hendersons of Glencoe passed through an heiress to her son, *Iain Fruoch* (Heather John), progenitor of the unfortunate McIans of Glencoe.

Other Hendersons in Caithness are descendants of Hendry, son of 'Crowner George' Gunn. Alexander Henderson (1583-1646), the Covenanter and Presbyterian divine who drafted the Solemn League and Covenant in 1643, was a Henderson of Fordell, with descent from James Henderson, 1st Laird of Fordell, Lord Advocate in 1494.

HENDERSON

HEPBURN, EARL OF BOTHWELL

HEPBURN

Tartan: *Hepburn*

Motto: *Keep traist [trust]*

Hepburns are first heard of in Northumberland, and Adam de Hibburne was granted Hailes, in East Lothian, among other lands by the Earl of March, 'for good and faithful service', which appears to have included saving his life from an attack by a wild horse.

HEPBURN

Patrick de Hepburn of Hailes, who, with his father, fought at the Battle of Otterburn in 1388, was twice married. His great-grandson by his first wife was made Earl of Bothwell in 1488. James Hepburn (1536-78), 4th Earl of Bothwell, was the third husband of Mary, Queen of Scots. He died insane, a prisoner in Denmark, having forfeited all his titles and without legitimate issue.

From Patrick of Hailes by his second wife descended the Hepburns of Smeaton Hepburn, the estate passing to Sir George Buchan-Hepburn (1738-1819).

HERD

Tartan: *Herd*

The name means, simply, a herdsman of flocks or a shepherd, and the first significant person of that name was the attorney of Bernard, Abbot of Aberbrothoc in 1328. It is a name particularly associated with Angus and Galloway.

HOME, HUME

Branches: *Home of Blackadder, Home of Broomhouse, Home of Coldingknows, Home of Manderston, Home of Polwarth, Home of Simprin, Home of Wedderburn*

Tartan: *Home*

Slogan: *A Home, A Home, A Home!*

The Homes or Humes (the spelling seems to be a matter of personal preference) go back at least to Aldan de Home in the twelfth century, whose descendant, Sir Thomas Home, married the heiress of Dunglass. Sir Alexander Home of Dunglass, their eldest son, was killed at Verneuil in 1424, fighting against the English for a combined French and Scottish force, and his younger sons founded minor branches of the family, including

HOME

the Homes of Ninewells. His eldest son, Sir Alexander Home of Home (*d.* 1456), was Warden of the Marches in the Borders, and *his* eldest son, Sir Alexander (*d.* 1491) was made 1st Lord Home in 1473. The 3rd Lord was Lord Chamberlain of Scotland and Warden of the Marches in the reign of King James IV, and performed nobly at the Battle of Flodden in 1513, only to be executed the following year for rebelling against the Regent, John Stewart (1481-1536), 1st Duke of Albany. The 6th Lord was created Earl of Home in 1605.

The title descended via the Homes of Coldingknows (a branch stemming from John Home of Whiterings and Essilton, grandson of the 1st Lord) and a marriage with the heiress to the Douglas estates, to the 13th Earl (*b.* 1903), who renounced the title in 1963 to become Prime Minister as Sir Alec Douglas-Home, later being made Lord Home of the Hirsel, the family seat of the earls of Home.

From David Home of Wedderburn, younger brother of Sir Alexander Home of Dunglass, descended the Homes of Polwarth, of whom Sir Patrick Hume (1641-1724), 1st Earl of Marchmont, was the father of Lady Grisell Baillie (1665-1724), poet and first chatelaine of Mellerstain House, with which the Baillie-Hamiltons, present earls of Haddington, are so closely associated.

David Hume (1711-1776), the philosopher and historian, author of *An Enquiry Concerning Human Understanding* (1758) and *An Enquiry Concerning the Principles of Morals* (1751), was a son of Joseph Hume of Ninewells. The Homes of Blackadder, Broomhouse, Manderston, and Simprin are descended from Sir David Home, 3rd Laird of Wedderburn, who had seven sons, known as the 'Seven Spears of Wedderburn'.

HUNTER OF HUNTERSTON

Tartans: *Hunter of Hunterston, Hunter*

Motto: *Cursum perficio (Latin: I follow the chase)*

The name derives from the hunt, and therefore it occurs widely at an early stage. The Hunters of Hunterston appear to have held the lands in Ayrshire in the early part of the thirteenth century, and obtained a charter for them in 1375.

William Hunter (1718-1783), the anatomist, whose acquisitions of paintings, artefacts, fossils, coins, and anatomical and pathological specimens are still the basis of the collections at the Hunterian Museum, Glasgow University, and his brother John (1728-93), the surgeon, were descended from a younger son of Patrick

HUNTER OF HUNTERSTON

HUNTER OF HUNTERSTON

HUNTER

Hunter, great-grandson of Mungo, or Quentegern, Hunter of Hunterston, who fell at the Battle of Pinkie in 1547.

Neil Kennedy-Cochran-Patrick (*b.* 1926) was officially recognised by the Lyon Court in 1969 in the name of Hunter of Hunterston as being 29th Laird of Hunterston and Chief of Clan Hunter.

INGLIS

INGLIS

Tartan: *Inglis*

Motto: *Recte faciendo securus (Latin: Safe, by right doing)*

Inglis means 'Englishman', and the name occurs in a number of records of the twelfth and thirteenth centuries.

James Inglis (*d.* 1531), Abbot of Culross, chaplain and secretary to the royal family, was murdered by his neighbour and a priest, both of whom were beheaded for the deed.

Rear-Admiral Charles Inglis (1731-91), younger son of Sir John Inglis of Cramond, Bart, served at sea during the French and Spanish wars. Lieut-General Sir William Inglis (1764-1835), son of a surgeon descended from a landed family in Roxburghshire, fought in the Peninsular War.

John Inglis (1810-91), Lord Justice-General of Scotland, son of a minister in Perthshire, was created Lord Glencorse in 1867, the ensuing baronetcy devolving in 1958 on Sir Maxwell Inglis, 9th Baronet of Glencorse, great-great-grandson of Rev. John Inglis, of Edinburgh.

INNES OF   THAT ILK

INNES

Branches: *Innes of Balveny, Innes of Benwell, Innes of Coxton, Innes of Innermarkie*

Tartan: *Innes*

Motto: *Be traist [trustworthy]*

Slogan: *An Innes, An Innes!*

Bercowald the Fleming received the Barony of Innes in Moray from King Malcolm IV in 1160. 'Good Sir Robert', 8th Laird from 1364 to 1381, had three successful sons: Sir Alexander, 9th Laird, who married the heiress of Aberchirder; John, Bishop of Moray 1407-14, who restored Elgin Cathedral after it had been destroyed in 1390 by Alexander Stewart (1343-1405), Earl of Buchan (called 'Wolf of Badenoch' for this act of depredation);

INNES

and George, head of the Scottish Trinitarian friars.

'Ill Sir Robert', 11th Laird, founded the Greyfriars of Elgin in penance for a wild and wicked life. William Innes, 15th Laird, tried to assassinate the Prior of Pluscarden on the altar steps of Elgin Cathedral in 1554, and was a member of the Scottish Parliament in 1560 which repudiated Catholicism. Robert Innes, 19th Laird, was fascinated, as was his king, James VI, by witchcraft, and is reported as having seen, and entertained, the queen of the fairies. The 20th Laird was created 1st Baronet in 1625.

Sir James Innes (1738-1823), 6th Baronet, became 5th Duke of Roxburghe in 1805, taking the name of Ker-Innes, and his son was made also Earl Innes in 1836, the chiefship of the clan continuing to be vested in this line.

Sir Thomas Innes of Learney (1893-1971), of a line descended from the Inneses of Innnermarkie, from which the Balveny branch also stems, was Lord Lyon King of Arms 1945-69, a position held since 1981 by his youngest son, Sir Malcolm Innes of Edingight (*b.* 1938).

IRVINE

the outbreak of the Civil War prevented him from formally accepting it. The offer was renewed to his son by King Charles II after the Restoration of the Monarchy in 1660, but was refused.

IRVINE OF DRUM

IRVINE

Tartan: *Irvine*

Motto: *Sub sole sub umbra virens (Latin: Flourishing in the sun and in the shade)*

Irwins held lands in Dumfriesshire at the beginning of the thirteenth century. A member of that family, William de Irwin, was armour-bearer to King Robert I (the Bruce), who granted him the forest of Drum, Aberdeenshire, in 1324. From him descended the Irvines of Drum, the principal family of that name. Sir Alexander Irvine of Drum (*d.* 1658) was a confirmed royalist to whom King Charles I gave the earldom of Aberdeen, but

JARDINE OF APPLEGIRTH

JARDINE

Tartans: *Jardine, Jardine (new: with Chief's permission only)*

Motto: *Cave adsum (Latin: Beware my presence)*

Jardine is the French *jardin*, and means of (or in) 'the garden', the name being recorded in Scotland in the twelfth century. John Jardine of Applegirth, in Dumfriesshire, was granted a charter in 1476, and that family has been the principal one ever since, Alexander Jardine being created a baronet of Nova Scotia in 1672.

Robert Jardine (1825-1905), Member of Parliament for Dumfriesshire 1880-92, whose father was born in the

parish of Appplegirth, was made a baronet in 1885, his direct descendants having now assumed the name of Buchanan-Jardine.

JOHNSTON(E)

Branches: *Johnstone of Alva, Johnstone of Annandale, Johnston of Caskieben, Johnstone of Elphinstone, Johnston of Galabank, Johnston of Mylnefield, Johnston of Newbie, Johnston of Westerhall*

Tartan: *Johnstone*

Motto: *Nunquam non paratus (Latin: Never unprepared)*

This powerful Border clan, some of whose members used to sally forth from their Annandale fastness at the head of the river, and which from 1585 to 1623 waged open war against the Maxwells, probably originated with Sir Gilbert de Johnstoun in about 1200. At various times the chiefship has been vested in the line of Lord Johnstone (created 1633), who was made Earl of Hartfell

JOHNSTONE, EARL OF ANNANDALE

(1643), his son being made Earl of Annandale and Hartfell (1661), and his great-grandson Marquis of Annandale (1701). It has subsequently descended through the earls of Hopetoun, who acquired it through marriage. The Johnstons of Westerhall are descended from an early offshoot of the main stem, and the 3rd Baronet was made Lord Derwent in 1881.

A separate Aberdeenshire line claims descent from Steven de Johnston, a fourteenth-century scholar, whose grandson founded the branch of Caskieben, and whose representative was granted a Nova Scotia baronetcy in 1626. Sir John Johnston, 3rd Baronet, was hanged in 1690 for being present at the wedding of Capt. the Hon. James Campbell and Mary Wharton, an heiress whom Campbell was said to have abducted.

KEITH

Tartan: *Keith (also known as Keith and Austin and sometimes as Marshall)*

Motto: *Veritas vincit (Latin: Truth prevails)*

The story of the Keiths is not so much the feud with the Gunns in Caithness, as the progress of the marischals of Scotland, hereditary keepers of the royal horses.

Hervey, Sheriff of Haddington in 1170, who may have been an ancestor of the Keiths, held that office in the reign of King William I (the Lion). Sir Robert Keith (*d.* 1346), Great Marischal, commanded Robert the Bruce's cavalry at the Battle of Bannockburn in 1314, and was afterwards rewarded with the royal forest of Kintore. Sir William Keith was created 1st Earl Marischal of Scotland by James II in 1458. The 4th Earl founded Marischal College, Aberdeen.

After the Battle of Worcester was lost by Charles II, William (1617-71), 7th Earl Marischal, who was also Warden of the Regalia of Scotland, sent the royal crown,

JOHNSTONE

KENNEDY, MARQUIS OF AILSA

KEITH

KENNEDY

Branches: *Kennedy of Cassilis, Kennedy of Culzean, Kennedy of Dunure*

Tartan: *Kennedy*

Motto: *Avise la fin (French: Consider the end)*

The Kennedys emerged in Ayrshire. In the fourteenth century John Kennedy of Dunure, having acquired Cassilis by his first marriage, married as his second wife Mary of Carrick, with whom came to him the right to be chief of the men of Carrick. Their grandson, Sir James Kennedy of Dunure (*d.* 1409) was second husband of Mary Stewart, daughter of Robert III. Of their three sons, the youngest, James (1408-65), was Bishop of St Andrews and adviser to King James II, and Gilbert (1406-80), one of the regents during the minority of King James III, was

sceptre, and sword to his stupendous castle at Dunnottar, on the coast by Stonehaven, for safe keeping. They were secretly transported there in panniers on the back of an old horse, ridden by a minister's wife disguised as a peasant woman. The English realised they were there, and for eight months laid siege to the castle, which only capitulated after ten solid days of bombardment by cannon. Then they rushed in and tore the place apart. The Regalia were nowhere to be found. They had in the meantime been lowered over the battlements to the shore, where the maid from the nearby manse of Kinneff, who was often to be seen collecting seaweed, gathered them into her basket and took them away. Eight years later, at the Restoration of Charles II, the items were produced, and for his part in the operation, the 8th Earl Marischal, brother of the 7th Earl, was created Earl Kintore, with the Latin motto, *Quae amissa salva* (Save what has been lost).

KENNEDY

KERR

KERR, MARQUIS OF LOTHIAN

KERR HUNTING

made Lord Kennedy in 1457. The 3rd Lord was created Earl of Cassilis in 1509 and died in the Battle of Flodden in 1513. The 2nd Earl was killed by the Sheriff of Ayr in 1527, and the 3rd Earl was one of the members of the commission for the marriage of Mary, Queen of Scots, to the Dauphin of France, who were poisoned in 1558.

Gilbert (1541-76), 4th Earl, is notorious for 'roasting the Abbot of Crossraguel' in 1570, in an attempt to force the unfortunate man (who was commendator, or licensee of the abbey and its lands) to give up part of his concession. The 3rd Earl had married Margaret Kennedy of Bargany, and it was between the Kennedys of Cassilis and of Bargany that the fiercest of the great family feuds of the late sixteenth century was fought, culminating in a battle near Maybole in 1601 and several subsequent murders by way of reprisal.

The earldom of Cassilis passed to the Kennedys of Culzean in 1759, who became marquises of Ailsa in 1806. Culzean Castle, built round an ancient tower of the Kennedys, dates largely from 1777.

KERR

Branches:	*Kerr of Cessford, Kerr of Ferniehurst*
Tartans:	*Kerr, Kerr (hunting)*
Motto:	*Sero sed serio (Latin: Tardily but thoroughly)*

The first recorded Kerr (or Ker or Carr) is John Ker of Swinhope, near Peebles, in the twelfth century. The

great branches of Cessford and Ferniehurst are said to have descended from two brothers, who lived by Jedburgh in about 1330. Down the years there was the greatest rivalry between them, sometimes with bloodshed. The Cessford Kerrs received their grant of land in 1467, and built a castle on it. At about the same time, a younger son got by marriage the castle of Ferniehurst, a few miles away.

For some years the Warden of the Middle March was alternately a Cessford and a Ferniehurst. Andrew Kerr of Ferniehurst was made Lord Jedburgh in 1662, the title devolving on the marquises of Lothian, who were descended from Mark Kerr, commendator (licensee) of Newbattle Abbey in 1547, who was a second son of a Kerr of Cessford.

Sir Robert Kerr of Cessford (1570-1650) was made Lord Roxburghe in 1600, and Earl of Roxburghe in 1616. John Ker (*d.* 1741), 5th Earl, as a secretary of state for Scotland, was prominent in furthering the union of the two parliaments in 1707, and was created 1st Duke of Roxburghe.

KIDD

KILGOUR

KINCAID

LAMONT

LAMONT OF
LAMONT

KIDD, KYD

Tartan: *Kidd*

The name is probably a diminutive of Christopher, and is recorded in the twelfth and thirteenth centuries in Angus. Alexander Kyd held lands in Aberdeen in 1492, and William Kyd in Alloa in 1571.

KILGOUR

Tartan: *Kilgour*

The name derives from Kilgour, an ancient parish near Falkland, and is common in Fife and Aberdeenshire, and also in northern Australia, where there is a river of the same name.

KINCAID

Tartan: *Kincaid*

The name is from the lands of Kincaid in Stirlingshire, and is recorded in the fifteenth century. Jean Kincaid (1579-1600) incited a servant to batter to death with his fists her brutal husband, John Kincaid of Warriston, a descendant of the original Stirling family, and was beheaded for her part in the crime. Sir John Kincaid (1787-1902) served in the Peninsular War and at the Battle of Waterloo in 1815, and afterwards wrote a lively account of his experiences, *Adventures in the Rifle Brigade* (1840).

LAMONT

Branch: *Lamont of Knockdow*

Tartan: *Lamont*

Motto: *Ne parcas nec spernas (Latin: Do not be disrespectful or scornful)*

In about 1240 Laumun and his father, Malcolm, son of Ferchar, granted lands at Kilmun and Kilfinan to the monks of Paisley.

John Lamont of Inveryne, owner of Toward Castle, was knighted in 1539, and until 1646, when Ardlamont became the principal seat, the chiefs of the clan used the suffix 'of Inveryne'. That same year, 1646, saw the appalling revenge of the Campbells for the slaughter of their ranks by the Lamonts, who fought against them for the Marquis of Montrose. Toward was besieged and capitulated on promise of safe conduct for its occupants. Instead, according to the chief's own account, no one over the age of seven who was called Lamont was spared. The Lamonts of Knockdow are descended from Geoffrey Lamont, Laird of Knockdow in about 1430.

LAUDER

LAUDER

Tartan: *Lauder*

The name comes from Lauder in Berwickshire, and in the thirteenth century the Lauders owned Bass Rock in the Firth of Forth.

John Lauder (*d*. 1692), an Edinburgh merchant, who received the Barony of Fountainhall in 1681, was created a baronet in 1690. Sir John Lauder (*d*. 1722), 2nd Baronet, a judge of the Court of Session, was made Lord Fountainhall in 1689. The 5th Baronet married his cousin Isobel (*d*. 1758), heiress of William Dick of Grange. The

family name was changed to Dick-Lauder in the time of the 7th Baronet, Sir Thomas Dick-Lauder (1784-1848), author and antiquary, whom the Sobieski Stuart brothers enlisted as a supporter of the authenticity of their tartan theories and creations.

Sir Harry Lauder (1870-1950), the famous entertainer, was born in Musselburgh.

LEASK

Tartan: *Leask*

The name derives from lands in Aberdeenshire, and is first recorded in 1380. At a comparatively early date, people of that name sailed to Orkney and settled there.

LEITH

Tartan: *Hay and Leith*

Mottos: *Trusty to the end; Spare not*

The Leiths are said at one time to have held vast lands in Midlothian. William Leith of Barnis was Provost of Aberdeen in 1350, and his descendants acquired and held at various times the lands of Edingarrock, Kirkton de Rain, and New Leslie, on which Leith Hall was built. On the death of John Leith in 1778, Leslie Hall and Leith Hall passed to his brother, General Alexander Leith (1758-1838) who, on his succession to the estates of Andrew Hay of Rannes, adopted the name Leith-Hay.

LEITH

ABOVE: LENNOX

LENNOX

Tartan: *Lennox*

Mottos: *Avant Darnlie (French: Darnley to the fore);*
En la rose je fleuris (French: I flourish in the
rose); Bydand (Steadfast)

The name of the district of Lennox, which includes
Loch Lomond, comes from the Gaelic for the Vale of
Leven, where the Celtic earls of Lennox held sway from
the twelfth to the fifteenth centuries. Sir John Stewart of
Darnley (*d.* 1495) was created 1st Earl of Lennox of the
new line by King James III in 1473, and Henry Stuart
(1545-67), Lord Darnley, eldest son of the 4th Earl of
Lennox, was the second husband of Mary, Queen of
Scots, and father of King James VI, who promoted the
8th Earl to be Duke of Lennox in 1581.

On the death of the 6th Duke, who was drowned at
Elsinore in 1672, the title devolved on King Charles II,
who passed it on to Charles (1672-1723), his illegitimate
son by his mistress, the Duchess of Portsmouth. The
infant Charles, who was already 1st Duke of Richmond
(Yorkshire), thus in 1675 became also Duke of Lennox
and Earl of Darnley.

Lennox Castle, Lennoxtown, Stirlingshire, was at
one time the family seat of the Lennoxes of Woodhead,
who claimed descent from Donald, illegitimate son of
Duncan, 8th and last of the Celtic earls of Lennox, who
was beheaded on the orders of King James I in 1425.

LESLIE

Branches: *Leslie of Ballenbreich, Leslie of Balquhain,*
Leslie of Wardis, Leslie of Warthill

Tartans: *Leslie (red), Leslie (hunting)*

Motto: *Grip fast*

Bertolf, a Hungarian noble, chamberlain to Margaret
(St Margaret, wife of King Malcolm III), sister of Edgar
the Atheling, came with them to Scotland in 1070, and
claimed vacant lands in Aberdeenshire, which were
confirmed as the lands of Leslie to his son, Malcolm,
constable of the royal castle of Inverurie.

George Leslie of Ballinbreich, a descendant of the
6th Laird of Leslie, was made 1st Earl of Rothes by King
James II. John (1630-81), 7th Earl, carried the sword of
state at the Scottish coronation of King Charles II in
1651. At the Battle of Worcester that same year, he led
a regiment of horse in the King's army, which was

LESLIE, EARL OF ROTHES

LESLIE

LESLIE RED

commanded by David Leslie (*d.* 1682), of the Pitcairlie branch of the family, who was made Lord Newark in 1661. Rothes was imprisoned in the Tower of London for ten months, after which he was allowed a certain amount of freedom until 1658, when he was put in Edinburgh Castle for a year to prevent a duel between him and Viscount Morpeth, whose wife he desired. After the Restoration of Charles II in 1660 he held various positions of state, and progressed through the Scottish

countryside with his mistress, sister of the Duke of Gordon. His offices were removed from him in 1667, but he was appointed Lord Chancellor in 1670, and made Duke of Rothes, Marquis of Ballenbreich, and Earl Leslie in 1680. He had no sons. His daughter Margaret married Charles Hamilton (1650-1685), 5th Earl of Haddington: their elder son inherited from his mother the earldom of Rothes, while the younger became 6th Earl of Haddington.

Sir Alexander Leslie (1580-1661), David Leslie's predecessor as commander of the army of the Covenant, who was made Earl of Leven in 1641, came of the branch of Balquhain, from which stemmed the families of Wardis and Warthill.

LINDSAY, EARL OF CRAWFORD

LINDSAY

Branches: *Lindsay of Balcarres, Lindsay of the Byres, Lindsay of Crawford, Lindsay of Edzell, Lindsay of Glenesk*

Tartan: *Lindsay*

Motto: *Endure fast*

The first recorded Lindsay in Scotland, Sir Walter, arrived in the twelfth century from England, where his

Norman forebears had held lands since the Norman Conquest.

In about 1346 Sir David Lindsay of Crawford, in Lanarkshire, acquired Glenesk, in Angus, by marriage. His younger son was Sir William Lindsay of the Byres, Haddington. The elder was Alexander Lindsay of Glenesk, whose son Sir David Lindsay (1365-1407), famous for his sparing rather than despatching an opponent during a tournament at London Bridge in 1390, inherited from a cousin the Barony of Crawford and in 1398 was made Earl of Crawford.

LINDSAY

The sixteenth-century Crawfords were a fairly wild lot. The 8th Earl, known as the 'Wicked Master', forfeited his title to his cousin, David Lindsay of Edzell, for murdering a servant of Lord Glamis and committing other less mentionable acts, though it reverted to the original line through his grandson.

David Lindsay's younger son, John Lindsay of Balcarres, Fife, was father of David Lindsay, an alchemist and patron of literature, who was made Earl of Balcarres and hereditary Keeper of Edinburgh Castle by King Charles II in 1651. The two earldoms came together in 1808.

Sir David Lindsay of the Mount (1490-1555) was of the line of the Lindsays of the Byres. Tutor of the young King James V, Lord Lyon King of Arms, and poet, he wrote *The Satire of the Three Estates*, which was first performed before the royal court at Linlithgow in 1540 and is the first real Scottish drama. Robert Lindsay of Pitscottie (1532-80), who was related to the Lindsays of the Byres, wrote a vivid if not altogether reliable history of Scotland from 1436 to 1575. Lady Anne Lindsay (1750-1825), daughter of the 5th Earl of Balcarres, wrote the splendid romantic song *Auld Robin Gray* when she was 21, but did not herself marry until until she was 43.

John Lindsay (1702-49), 20th Earl of Crawford, was the first colonel of the Black Watch.

LIVINGSTONE, EARL   OF LINLITHGOW

LIVINGSTON(E)

Branches:	*Livingstone of Bachull, Livingstone of Barncloich, Livingstone of Bonton, Livingstone of Kinnaird, Livingstone of Westquarter*
Tartan:	*Livingstone*
Motto:	*Si je puis (French: If I can)*

Livingston, near Linlithgow, was the 'toun' or estate of a twelfth-century Saxon called Living, whose descendants took the name. By collecting for themselves offices of state (and with them castles), the family became enormously powerful in the fifteenth century, until the young King James II decided in 1449 that he had had enough of them, whereupon he imprisoned his former guardian, Sir Alexander Livingstone of Callander (*d.* 1450), and others of his family, and executed two of his sons. The Livingstones of Barncloich, Bonton, Kinnaird, and Westquarter descended from Sir Alexander's brothers. His elder son, James (*d.* 1467), was made 1st Lord Livingstone. Alexander (*d.* 1622), 7th Lord, was created Earl of Linlithgow in 1600, his younger son, James (*d.* 1674) being made 1st Earl of Callander.

LOGAN OF THAT ILK

LIVINGSTONE

Sir James Livingstone of Barncloich (1616-61) was made Viscount Kilsyth at the Restoration of the Monarchy in 1660. Both the 5th Earl of Linlithgow and the 3rd Viscount of Kilsyth lost their titles for their part in the 1715 rising.

The Livingstones from Argyll and the Hebrides claim descent from a physician to the Lord of the Isles, the name *Mac-an-leigh* (son of the physician) becoming in English Livingstone. This family was called the Barons of Bachull, being hereditary keepers of the *baculum*, or crozier, of the bishops of Lismore, an island in the Hebrides. A very distant and, by birth, humble descendant was Dr David Livingstone (1813-73), the explorer of Africa and missionary (though latterly he was more concerned with commerce than converts).

LOGAN

Tartan: *Logan*

Motto: *Hoc majorum virtus (Latin: This is the valour of my ancestors)*

Slogan: *Druim-nan-Deur (Gaelic: The Ridge of Tears)*

The early Lowland Logans, who originated in Galloway, were on the whole solid citizens, two of whom were killed in Spain in 1329 on their way to the Holy Land with the heart of King Robert I (the Bruce). An exception was Sir Robert Logan of Restalrig (d. 1606), whose bones

were exhumed and paraded in Parliament so that he could personally if posthumously be convicted of treason.

The Highland Logans claim descent from the Logans of Drumderfit in Easter Ross. See also MacLennan, with whom the Highland Logans are closely linked

LUMSDEN

LUMSDEN

Tartan: *Lumsden*

Motto: *Dei dono sum quod sum (Latin: By the gift of God I am what I am)*

The name is that of a manor in Berwickshire, and is recorded in the twelfth century.

Thomas Lumsden of Conland (Fife) and Medlar (Aberdeenshire), who died in about 1470, founded the

MACALISTER

MACALISTER OF   THE LOUP

MacALISTER

Branches: *MacAlister of Glenbarr, MacAlister of Loup, MacAlister of Tarbert*

Tartans: *MacAlister, MacAlister of Glenbarr (also known as hunting MacGillivray)*

Mottos: *Fortiter (Latin: Bravely); Per mare et terram (Latin: By sea and land)*

The clan is generally held to have branched off from Clan Donald through Alastair *Mór*, grandson of Somerled, ruler of the Isles. Its members settled in Kintyre, and in 1481 King James II gave the Stewartry of Kintyre to Charles MacAlister, whose son became known as John of the Loub (*lùb* is Gaelic for a bend or loop in the coastline).

One branch of his descendants became hereditary constables of the royal castle of Tarbert, and another family settled in Glenbarr, Argyll. The lands of Kennox, in Ayrshire, came to the family of Loup by marriage in 1805.

branch of Cushnie (Aberdeenshire), which was granted to the family by King James IV. Another branch is that of Lumsden (or Burges-Lumsden) of Pitcaple, owners of Pitcaple Castle, Aberdeenshire, where the Marquis of Montrose was lodged for a night in 1650 on his sad journey as a prisoner after his defeat at Carbisdale and subsequent betrayal. The Laird was away, but his wife obtained permission from the guards to see Montrose alone, and showed him the entrance to a secret tunnel which led to the outside. He refused to escape, knowing what would happen to her if he did.

MACALISTER

MacALPINE

Tartan: *MacAlpine*

The MacAlpines are not so much a clan as members of other clans, including the Grants, the MacGregors, and the MacNabs, known collectively as *Siol Ailpein*, meaning the descendants of Alpin, King of the Scots, who was killed fighting the Norsemen in the ninth century. His son, Kenneth MacAlpin, either by conquest, treachery, or a claim to the throne through one of the line of royal women, became King of the Picts as well as of the Scots, and thus as Kenneth I the first ruler (from 843 to 859) of Scotia, which in due course grew into the kingdom of Scotland.

MacARTHUR

Branches: *MacArthur of Milton, MacArthur of Proaig, MacArthur of Strachur*

Tartan: *MacArthur*

Motto: *Fide et opera (Latin: By faith and service)*

Slogan: *Eisde! O Eisde! (Gaelic: Listen! O Listen!)*

Clann Artais first appears in Argyll, on the shores of Loch Awe, and there is as little reason to doubt its descent from the mythical (not the historical) King Arthur as there is to question the claims of other clans to have as ancestors equally shadowy heroes of legend. The name of Arthur's Seat, the extraordinary hill which looms over the Abbey and Palace of Holyroodhouse in Edinburgh, has a similar provenance.

Ian, chief of the clan, was one of the many Highland leaders King James I disposed of in the interests of good government, and the MacArthurs of Strachur, in Cowall, Argyll, then emerged as the chiefly branch. The MacArthurs of Proaig, Islay, were once armourers to the MacDonalds of Islay, while members of a MacArthur sept were hereditary pipers to the MacDonalds of the Isles.

MacAULAY

Branches: *MacAulay of Ardincaple, MacAulay of Lewis*

Tartans: *MacAulay, MacAulay (hunting)*

Motto: *Dulce periculum (Latin: Danger is sweet)*

There are two distinct families, or branches, of the name. The MacAulays of Ardincaple, Dumbartonshire, were one of the clans of MacAlpine, and the name of MacAulay appears in the Ragman Roll of 1296, by which

MACAULAY

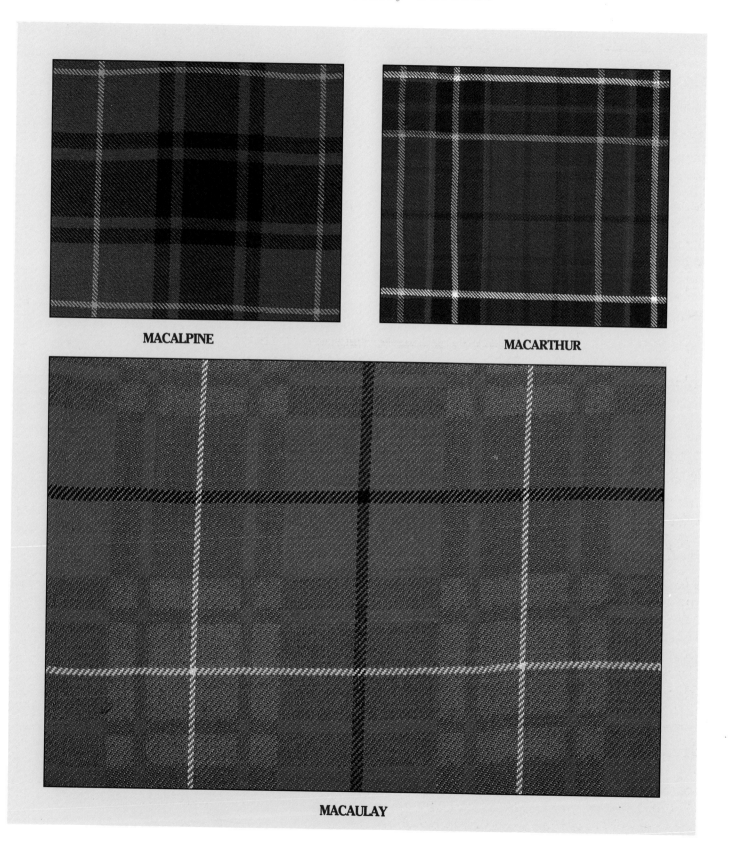

MACALPINE

MACARTHUR

MACAULAY

signatories acknowledged their homage to King Edward I of England. The lands of Ardincaple were sold to the 4th Duke of Argyll in 1767.

The MacAulays of Lewis claim descent from Aula, or Olaf the Black, a thirteenth-century king of the Isles. From this family, and from a line of Calvinist ministers, descended Thomas Babington Macaulay (1800-59), 1st Lord Macaulay, poet, critic, and the first historian to popularise the subject.

MacBEAN, MacBAIN

Branches: *MacBean of Kinchyle, MacBean of Tomatin*

Tartan: *MacBean*

Motto: *Touch not the cat bot [without] a targe [shield]*

Slogan: *Kinchyle!*

MacBeans came to Dores, Invernessshire, from Lochaber with an heiress of Clan Chattan, with which the clan, whose leading family became MacBean of Kinchyle, on the shores of Loch Ness, was associated.

MacBeans were fearless soldiers. Lieutenant-General Forbes MacBean (1725-1800) was in charge of two guns at the Battle of Fontenoy (1745), and in 1778 was appointed commander of the British artillery in Canada. At the Battle of Culloden in 1746, Gillies MacBean stood at a breach in the wall and despatched fourteen Hanoverian soldiers before he himself fell. Major-General William MacBean won the Victoria Cross at Lucknow in 1858. Colonel MacBean upheld the honour of the Gordon Highlanders at the dreadful battle against the Boers at Majuba Hill in 1881. Major Forbes MacBean, of the same regiment, was severely wounded in the assault on the Afridis holding the Dargai ridge on the Indian northwest frontier in 1897.

The MacBeans of Tomatin, Strathdearn, by contrast, were prominent merchants in the eighteenth century.

MACBEAN

MACBETH

MACCALLUM

Kinchyle and other lands were sold in 1760.

A chiefly line of the family flourished in Canada, the MacBean of Glen Bean, Saskatchewan, resigning his title to his American cousin, Hughston M. MacBain, who was officially recognised as chief by the Lyon Court in 1959, and who retrieved some of the Kinchyle lands and established the MacBean Memorial Park on the shores of Loch Ness.

MacBETH

Tartan: *Macbeth*

The presumed ancestor of the clan is Macbeth (1005-1057), Mormaer (High Steward) of Moray, whose mother was said to have been a daughter of King Kenneth II. He married, as her second husband, Gruoch, daughter of a son of King Kenneth III. Under the ancient law of the Scots he had as much claim to the throne of Scotland as King Duncan I, against whom he rebelled, and whom he defeated and killed in battle in 1040. He was proclaimed king, and Scotland prospered during his reign.

He and his wife granted lands to monks, and he went on a pilgrimage to Rome, where he distributed alms to the poor. Duncan's son Malcolm (later King Malcolm III), with the help of an army from England, defeated him between Birnam Wood, near Perth, and Dunsinane Hill, on which was Macbeth's castle. Macbeth escaped and was finally killed three years later in a battle at Lumphanan, twenty-five miles inland from Aberdeen. A cairn marks the spot where he was buried before his body could be taken to Iona for a royal funeral. Even so, Malcolm only became king in 1058 after ambushing and killing Lulach, Macbeth's stepson, whom many preferred to see on the throne.

In 1369 King David II granted a charter for lands in Angus to a family of Macbeths, who were descended from the major Fife family of Bethune. A further family, called *MacBeatha*, practised as physicians to the lords of the Isles and then to the Macleans of Mull at much

the same time as a family of Bethunes were notable physicians in Skye. This has caused confusion in the light of the fact that in the Highlands the names Macbeth, Bethune, and Beaton were often interchangeable. The name Macbeth has also become MacVeigh (especially in Mull), and Leech or Leitch, from one of the original descriptions of the craft of the doctor.

MacCALLUM (see also MALCOLM)

Branches: *MacCallum of Colgin, MacCallum of Glen Etive, MacCallum of Kilmartin, Malcolm of Poltalloch*

Tartan: *MacCallum*

Mottos: *Deus refugium nostrum (Latin: God is our refuge); In ardua tendit (Latin: He takes on difficulties)*

MacCallum is said to be derived from the Gaelic name of St Columba, and the home of Clan MacCallum is in Argyll, the nearest part of the mainland to Iona, where Columba landed in 561.

The MacCallums of Colgin were at one time the family of the chief. The story goes that the three sons of one of the chiefs decided to leave home. Their horses were equipped for the journey, and their father advised each of them to settle wherever his panniers should come apart from the straps holding them. One son's panniers fell off before he was out of the gate, so he stayed at home. The panniers of the other two fell off at Glen Etive in one direction and Kilmartin. south of Loch Awe, in the other, and there they each founded a branch of the clan.

In 1562 Donald McGillespie mac O'Challum was granted the property of Poltalloch, on the eastern shore of the Bay of Craignish, a few miles from Kilmartin. Dugald MacCallum of Poltalloch, who inherited the estate in 1779, seems to have been the first of that name to call himself Malcolm.

ABOVE: MACCASKILL

MacCASKILL

Tartan: *MacCaskill*

The Gaelic of the name is MacAsgaill, derived from the Old Norse *askell* (sacrificial vessel). The clan is a sept of the Macleods of Lewis, whom William MacAskill led against the Clanranald fleet in the sixteenth century.

Angus McAskill, seven-feet-nine-inches tall and known as the Cape Breton Giant, was born in Lewis and died in Canada in 1863.

MacCOLL

Tartan: *MacColl*

The MacColls were originally a branch of the MacDonalds, and made their home by Loch Fyne. Being so close to Campbell territory, they tended for political reasons, as well as those of proximity, to follow that clan, and thus found themselves in opposition to the Macphersons, who supported the MacGregors. Matters came to a head in 1602 with a fight at Drum Nachder, in which the MacColls lost their chief and many other

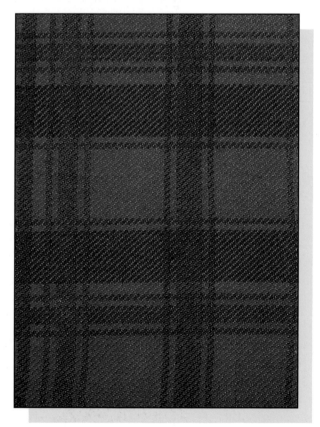

MACCOLL

men. Other MacColls settled in Appin, in Lorn, and followed the Stewarts of Appin in the '45 Rebellion.

Evan MacColl (1808-98), Gaelic poet, was born in Kenmore, Loch Fyne. Ewan MacColl (1915-89), dramatist, folklorist, and folk singer, was born in Auchterarder, Perthshire.

MACCORQUODALE   OF PHANTILLANS

MacCORQUODALE

Tartan: *MacCorquodale*

Motto: *Vivat Rex (Latin: May the King live)*

The name is Old Norse *Thorketill* (Thor's kettle), in Gaelic *MacCorcadail*, and the clan held lands in Argyll in the fourteenth century. From Ewen Makcorquydill of Phantelan, of whom there is a record in 1434, descended Duncan MacCorquodale of Phantillans, and from him Sir Malcolm MacCorquodale (1901-71), 1st and last Lord MacCorquodale of Newton, created in 1955.

MACCORQUODALE

MacDIARMID

Tartan: *MacDiarmid*

All spellings of the name derive from the Gaelic *MacDhiarmaid*, 'son of Dermid', who is variously one of St Columba's attendants, son of a king of the Scots, and a Celtic hero. The MacDiarmids claimed to be the oldest inhabitants of Glenlyon, and many of them enlisted in the company raised by the Duke of Atholl in 1706. There is a strong representation in Argyll.

MacDONALD

Branches: *MacDonald of the Isles; MacDonald of Clanranald, from which MacDonald of Knoidart, MacDonald of Moidart, MacDonald of Morar; MacDonell of Glengarry, from which MacDonell of Scotus; MacDonell of Keppoch; MacDonald of Sleat*

Tartans: *MacDonald, MacDonald (dress), MacDonald of Kingsburgh; MacDonald of the Isles, MacDonald of the Isles (hunting); MacDonald of Ardnamurchan (see also MacKeane); MacDonald of Boisdale; MacDonald of Clanranald; MacDonell of Glengarry; MacDonnell of Keppoch; MacDonald of Sleat; MacDonald of Staffa*

Mottos: *Per mare per terras (Latin: By lands and by sea); (Clanranald) My hope is constant in thee,*

MACDIARMID

Slogans: *Fraoch Eilean (Gaelic: The Heathery Isle);*
(Clanranald) Dh'aindeoin co' theireadh e
(Gaelic: Gainsay who dare); Creagan-an-Fhitich
(Gaelic: The Raven's Rock)

Somerled (*d.* 1164), ruler of the Isles, had three sons, who divided up his territory between them. The second son, Reginald (*d.* 1207), also had three sons, of whom Donald (*d.* 1289) gave his name to the clan. Donald's grandson, John (*d.* 1386), took the formal title of Lord of the Isles in 1354. He also married, as his second wife, Margaret, one of the thirteen children of King Robert II's first marriage. Their son, Donald (*d.* 1423), 2nd Lord of the Isles, became through his wife, Mary Leslie, uncle by marriage of Euphemia, who had inherited the earldom of Ross from her mother in 1402 but had inconveniently become a nun, and thus was legally counted as dead. Donald wanted the earldom of Ross, and in 1411 decided to invade the Lowlands as a means of persuading the Regency (King James I being in captivity in England) to let him have it. The plan came unstuck twenty miles from Aberdeen, at Harlaw, from which he was forced to withdraw, unable to break through the ranks of the opposition. His son, Alexander (*d.* 1449), 3rd Lord of the Isles, did succeed to the earldom of Ross. He also made all kinds of trouble for King James I, including the burning of Inverness in a fit of pique. Thus it came about that the 4th Lord of the Isles, John (*d.* 1498), was also the last. Alexander's youngest son, Hugh (*d.* 1498), got as his inheritance the region of Sleat in Skye, and is the founder of the MacDonalds of Sleat. Donald (*d.* 1643), 8th Chief of the MacDonalds of Sleat, was granted a baronetcy in 1617. His son, 2nd Baronet of Sleat, supported the Marquis of Montrose and supplied troops to King Charles II in England in 1651, which made it predictable that the 4th Baronet should have supported the Jacobite cause in 1715, and forfeited his estates for doing so, though they were restored to the family shortly afterwards.

The MacDonalds of Clanranald are descended from Ranald, younger son of the first marriage of John, 1st Lord of the Isles. Ranald received the northern islands and other lands in 1373 and was the ancestor of the branches of MacDonalds of Knoidart, Moidart, and Morar. The MacDonalds of Clanranald, under their sixteen-year-old chief, were among the first of the clans to rally to Viscount Dundee at Lochaber in 1689, and

MACDONALD OF
CLANRANALD

CLANRANALD

MACDONALD
OF MACDONALD

MACDONALD

MACDONALD DRESS

MACDONALD OF BOYSDALE

MACDONALD OF STAFFA

MACDONALD OF THE ISLES

were in continuous support of Bonnie Prince Charlie from the moment he set foot on the mainland in 1745 to his final departure over a year later. Flora MacDonald (1722-1790), chief heroine (but by no means the only heroine) of the escape, was of Clanranald through her father's line, though after her father's death her mother married a cousin of Sir Alexander MacDonald of Sleat (1711-46), who supported the Government in 1745-6, while his wife was an active Jacobite and accomplice of Flora. Alexander MacDonald of Kingsburgh, who played such a part, too, and whose son Flora married in 1750, was factor to Sir Alexander. Alexander MacDonald of

Boisdale, brother to the chief of the MacDonalds of Clanranald, was one of those who tried to persuade Bonnie Prince Charlie to go home. In spite of not joining the rising himself, he was imprisoned in 1746, though his wife assisted the Prince by sending him brandy and other necessary supplies.

Donald of Glengarry was a son of the 1st Lord of the Isles and younger brother of Allan MacDonald, 1st of Clanranald. The MacDonells of Glengarry were always supporters of the Crown, and thus also of Bonnie Prince Charlie, whom they regarded as the rightful heir to it. The 9th Chief was created Lord MacDonell and Aros at the Restoration of the Monarchy in 1660, but on his death without issue the chiefship went to the Scotus branch of Glengarry. Duncan, 14th Chief, raised a whole company of infantry, mainly men from his own estate, in 1794-5. When it was disbanded in 1801, most of the men emigrated with their families to Canada, where they founded Glengarry, Ontario. Alistair MacDonell (d. 1828), 15th Chief, was a romantic who, according to Sir Walter Scott, 'lived a century too late', and who always wore full Highland dress, insisting that his followers and servants did the same, which on one occasion so frightened the inhabitants of a convent he was visiting that nuns fled in all directions. He was also rather a disgrace. He had a foul temper, and was

MACDONALD OF THE ISLES

acquitted of murder after killing Flora MacDonald's grandson in a duel after a ball at Fort William. He was drowned in the shipwreck of a passenger steamer, his son being forced to sell the estates, which had fallen into ruin, and then to emigrate. His younger brother, General Sir James MacDonell (d. 1857), somewhat restored the family reputation by serving with

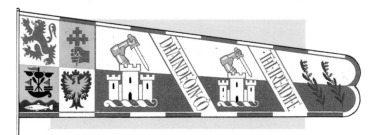

MACDONALD OF CLANRANALD

MACDONELL OF KEPPOCH

MACDONALD OF KINGSBURGH

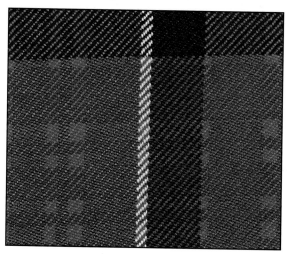

MACDONALD OF CLANRANALD

MACDONALD

distinction at the Battle of Waterloo in 1815, and in Canada 1838-41, where he commanded the troops after the disturbances of 1837.

The MacDonells of Keppoch are descended from the third son of John, 1st Lord of the Isles, and Princess Margaret. Alexander, 16th Chief, was so impressed by Bonnie Prince Charlie's determination that he threw in his lot with him. It was a party from his clan which fired the first shots of the campaign, but at the Battle of Culloden in 1746 his men were reluctant to charge. Crying in Gaelic, 'My God, have the children of my clan abandoned me?', he rushed out in front of them, alone, with a pistol in one hand and his sword in the other, and was instantly shot down by musket fire.

There is a Clan Donald Centre at Armadale, Skye.

MACDOUGALL OF MACDOUGALL

MacDOUGALL

Tartan: *MacDougall*

Motto: *Buaidh no bàs (Gaelic: Victory or death)*

The MacDougalls are descended from Dugall, eldest son of Somerled (*d.* 1164), ruler of the Isles. Dugall's son appears in a record as 'Duncan of Argyll' in 1244, and his lands included Lorn(e), a fertile area opposite the island of Mull, where the clan built the castles of Dunollie and Dunstaffnage. Duncan's grandson, Alexander of Lorn (*d.* 1310), married a sister of John Comyn, whose son was slain in the church by Robert the Bruce. There was thus extreme enmity between the MacDougalls and the King, who was hunted by them and in 1306 escaped from an encounter with them at the expense of his cloak, with its elaborate fastening, known as the 'Brooch of Lorn'.

LEFT AND ABOVE: MACDOUGALL

On the death of John of Lorn in 1388, the lands of Lorn passed through his daughters to the Stewarts, who in 1457 granted Dunollie to John MacAllan MacDougall, 10th Clan Chief. Shortly afterwards, Lorn passed into the family of the Campbells of Argyll by the marriages of the daughters of the last Stewart of Lorn. Thus it is that the title of the eldest son of the Duke of Argyll is Marquis of Lorne, while the eldest daughter of the chief of Clan MacDougall, as long as she is unmarried, is known as the 'Maid of Lorn'.

The MacDougalls fought for the Jacobites at Sheriffmuir in 1715, while the chief's wife defended Dunollie Castle against the government forces, and they afterwards forfeited their estates, except for Dunollie. They were returned after the '45 Rebellion, during which the MacDougalls sided with the Government.

MacDUFF

Branch: *Duff of Braco*

Tartans: *MacDuff, MacDuff (hunting)*

Mottos: *Deus juvat (Latin: God helps); Virtute et opera (Latin: By virtue and service)*

Shakespeare, as we have seen from the difference between his portrait of Macbeth in his tragedy of that name and the historical king of Scotland who reigned from 1040 to 1057, was somewhat hazy about Scottish history. In *Macbeth*, however, he does present us with a MacDuff who is 'Thane of Fife', and it is historical fact that at the beginning of the twelfth century the family name of the earls of Fife was MacDuff.

The first recorded Earl of Fife was Ethelred, born in about 1073. He was a son of King Malcolm III, whose father was the King Duncan who was killed (in battle) and displaced by Macbeth. Constantine, Earl of Fife, who died in about 1129, is said to have been of the family of MacDuff, and his successor, who may have been his brother, was called Gillemichael MacDuff, and from this point at least the earldom was hereditary.

MACDUFF

That the family had royal connections may be divined from the 'Law Clan MacDuff', which is mentioned in 1384. The clan's representative had the right to place the King on the throne at his coronation; the clan should be in the front line of any battle fought by the King; and a fixed payment would secure remission from an act of murder.

William Duff of Braco, in Banffshire, who inherited the chiefship, was created Lord Braco in 1725, and Earl of Fife in the Irish peerage in 1759. Alexander W.G. Duff, 6th Earl, was made Duke of Fife in 1889 on his marriage to Princess Louise, daughter of King Edward VII.

MacEWEN

Branches: *MacEwen of Bardrochat, MacEwen of Marchmont*

Tartan: *MacEwen*

Motto: *Reviresco (Latin: I flourish again)*

The clan was known as the MacEwens of Otter, from a mile-long sandbank which jutted out into Loch Fyne, near Kilfinan in Argyll. A Ewen of Otter is known at the beginning of the thirteenth century. Swene, last of the chiefs of Otter, gave over the lands to the Campbells in 1432, and the ownership was later confirmed to the Earl of Argyll by King James V. The MacEwens who remained became hereditary bards to Clan Campbell, and the rest, having lost their home base, scattered through Scotland, some of them acquiring the lands of Bardrochat in Ayrshire and Marchmont in Berwickshire.

MACEWEN

MACFADYEN

MacFADYEN

Tartan: *MacFadyen*

All variants of this name derive from the Gaelic *Macphaidein*, 'little Pat', and it is first recorded in Kintyre in 1304. There is a tradition that the clan was the first owner of Lochbuie, and subsequently became itinerant goldsmiths. The name was common in Islay, Mull, and Tiree.

MacFARLANE

Branch: *MacFarlane of Keithton*

Tartans: *MacFarlane, MacFarlane (black and white), MacFarlane (hunting)*

Motto: *This I'll defend*

Slogan: *Loch Sloy!*

The MacFarlanes are descended from the ancient earls of Lennox through Gilchrist, younger brother of Malduin, Earl of Lennox in the mid-thirteenth century, who gave him the lands of Arrochar on the west side of Loch Lomond.

The name derives from Bartholomew (Gaelic *Parlan*), 4th Chief, and the clan slogan from the loch of that name below Ben Vorlich to the north, which is now part of a hydro-electric scheme. The last of the former line of the earls of Lennox was executed by King James I in 1425 without there being a male heir, but instead of the title going to the chief of Clan MacFarlane, it was

MACFARLANE   MACFARLANE OF MACFARLANE   MACFARLANE HUNTING

finally awarded to Sir John Stewart of Darnley (*d.* 1495), whose grandmother had been the old Earl's daughter. Sir John, who became 1st Earl of Lennox of the new line, was the great-grandfather of Matthew Stuart (1516-71), 4th Earl of Lennox and father of Lord Darnley (1545-67), second husband of Mary, Queen of Scots.

That the MacFarlanes did not take kindly to being overlooked is demonstrated by their opposition to the earls of Lennox, for which they lost most of their lands, and would have lost all of them if a MacFarlane had not married a daughter of the Lennox line. So it came about that at Langside in 1568, the MacFarlanes were well to the fore in the rout, after a battle of only 45 minutes, of the army of Mary, Queen of Scots, by the nobles opposing her, among whom was the 4th Earl of Lennox, who believed she had been a party to his son's murder. Regrettably, the aggressive nature of the MacFarlanes was prominent also in their daily lives, and various acts had to be passed to curb their unlawful excesses, culminating in 1624 in many of them being deported to other parts of Scotland and taking different names.

MacFIE, MacPHIE

Branches: *MacFie of Colonsay, MacFie of Dreghorn, MacFie of Langhouse*

Tartan: *MacFie*

Motto: *Pro rege (Latin: For the king)*

The MacFies, or MacDuffies, as they may originally have been known, are a branch of Clan Alpin, and were

the most ancient inhabitants of Colonsay, though the earliest reference to one of them is as a witness to a charter in 1463.

In the middle of the seventeenth century, the island came into the possession of the MacDonalds. Some of the native MacFies followed the MacDonalds of Islay, others settled in Lochaber and supported the Camerons, while those who went as far afield as Galloway became known as MacGuffie or Mahaffie. The MacFies of Dreghorn, Ayrshire, are descended from those of Langhouse, Renfrewshire.

MACFIE

MacGILL

Tartan: *MacGill*

The name is the Gaelic *Mac an Ghoill*, 'son of the Lowlander (or stranger)', and it was especially common in Galloway. In Jura the family was known in 1702 as *Clann a'ghoill*.

MACGILLIVRAY OF DUNMAGLASS

MacGILLIVRAY

Tartans: *MacGillivray, MacGillivray (hunting, also known as MacAlistair of Glenbarr)*

Mottos: *Be mindful; (Dunmaglass) Touch not this cat*

Slogan: *Dunmaglass*

The MacGillivrays, a west-coast clan with a firm base in Mull, were among the first members of Clan Chattan. Some of the clan pushed northwards to Dunmaglass, Strathnairn, and founded a branch there. The Laird of Dunmaglass and his brother fought on the Jacobite side in 1715, and the clan was led at the Battle of Culloden in 1746 by its chief, whose death near a well is marked today by a memorial stone.

MacGREGOR

Branches: *MacGregor of Glengyle, MacGregor of Glenlyon, MacGregor of Glenorchy, MacGregor of Glenstrae*

Tartans: *MacGregor, MacGregor (Rob Roy)*

Motto: *'S rioghal mo dhream (Gaelic: Royal is my race)*

Slogan: *Ard-choille (Gaelic: The High Wood)*

Something of the violent and unhappy history of the clan and of the exploits of its most celebrated member

MACGILLIVRAY

MACGILLIVRAY

MACGILLIVRAY HUNTING

MACGREGOR
OF
MACGREGOR

MACGREGOR

ROB ROY

MACHARDY

appears on pages 16 and 17. The 'royal' descent in its motto refers to a tradition that the clan's founder was Gregor, brother of King Kenneth I, the first ruler of a combined Scottish and Pictish kingdom. The earliest clan lands were in Glen Orchy, in Lorn, and after their chief had died childless, a prisoner of King Edward I of England, he was succeeded by his nephew, Gregor. A daughter of the clan married into Clan Campbell, which then included all the MacGregor territories in its policy of expansion, taking over the glens of Orchy, Strae, and Gyle, so that the landless MacGregors became known as the 'Children of the Mist'. Rob Roy MacGregor (1671-1734) was the third son of Donald Glas (*d.* 1702), 5th Chief of Glengyle.

MacHARDY

Tartan: *MacHardy*

The name is the Gaelic *MacCardaidh*, 'son of the sloe', and the clan, notably the MacHardies of Strathden and Braemar, became very influential in and around the mountainous districts of Aberdeenshire.

MacINNES

Branches: *MacInnes of Kinlochaline, MacInnes of Malagawatch, MacInnes of Morven, MacInnes of Rickersby*

Tartan: *MacInnes*

Motto: *Irid ghibht Dhé agus an Righ (Gaelic: Through the grace of God and the King)*

MacInnes is from the Gaelic *aonghais* (unique choice), and members of the the clan are said to have been the original inhabitants of the region of Morven, on the mainland opposite the northwest coast of Mull, and to have been constables of Kinlochaline Castle. During the seventeenth century the lands came under the control of the Campbells, which is why in 1644 Sir Alasdair MacDonald (*d.* 1647), nicknamed *Coll Keitach* (Coll the Ambidextrous) after his father, came from Antrim, ravaged Morven, and burned the castle as a part of the overall battle plan of the Marquis of Montrose. The MacInneses now spread in all directions, and served different causes depending on where they settled.

MACINNES

MacINROY

Tartan: *MacInroy*

The name in Gaelic means 'son of Ian Roy', and the clan is associated with Clan Robertson, by descent from the Reid-Robertsons of Straloch.

MACINROY

MacINTYRE

Branches: *MacIntyre of Badenoch, MacIntyre of Glenoe, MacIntyre of Rannoch*

Motto: *Per ardua (Latin: Through difficulties)*

Slogan: *Cruachan (name of a mountain by Loch Awe)*

The Gaelic *Mac-an-t-saoir* means 'son of the carpenter', the carpenter in question, according to tradition, cutting off his thumb, which he used to plug a leak in a galley.

It was in a galley, too, that it is said that members of the clan came from the Hebrides to Argyll, becoming foresters to the Stewarts of Lorn and then to the Campbells, from whom they leased the lands of Glen Noe for an annual payment in the summer of a white cow (born of the stock they had brought with them originally) and a snowball (readily obtainable from the upper slopes of Ben Cruachan). The arrangement appears to have lasted until the eighteenth century, when the chief of the MacIntyres of Glenoe agreed to compound kind into cash, which with inflation grew to a rent of such proportions that his people had to abandon their homeland.

The MacIntyres of Badenoch were admitted as a sept of Clan Chattan in 1496, while the MacIntyres of Rannoch were hereditary pipers to the chief of Clan Menzies. Duncan ban MacIntyre (1724-1812), born in Glen Orchy, was a gamekeeper who, though he never learned to write, became one of the finest, and certainly the jolliest, of all Gaelic poets.

MACINTYRE

MacIVER

Branches: *MacIver of Asknish, MacIver of Lergachonzie, MacIver of Stronshiray*

Tartans: *MacIver, MacIver (hunting)*

Motto: *Nunquam obliviscar (Latin: I will never forget)*

Clan Iver, which had its base in Glen Lyon, Perthshire, is supposed to have accompanied King Alexander II in 1221 on his expedition against Argyll, which landed from the sea. As a reward for their service, its members were given lands in Argyll, notably Asknish and Lergachonzie. From Argyll, the clan spread once again, to Lochaber, Glenelg, Ross, and the island of Lewis. In 1685 Iver of Asknish lost his lands for supporting the rebellion against King James VII (II of England), in the aftermath of which the 9th Earl of Argyll was executed.

Archibald (1658-1703), 10th Earl of Argyll, who was instrumental in bringing William and Mary from Holland to the throne in 1689, restored the lands to Iver's son, Duncan McIver, on condition that he and his heirs took the name of Campbell.

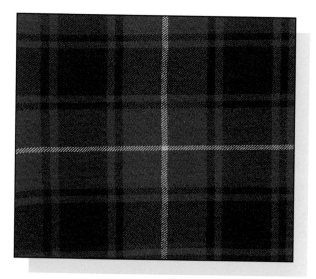

MACIVER

MACIVER HUNTING

MACKAY   LORD REAY

MACKAY

Branches: *Mackay of Farr, Mackay of Scourie, Mackay of Strathnaver*

Tartan: *Mackay*

Motto: *Manu forti (Latin: With strong hand)*

Slogan: *Bratach Bhan Chlann Aoidh (Gaelic: The White Banner of Clan Mackay)*

The region of Strathnaver not only comprises most of the northernmost coast of Britain, but it is also the farthest removed on the mainland from the seat of government. In 1415 the Lord of the Isles formally granted Strathnaver to Angus (*d.* 1433), Chief of Mackay, and also gave him his sister in marriage. The chiefs of

Mackay made a regular habit of matches with aristocratic members of other clans. It was not, however, enough to prevent Uisdean Mackay (1561-1614) from being forced to become a vassal of the Earl of Sutherland, who then, and only then, offered him his daughter as wife.

The Barony of Farr had come to the clan by charter of King James V in 1539. Uisdean Mackay, when he became chief, had settled the property of Scourie on his younger brother. The eastern coastal boundary of the clan's territory was extended for a few miles in 1624 by the acquisition of Reay by Donald Mackay (1591-1649), who in 1626 recruited an army of three thousand men

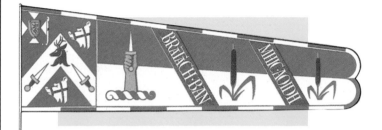

to fight for the Protestant cause in Europe. A year later he was commissioned by King Christian IV of Denmark and Norway to raise a further thousand men, the bill to

MACKAY

MACIAN

There is a separate family of Mackays in the south, where in 1408 a Mackay of Islay was granted a charter by the Lord of the Isles.

MacKEANE, MacIAN

Tartan: *MacKeane/MacIan*

The name MacKeane is a variant of MacIan, 'son of John'. The MacIans of Ardnamurchan, who sometimes, wrongly, called themselves Johnstone, claimed descent from a son of Angus *Mór*, Lord of the Isles in the fourteenth century. In the seventeenth century some of them settled on the east coast and became prominent merchants in Elgin, where they called themselves MacKeane. The MacIans of Glencoe, victims of the Massacre of Glencoe in 1692, were a branch of the MacDonalds.

MACKELLAR

Tartan: *MacKellar*

MacKellar is the Gaelic *Mac Ealair*, 'son of Ealair', from Hilarius, Bishop of Poitiers in about 1230, and the main family was in Argyll from the thirteenth century, before spreading to other parts of Scotland and overseas.

be paid by King Charles I, who created Mackay 1st Lord Reay in 1628. The machinations involved in these transactions came to an unfortunate head in 1631, when Mackay laid formal charges in London before the King against an agent of James (1606-49), 1st Duke of Hamilton, of procuring him to raise forces which would be used against the Crown. The matter was commuted to trial by hand-to-hand combat in public, which was postponed indefinitely by the King himself, who had probably connived at the recruitment of the men to assist in the imposition on Scotland of the episcopal faith.

In 1642 a bankrupt first lord Reay sold Strathnaver to the Sutherlands, who got the rest of the clan's territory in 1829 in the aftermath of the clearances. In the meantime General George Mackay of Scourie (1640-92), on the accession of William and Mary in 1689, had become commander of the English and Scottish forces of the Crown, and lost in the same year the Battle of Killiecrankie, in which Viscount Dundee was killed. On the general's death in action in Europe, his nephew, Aeneas Mackay (*d.* 1697), a grandson of the 1st Lord Reay, assumed command of the Mackay regiment. He married a Dutch countess and settled in Holland, where his descendants were made barons. So it was that in 1875, on the lapse of the direct line in Scotland, Baron Eric MacKay van Ophemert succeeded as 12th Lord Reay.

MACKENZIE, EARL OF CROMARTIE

MACKENZIE

Branches:	*See below*
Tartans:	*Mackenzie, Mackenzie (dress)*
Mottos:	*Luceo non uro (Latin: I shine, not burn); Cuidich 'n righ (Gaelic: Help the king)*
Slogan:	*Tulach Ard (Gaelic: The High Hill)*

It is generally accepted that the ancient earls of Ross, who held vast sway in Moray, descended from an elder son of Gilleoin of the Aird, and the Mackenzies from a younger son. Mackenzie means 'son of Kenneth', and in 1267 a Kenneth was inhabiting the strategic stronghold of Eilean Donan, at the mouth of Loch Duich, in what became the Mackenzie heartland of Kintail. From here the clan spread out to occupy territory which encompassed stretches of both the east and west coasts of the mainland. At the same time the chiefly family was multiplying. The two younger sons of Alexander (*d.* 1488), Chief of Kintail, Duncan of Hilton and Hector of Gairloch, and four grandsons, Alexander of Davochmuluag, Roderick of Achilty, Kenneth of Gilchrist, and Roderick of Redcastle, between them founded twenty-five branches of the clan, and another sixteen emerged in the seventeenth century. Kenneth Mackenzie (*d.* 1611) was made Lord Mackenzie of Kintail in 1609, and his son Colin (*d.* 1633) Earl of Seaforth in 1623. Roderick of Coigach, brother of Lord Mackenzie, was known as the 'Tutor of Kintail' for his office as administrator of the affairs and estates of the young Earl, and his grandson George (1630-1714) was ennobled first as Viscount Tarbat and then as Earl of Cromartie.

Clan Mackenzie illustrates the perplexities of loyalty. It took neither side during the campaign of the Marquis of Montrose in 1644-5, but in 1649 George (*d.* 1651), 2nd Earl of Seaforth, joined King Charles II in Europe, and his family fought for the King at the Battle of Worcester in 1651. Kenneth (*d.* 1678), 3rd Earl, was pardoned by Cromwell for his active opposition to his regime, but had much of his land burned as punishment. The 4th and 5th earls were likewise confirmed Jacobite plotters and activists, with such disastrous results to family, lands and titles, that the clan itself had not the resources to support Bonnie Prince Charlie in 1745. George (*d.* 1766), 3rd Earl of Cromartie, managed to raise a small force, but it was occupied on duty elsewhere during the Battle of Culloden in April 1746. Even so, two Mackenzies were executed, 79 were transported in unbelievable conditions, and the Earl himself was condemned to death but reprieved on condition that he went to live in England. Needless to say, he lost his title, which was not revived until 1861.

SIR GEORGE MACKENZIE 1636-91

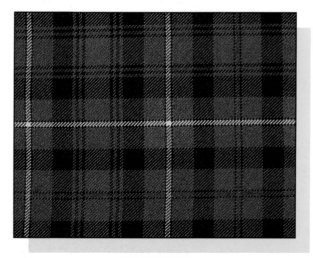

MACKENZIE

Kenneth Mackenzie (*d.* 1781) was able to recover the forfeited earldom of Seaforth, and in 1778 raised the 78th Regiment, afterwards known as the Seaforth Highlanders, for service in the American War of Independence (today the Queen's Own Highlanders, formed of the Seaforths and Camerons, wear the Mackenzie tartan). After his death, the chiefship devolved to a cousin, Lieut-General Francis Humberstone Mackenzie (1754-1815), Lord Seaforth and Mackenzie, soldier, politician, statesman, and naturalist, whose outstanding qualities are even more extraordinary in that he was completely deaf from childhood. After the deaths of his four sons he went dumb as well, all of which fulfilled explicitly the two-hundred-year-old prophecy of the 'Brahan Seer' about the disasters which would befall the line of the chief of Mackenzie. Though the Seer himself is more likely to have been not so much a person as a convenient and collective mouthpiece for a series of prophecies made and brought together towards the beginning of the seventeenth century, there was nothing inaccurate, either, in the precise predictions about the subsequent and continuing doom of the family.

MacKERRELL OF HILLHOUSE

Tartan: *MacKerrell of Hillhouse*

Motto: *Dulcis pro patria labor (Latin: Sweet is toil for one's country)*

The name, which means 'son of Fearghal', is recorded in the twelfth century. Sir John Makirel fought at the Battle of Otterburn in 1388, capturing the brother of Sir Harry Percy (Hotspur). Sir John's descendant, Martin McKerrell, is described as 'in Hillhouse' at the end of the fifteenth century. The estate, among others in Ayrshire, was formally confirmed to William MacKerrell, 1st Laird of Hillhouse, by King James VI in 1589.

MacKILLOP

Tartan: *MacKillop*

The name in Gaelic means 'son of Philip', and members of the clan are said to have been standard-bearers to a branch of the Campbells. Others became septs of the MacDonalds of Glencoe and the MacDonells of Keppoch. The name was also well known in Arran.

MACKERRELL OF HILLHOUSE

MACKILLOP

MACKINLAY

Tartan: *Mackinlay*

The Mackinlays who first inhabited Lennox were descended from Finlay, son of Buchanan of Drumikill (and there was a Miss Buchanan still living at Drumkill, Kilmarnock, in 1811). The Finlaysons of Lochalsh claim the same descent as the Farquharsons of Braemar, from *Fionnlagh Mór*. John MacKinlay (1819-72), the Australian explorer, was born by the River Clyde and emigrated to New South Wales in 1836 to join his uncle. It was an emigrant in the other direction who gave his name to Mount McKinley in Alaska, unconquered until 1913, when it was climbed by an archdeacon.

William McKinley, (1843-1901), 25th President of the USA, was descended, via Ireland, from another line of MacKinlays who claim descent from the Farquharsons. Their homeland was Anie, to the northwest of Callendar, and many of them are buried in the nearby grounds of St Bride's Chapel.

MACKINNON OF   MACKINNON

MACKINNON

Branches: *Mackinnon of Corryatachan, Mackinnon of Strathardal*

Tartans: *Mackinnon, Mackinnon (hunting)*

Motto: *Audentes fortuna juvat (Latin: Fortune favours the bold)*

Slogan: *Cuimhnich bás Ailpein (Gaelic: Remember the death of Alpin)*

The Mackinnons, a branch of Clan Alpin, claim descent from Fingon, known variously as the younger son and the great-grandson of Alpin, King of the Scots. In 1409 Lachlan MacFingon witnessed a charter for the Lord of the Isles, and the same name recurs as Clan Chief in

MACKINLAY

MACKINNON

MACKINNON HUNTING

documents of 1606 and 1671, Lauchlan Mackinnon and Lauchlan MacFingon, both of Strathardal in Skye. John Mackinnon (*d.* 1500) was the last Abbot of Iona, an incumbency which seems to have been a family tradition.

The clan fought for Bonnie Prince Charlie at the Battle of Culloden in 1746, and its elderly chief personally conducted the Prince from Skye to the mainland in an open boat during the escape, being captured on his way home and imprisoned at Tilbury. His son was forced to sell Strathardal, the last of the clan lands, in one of whose numerous caves the Prince had sheltered. When his son died in 1808, the chiefship was successfully claimed by William Mackinnon (1789-1870), later Member of Parliament for Dunwich, a descendant of William Mackinnon of Antigua, who in 1756 obtained arms as a branch of the main family. A chiefship of the branch of Corryatachan, Skye, was recognised in 1947.

chief', and the founder of the clan is said to be a younger son of the MacDuff from whom the earls of Fife descended. The 6th Chief became also Chief of Clan Chattan through his marriage in 1291 to Eva, heiress of

the 6th Chief of that clan. The 7th Chief acquired the Barony of Moy, Invernessshire, now the home of the present, and 30th, Chief.

For most of the sixteenth and seventeenth centuries the Mackintoshes were at variance, and often at war,

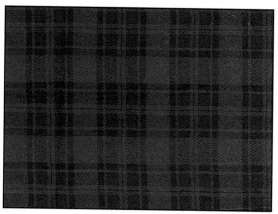

MACKINTOSH

MACKINTOSH HUNTING

MACKINTOSH

Branch: *Mackintosh of Borlum*

Tartans: *Mackintosh, Mackintosh (hunting)*

Motto: *Touch not the cat bot [without] a glove*

Slogan: *Loch Moigh [Moy]*

Mackintosh is the Gaelic *Mac-an-Toisich*, 'son of the

with the Gordons (earls of Huntly), the Camerons, and the MacDonells of Keppoch, against whom in 1688 they fought the last clan battle. They supported the Government, not Viscount Dundee, in the revolution of 1689, but Brigadier William Mackintosh of Borlum (1662-1743) and his regiment of seven hundred officers and men played a notable part on the Jacobite side in 1715.

In 1746 the 22nd Chief of Clan Mackintosh was serving the Government as an officer in the Black Watch, while his wife, a Farquharson by birth, was raising a contingent for the other side and personally assisting Bonnie Prince Charlie.

Since 1938, the chiefships of Clan Mackintosh and Clan Chattan have been held by different lines of the family.

McKIRDY

Tartan: *McKirdy*

All the earliest records of the name are in connection with the islands of Arran or of Bute.

MacLACHLAN

Branches: *MacLachlan of Coruanan, MacLachlan of Cowal, MacLachlan of Kilchoan*

Tartans: *MacLachlan (old), MacLachlan (dress), MacLachlan (hunting)*

Motto: *Fortis et fidus (Latin: Brave and trustworthy)*

The lands of Gilespic Maclachlan, Clan Chief, were incorporated in the Sheriffdom of Argyll, or Lorn, established in 1292 by King John (Balliol), and were formally designated the Barony of Strathlachlan, Loch Fyne, in 1680.

Lachlan MacLachlan, 15th Chief, brought 260 men right out of the Hanoverian heartland of Argyll to the support of Bonnie Prince Charlie, and performed military wonders at the battles of Prestonpans and Falkirk, before falling at Culloden in 1746, so furious being the charge he led that his body was later found, cut to pieces, well behind the government lines. His son, aide-de-camp to the Prince, was killed by a cannon ball as he took along the Jacobite line the order to advance.

The MacLachlans of Coruanan were hereditary standard bearers to the Camerons of Lochiel in Lochaber. The MacLachlans of Cowal, who held lands between Loch Fyne and Loch Long, usually followed the Campbells. The MacLachlans of Kilchoan inhabited a district of Ardnamurchan, and Rev. John MacLachlan of Kilchoan was chaplain to the Jacobite forces during the '45 Rebellion. MacLachlans were also settled at Auchentroig, Stirlingshire.

MacLAINE OF LOCHBUIE

Tartans: *MacLaine of Lochbuie, MacLaine of Lochbuie (hunting)*

Motto: *Vincere vel mori (Latin: To conquer or die)*

The MacLaines of Lochbuie, Mull, claim descent from Hector Reaganach, brother of the ancestor of the Macleans of Duart, who received his lands from John,

MACLACHLAN OF
MACLACHLAN

MACLAINE OF
LOCHBUIE

MCKIRDY

MACLACHLAN

MACLACHLAN DRESS

MACLAINE OF LOCHBUIE

MACLAINE OF LOCHBUIE HUNTING

1st Lord of the Isles, during the fourteenth century. John Og, 5th Chief of Lochbuie, had them confirmed to him by King James IV, but it is said that after his only son had rebelled against him and been killed, he was incarcerated on an island by Maclean of Duart, with an elderly female retainer as company. She gave birth to Murdoch (known as 'the Short'), who escaped to Ireland, from where he returned in due course to recover by arms the estate and castle of his now dead father, his birth being officially legitimised in 1538.

The MacLaines of Lochbuie and the Macleans of Duart, seven hundred men all told, joined the Marquis of Montrose in time for the Battle of Kilsyth in 1645.

Hector MacLaine brought two hundred raw Highlanders to bolster the cause of Viscount Dundee in 1689. They were intercepted en route by three hundred cavalry of Berkeley's Dragoons, whom they duly defeated after enticing them to dismount and attack up the slope of a hill on foot.

On their visit to Mull in 1773, James Boswell and Samuel Johnson were entertained by the Chief of Lochbuie, whom Johnson calls 'a true Highland Laird, rough and haughty, and tenacious of his dignity'. Boswell takes up the story: 'Being told that Dr Johnson did not hear well, Lochbuie bawled out to him, "Are you of the Johnstons of Glencro, or of Ardnamurchan?" Dr Johnson gave him a significant look, but made no answer; and I told Lochbuie that he was not John*ston*, but John*son*, and that he was an Englishman.'

Donald, 20th Chief of Lochbuie, made a fortune in Java in the nineteenth century with which he cleared the estate of debt, but in the 1920s it was claimed and appropriated by an English bondholder, in whose hands it remained.

MACLAREN

Branches: *Maclaren of Achleskine, Maclaren of Ardveche, Maclaren of Invernenty, Maclaren of Struthill*

Tartans: *Maclaren, Maclaren (dress)*

Motto: *Creag an Tuirc (Gaelic: The Boar's Rock [an eminence by Achleskine, Balquhidder])*

Maclarens held lands in Perthshire in the thirteenth century, and the MacLaurins possessed and occupied the island of Tiree from a date which may be even

MACLAREN

earlier. That the two families are connected was confirmed in 1781, when the claim of John MacLaurin (1734-96), Lord Dreghorn, judge and man of letters, to the chiefship of Clan Maclaren was established by the Lyon Court. The chiefship now resides with the Maclarens of Achleskine, who claim descent from Laurin, or Lawrence, hereditary Abbot of Achtus, Balquhidder.

MACLEAN OF DUART

Tartans: *Maclean of Duart, Maclean (hunting)*

Motto: *Virtue mine honour*

Slogans: *Bàs no beatha (Gaelic: Death or life); Fear eile airson Eachainn (Gaelic: Another for Hector)*

The Macleans of Duart, descended from Gillean of the Battleaxe, who flourished in the thirteenth century, are chiefs of Clan Maclean. The castle and lands of Duart, on the island of Mull, were granted to them by royal

Sir Hector Maclean of Duart, 2nd Baronet, died for the cause at Inverkeithing in 1651, alongside his seven brothers, each of whom in turn, as he stood protecting his chief, crying, 'Another for Hector!' Sir John Maclean, 4th Baronet, fought, with his clan, on the extreme right of the line for Viscount Dundee at the Battle of Killiecrankie in 1689. Shortly afterwards the estates were forfeited to the Campbells, and in 1750 the Duart line became extinct.

In 1912, however, Sir Fitzroy Maclean, 10th Baronet and 26th Chief, having recovered the lands and restored the castle of Duart, was re-established in the traditional seat of the clan.

MACLEAN OF DUART

MacLELLAN

Tartan: *MacLellan*

Mottos: *Think on; Superba frango (Latin: I break down proud things)*

Patrick, son of Gilbert M'Lolane, was one of the band of landed gentry who took Dumfries Castle from the supporters of King Robert I (the Bruce) in 1306 after the murder of John Comyn. The family was prominent in Galloway, and a William MacLellan of Bombie is recorded in 1467.

Sir Robert MacLellan of Bombie (*d.* 1639), who had been knighted at an early age, was Provost of Kirkcudbright in 1607, whereupon he embarked on a

MACLEAN

charter in 1390. One of the dynastic marriages of the clan was between Lachlan Maclean of Duart and a sister of the Earl of Argyll, but finding, or suspecting, her to be barren, in about 1520 Maclean tied her to a rock (today called Lady's Rock) in the sound between Lismore and Mull and left her to drown when the tide rose. He reported her death as being by misadventure, and travelled to Inveraray to pay his respects to her family, only to find her there, flanked by stony-faced relations. She had been rescued by a passing fishing boat.

The Macleans were staunch royalists, Lachlan Maclean of Morvern, heir to his brother, Hector of Duart, being created a baronet by King Charles I in 1632.

MACLELLAN

MACLEOD RED

MACLEOD OF RAASAY

MACLEOD OF MACLEOD

MACLELLAN, LORD
KIRKCUDBRIGHT

MACLENNAN

MACLEOD OF MACLEOD

career of riotous (and violent) living and profligacy, though in 1633 he was made Lord Kirkcudbright, possibly for being useful to the Government while tending his estates in Ireland. After his death the title passed through the MacLellans of Glenshinnoch, Auchlane, and Balmangan to William MacLellan of Borness, 6th Lord, who was an Edinburgh glover and died in about 1765.

The title became dormant in 1832.

MacLENNAN

Tartan: *Logan and MacLennan*

Motto: *Dum spiro spero (Latin: While I breathe, I hope)*

At Drumderfit, Easter Ross, in 1372, in a battle with the Frasers, Gilliegorm, chief of the Logans, and many of his followers were slaughtered, and his pregnant wife was captured. She gave birth to a deformed son, who was known as *Crotair* (Hunchbacked) MacGilligorm. Though he took Holy Orders, he had several children, one of whom he named, or was called, *Gille Fhinnein* (Devotee of St Finnan). The descendants of *Gille Fhinnein* called themselves *Mac Gillinnein*, which roughly transliterates into MacLennan. Many of the clan settled in Kintail, where they became standard bearers to the chief of the Mackenzies. Another historical record makes the MacLennans the original inhabitants of Kintail as early as the sixth century.

MACLEOD

Branches: *Macleod of Harris and Dunvegan, from which Macleod of Glenelg, Macleod of Waternish; Macleod of Lewis and Raasay, from which Macleod of Assynt*

Tartans: *Macleod of Macleod (also known as hunting Macleod), Macleod (red), Macleod of Lewis and Raasay (also known as dress Macleod)*

Mottos: *Hold fast; Murus aheneus esto (Latin: Let there be a wall of brass); (Raasay) Luceo non uro (Latin: I shine, not burn)*

Leod, son of Olaf the Black, Norse King of Man in 1230, had two sons. From Tormod (or Norman) descended the Macleods of Harris and Dunvegan, and from Torquil the Macleods of Lewis and Raasay.

At Dunvegan in Skye the Macleods built the present stronghold, which dates from the fourteenth century. It is the seat of the chief, and it houses, among other relics, the Fairy Flag, said to have been given to John, 4th Chief, by his wife, a fairy princess, but more probably a battle standard of his Norse ancestors, plundered during one of their fearsome raids in the East. The Fairy Tower was built by Alastair Crotach, or Hunchback (*d.* 1547), 8th Chief, a master of diplomacy and a patron of the arts, to whom is credited the establishment of the MacCrimmons not only as hereditary pipers par excellence, but also as significant composers of traditional Highland music. It is said that because of his appearance Alastair was accepted in marriage only by the tenth daughter of Cameron of Lochiel, the other nine having turned him down. After the death of his son William in 1552 without a male heir, the chiefship passed by usurpation and murder swiftly through several hands until it reached Alastair's grandson, Roderick (*d.* 1626), 16th Chief, known as Rory *Mór*. Knighted by King James VI, he maintained the unenviable balance between political expediency and traditional values, while enlarging Dunvegan Castle and his estates (he also devised the exchange which restored Waternish to his line of the family), and establishing within his home an atmosphere in which poetry as well as music could flourish. Dame Flora Macleod, 28th Chief, died in 1976 at the age of 98, having travelled the world several times to visit and encourage members of her clan.

The island and chiefship of Lewis passed by marriage to the Mackenzies, earls of Cromartie, at the beginning of the seventeenth century, though the male line continued through the Macleods of Raasay, that island having come to Malcolm, younger brother of the 10th Chief of Lewis, in the fourteenth century from his father. The lands and castle of Assynt in Sutherland came to the Macleods of Lewis by marriage and were vested in the second son of the 5th Chief. It was Neil Macleod, the 22-year-old Laird of Assynt, who betrayed the Marquis of Montrose in 1650, for which he was awarded £25,000 Scots, of which a fifth was to be paid in oatmeal. He only got the oatmeal, and most of that had gone bad.

Norman Macleod (1780-1865), born in Assynt, organised the most extraordinary of all emigration pilgrimages. In 1817, 'to the wail of the bagpipes and the singing of MacCrimmon's Lament', he and his flock set out from Skye for Nova Scotia. Some settled in Pictou, others, after several years, decided to move on with him to Ohio, but they were blown off course and made their homes instead at St Ann's, Cape Breton. In 1851 he moved on to Adelaide, Australia, then to Melbourne, and finally to Auckland, New Zealand, where with the survivors of the original group he founded the Waipu Highlanders.

MACLINTOCK

MACLINTOCK

Tartan: *MacLintock*

Motto: *Virtute et labore (Latin: By virtue and hard work)*

The name is from the Gaelic *MacGillcondaig*, 'son of the gillie of [St] Findon', and the clan is known to have inhabited the regions of Luss and Lorn, Argyll, from about 1500. William McLintock (1873-1947), accountant and industrialist, was created a baronet in 1934.

MACMILLAN

Branches: *Macmillan of Dunmore, Macmillan of Knap, Macmillan of Laggalgarve*

Tartans: *Macmillan, Macmillan (old), Macmillan (hunting)*

Motto: *Miseris succurrere disco (Latin: I learn to help the unfortunate)*

The Gaelic *MacMhaolain* means 'son of the tonsured one', which in this case would be a cleric of the ancient Celtic Church. A ringed stone cross, carved in a style of the ninth century, with a Latin inscription which reads

MACMILLAN OLD   MACMILLAN OF MACMILLAN AND KNAP   MACMILLAN

'This is the cross of Alexander Macmillan', still stands today in the churchyard of Kilmory Knap, Loch Sween, Argyll. The Macmillans of Knap lost the chiefship of the clan to the family of Dunmore, Loch Tarbert, in the 1660s, through whom it passed eventually to the Laggalgarve branch. Very early on, Macmillans settled in Lochaber, from where two hundred of them emigrated to Ontario, Canada, in 1802.

Kirkpatrick Macmillan (1813-78), inventor of the pedal bicycle, was a Dumfriesshire blacksmith.

The two brothers who in 1844 founded the publishing firm of Macmillan came from Arran, and share the same family descent as Harold Macmillan (1894-1986), 1st Earl of Stockton, who was Prime Minister 1957-63.

MacNAB

Branches: *MacNab of Arthurstone, MacNab of Bovain*

Tartan: *MacNab*

Motto: *Timor omnis abesto (Latin: Let all fear be absent)*

Clann-an-Aba is Gaelic for 'children of the abbot', and the MacNabs are descended from the hereditary abbots of Glendochart, Loch Tay. They opposed the cause of King Robert I (the Bruce), and after the Battle of Bannockburn in 1314 lost their lands, though in 1336 Gilbert MacNab received a charter of the Barony of Bovain, Glendochart, from King David II.

The clan, led by 'Smooth John' MacNab, fought for the Marquis of Montrose in 1644-5, using local knowledge

ARCHIBALD, 13TH LAIRD OF MACNAB

THE MACNAB

and some trickery to capture the island castle of Loch Dochart.

Francis MacNab (*d.* 1815), 16th Chief, lost much of the family fortunes, and dissipated a great deal of sexual energy without producing a legitimate heir. The chiefship passed to his nephew Archibald (1777-1860), who in 1824 obtained a territorial grant of land in Ontario, Canada. Here, with the several hundred MacNabs who had emigrated earlier, and more whom he persuaded to follow him from Scotland, he established MacNab as a feudal township, but he was forced to leave the country

MACNAB

in 1853. Before his death he made a written statement that his cousin Sir Allan MacNab (1798-1862), Prime Minister of Canada 1854-7, was representative of the line nearest to his own, which became extinct on the death of his daughter in 1894. The dormant chiefship was revived in 1955 in the person of the head of the branch of MacNab of Arthurstone.

MacNACHTAN, MacNAUGHTEN

Branch: *MacNachtan of Dunderave*

Tartan: *MacNachtan*

Motto: *I hope in God*

Slogan: *Fraoch Eilean (Gaelic: The Heathery Isle)*

Nectan is a Pictish name which was borne by several kings, and MacNachtans held lands by Loch Tay in the

MACNACHTAN

MACNAGHTAN OF　　DUNDERAVE

MacNEIL(L)

Branches: *MacNeil of Barra, from which McNeil of Ersary; MacNeil of Gigha, from which MacNeill of Taynish, from which McNeill of Colonsay and McNeill of Raploch*

Tartans: *MacNeil of Barra, McNeill of Colonsay*

Mottos: *(Barra) Vincere vel mori, (Gigha) Vincere aut mori (Latin: To conquer or die)*

Slogan: *Buaidh no bàs (Gaelic: Victory or death)*

twelfth century, which they soon extended to other parts of Argyll, including Dunderave, Loch Fyne.

In 1267 King Alexander III gave Sir Gilchrist MacNachtan the island of Fraoch Eilean in Loch Awe, on condition that the King of Scotland should have free hospitality in the castle whenever he was in the vicinity. John MacNachtan of Dunderave, 16th Chief, fought for Viscount Dundee at the Battle of Killiecrankie in 1689, after which his estates were forfeited. His son John might have got the lands back when he became engaged to the second daughter of Sir James Campbell of Ardkinglas. Unfortunately, he indulged rather too freely before the ceremony with his future father-in-law, who succeeded in marrying him instead to his eldest daughter. The next morning MacNachtan fled to Ireland with the second daughter, having during the night consummated the marriage. A furious Campbell of Ardkinglas had MacNachtan 'condemned' for incest, obtained possession of the forfeited estates, and drowned the baby girl who was the outcome of the wedding night.

The chiefship of MacNachtan then lapsed until 1818, when, on the evidence of four hundred members of the clan, Edmund A. MacNaughten, of Antrim, was officially declared chief, as the direct descendant of John Dhu MacNachtan of Dunderave, who had emigrated to Ireland in about 1580 and was the grandson of Sir Alexander MacNachtan, who fell at the Battle of Flodden in 1513.

The MacNeils claim that they are descended from 'Niall of the Nine Hostages', King of Ireland, and that Niall, 21st of the line, came to Barra in the Outer Hebrides in 1049. The island was confirmed to the family by royal charter in 1495. In the meantime, on the loss of power and status of the Lord of the Isles in 1493, the MacNeills of Gigha, one of the Western Isles, had gone their own way.

MACNEIL OF BARRA

MACNEILL OF COLONSAY

MACNICOL

MACNICOL HUNTING

MCPHAIL

MACNEIL OF BARRA

JOHN MACNEILL, AGRICULTURIST

MACNICOL

The chiefs of MacNeil of Barra did themselves well in their island fortress of Kismull, whose tower dates from 1120 and which has now been restored. Rory the Turbulent, 15th Chief, arrested for the piracy of English ships, pleaded that he felt himself justified in embarrassing those who had executed the mother of his sovereign, King James VI. Subsequently the chiefship was passed down by men with equally interesting sobriquets, Black Roderick, Roderick the Dove of the West, Roderick the Peaceful, and Roderick the Gentle, to the Ersary branch, descended from the younger brother of the Dove of the West.

Gigha was sold in 1544, and after passing through various hands was repurchased by the Taynish branch, and then sold again to McNeill of Colonsay in 1780. In the meantime a chief had married the heiress of the Hamiltons of Raploch, Lanarkshire.

Duncan MacNeill (1793-1874), the judge, who was born in Oronsay, and bought Colonsay from his brother, Alexander, 6th Chief of Colonsay, was created Lord Colonsay and Oronsay in 1867.

MacNICOL, NIC(H)OLSON

Branches: *Nicolson of Lasswade, MacNicol of Scorrybreck*

Tartan: *MacNicol, MacNicol (hunting)*

Motto: *Generositate non ferocitate (Latin: By generosity not ferocity)*

Slogan: *Sgorr bhreac [Scorrybreck] (Gaelic: The Speckled Rock)*

There are many MacNicols in Argyll, while further north the Nicolsons emerged in the fifteenth century as tenants of the lands of Scorrybreck in Skye. The Nicolsons of Lasswade, Midlothian, are descended from a dean of Brechin, Angus. Today there are two distinct chiefs, the one for the Nicholsons, and the other for the Highland MacNicols and Nicolsons (the latter mainly in Skye).

McPHAIL

Tartan: *MacPhail*

The name means 'son of Paul' in Gaelic, and is first recorded in 1414. Members of the clan were associated

with the Camerons, Clan Chattan, the Mackintoshes, and the Mackays, a number of MacPhails appearing on a list of tenants on the Reay (Mackay) estates in 1678.

James MacPhail, who was born in Aberdeenshire in 1754, son of a humble Highlander, became a farm labourer earning £2. 6s. 8d a year. Not thinking much of this, he emigrated to England, where in 1785 he became gardener to Lord Hawkesby in Surrey. He pioneered a new way of growing vegetables, which he explained in *A Treatise on the Culture of the Cucumber* (1794).

CLUNY   MACPHERSON

MACPHERSON

MACPHERSON

Branches: *Macpherson of Cluny, Macpherson of Inverestine, Macpherson of Pitmain*

Tartans: *Macpherson (red), Macpherson (hunting), Macpherson (dress)*

Motto: *Touch not the cat bot [without] a glove*

Slogan: *Creag Dubh (Gaelic: The Black Craig, a hill near Cluny)*

The clan, but not the name, goes back traditionally to the chief of Clan Chattan in 1173, whose second son, Ewan *Ban*, had three sons, from whom descended the branches of Cluny, Inverestine, and Pitmain.

The first to bear the name was Donald Macpherson, son of Duncan, who was the Parson of Laggan in 1438. Ewen MacPherson of Cluny (*d.* 1756), Clan Chief, raised a company of three hundred men to fight against Bonnie Prince Charlie in 1745, and then, after the Battle of Prestonpans, brought them over to the Jacobite side. In June 1746 government soldiers burned down his 18-roomed mansion, built only two years before, and all the other houses in the vicinity. He set up residence in his 'cage', a cave in the mountain face of Ben Alder, from which he emerged to give personal assistance to the

MACPHERSON DRESS

Prince until his final escape, after which Macpherson lived in hiding for nine years, protected by his clansmen and tenants, before getting away to France. His estates were forfeited, but in 1784, after they had been offered to and refused by James Macpherson (1736-96), the perpetrator of the 'Ossian Poems', they were returned to Ewen's son, Duncan (1750-1817), who had been born in a corn kiln during his father's period of hiding, and who became a colonel in the 3rd infantry regiment. There is a Clan Macpherson Museum at Newtonmore.

ANDREW MACPHERSON OF CLUNY, 15TH CHIEF

MACQUARIE — OF ULVA

MACQUARRIE

Tartan: *Macquarrie*

Slogan: *An t'Arm Breac Darg (Gaelic: The Red-Tartaned Army)*

Guaire means 'noble' in Gaelic, and Guaire was the brother of Fingon, ancient ancestor of the Mackinnons. The Macquarries, one of the members of Clan Alpin, held the tiny island of Ulva, off Mull, being dependant first on the Macdonalds, lords of the Isles, and then on the Macleans of Duart.

Lachlan Macquarrie (1715-1818), 16th Chief, was in 1773 host to Samuel Johnson and James Boswell, who learned from him that the practice of *Mercheta Mulierum*, the right of a laird to have the wife of a tenant on her wedding night, was still an Ulva tradition.

MACQUARRIE

MACQUARRIE

Lachlan was forced to sell his island estates in 1778, when he was 63, whereupon he joined the army as an officer in the Argyll Highlanders. He died at the age of 103. His cousin, Major-General Lachlan Macquarie (1762-1824), born in Ulva, was Governor of New South Wales 1809-21, during which time he laid out the city of Sydney and performed other notable acts.

MACQUEEN

Branch: *Macqueen of Corrybrough*

Tartan: *Macqueen*

Motto: *Constant and faithful*

The Macqueens, or MacSweens, derive their name from the Norse *Sweyn*. They are also known as Clan Revan, under which name they were one of the traditional

MACQUEEN

seventeen members of Clan Chattan. The clan obtained the lands of Corrybrough, Strathdearn, at the beginning of the seventeenth century. Robert Macqueen (1722-99), Lord Braxfield, the 'hanging judge', was of a Lanarkshire family.

MacRAE

Branches: *MacRae of Conchra, MacRae of Inverinate*

Tartans: *MacRae, MacRae (hunting), MacRae of Conchra*

Motto: *Fortitudine (Latin: By fortitude)*

Slogan: *Sgur Urain (Mountain in Kintail)*

MacRath in Gaelic means 'son of grace', and it is a personal name which first appears in Scottish records in the twelfth century.

The family known as MacRae is said to have originated in the territory of the Frasers of Lovat, on the Beauly Firth. Three sons left home at the beginning of the fourteenth century, and founded dynasties at Brahan (near Dingwall), in Argyll, and in Kintail, where they became bodyguards to the chief of the Mackenzies of Kintail and ultimately pall-bearers to the lords of Seaforth.

Duncan MacRae, 5th Chief of Kintail, was granted the lands of Inverinate in about 1557. The MacRaes of Conchra are descended from Rev. John MacRae (1614-1673) of Dingwall. Many MacRaes left Kintail in the wake of the Clearances in the early years of the nineteenth century, to settle in Nova Scotia. After the potato famines of 1846-7, of a boatload of a hundred emigrants going to join a ship for Montreal, fifty were called MacRae. By 1852 there were 465 MacRaes in Glengarry, Ontario, and today there are more than a thousand in British Columbia.

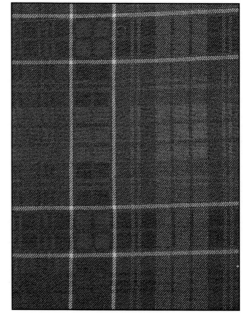

MACRAE

MACSPORRAN

MACTAGGART

MacSPORRAN

Tartan: *MacSporran*

The Gaelic *Mac-an-sporain* means 'son of the purse', and the clan is said to have been hereditary purse-bearers to the lords of the Isles.

MacTAGGART

Tartan: *MacTaggart*

The Gaelic *Mac-an-t-sagairt* means 'son of the priest', which in the case of Ferquhard Macintaggart meant the lay abbot of the monastery of Applecross. In 1215 he put down a rebellion, beheaded its leaders, and presented their heads to King Alexander II, who knighted him and later made him Earl of Ross. The name recurs in Dumfries in 1459. Elsewhere, in 1583 three MacTaggarts were charged with arson, and in 1688 Catherine McTarget was accused of witchcraft.

John Mactaggart (1867-1956), grandson of John Mactaggart of Campbeltown, was created a baronet in 1938.

MacTAVISH

Tartan: *MacTavish*

Motto: *Non oblitus (Latin: Not forgotten)*

The name means 'son of Tammas', the Scots form of Thomas, and is common in Argyll, where the estate of Dunardarie was granted to the family by the Duke of Argyll in 1533, and was the seat of the chief until 1785.

MACTAVISH

The MacTavishes of Stratherrick, Invernessshire, are considered to be a sept of the Frasers.

Simon McTavish (1750-1804) was born in Stratherrick, son of John McTavish of Garthbeg, a lieutenant in the 78th Regiment of Foot. Simon left Scotland for New York when he was fourteen. Twelve years later he was ensconced in Montreal, preparing to leave for London with a cargo of furs worth £15,000. Nicknamed 'The Marquis', for his elegance, personality, and business acumen, he became the most influential Canadian businessman of his time, and in 1799 he bought back for his clan the original estate of Dunardarie. His cousin Donald McTavish (1771-1814), also born in Stratherrick, started in 1790 as an apprentice clerk in the North West Company, of which Simon was the principal director. He would have become the company's agent had he not drowned at the mouth of the Columbia River while on his way to board a ship whose commission was to destroy American settlements on the northwest coast. Impressed into the British navy, he had travelled to England to join the ship, and during the thirteen-month voyage back again from Portsmouth he consoled himself with the charms of a local barmaid, whom he had persuaded to come with him.

MacTHOMAS

Branches: *MacThomas of Finegand, MacThomas of Glenshee*

Tartan: *MacThomas*

Motto: *Deo juvante invidiam superabo (Latin: With God's help I will rise above envy)*

Slogan: *Clach na coileach (Gaelic: 'The Cockerel's Crest')*

The fourteenth-century founder of the clan was Thomas, illegitimate son of Angus, 6th Chief of Clan Mackintosh, and it emerges later as a member of Clan Chattan.

In 1587 there is a reference to 'Clan MacThomas in Glenshee', whose representative was adjudged Clan Chief in 1968. In about 1600, on the murder of the then

MACTHOMAS

WILLIAM MAITLAND OF LETHINGTON

chief, the chiefship had passed to his brother, John MacComie of Finegand, a few miles further down the glen, in which branch the chiefship of the clan is now vested.

McWHIRTER

Tartan: *McWhirter*

The old form of the name is MacChruiter, meaning 'son of the harper', and it is first found in Ayrshire.

McWILLIAM

Tartan: *McWilliam*

The name McWilliam occurs in the Highlands in the twelfth century, and a formidable dynasty descended from William, an illegitimate, or unrecognised, son of King Duncan II, who died in 1094. Its members made repeated efforts to obtain the crown by force, but were finally defeated in 1215 at the beginning of the reign of King Alexander II, the line being effectively and drastically extinguished by the infant daughter of the McWilliam chief being battered to death against the market cross in Forfar. As William was a popular baptismal name, many of those who came to be called McWilliam ('son of William') or Williamson (which first appeared as a name in the fourteenth century) can claim no clan descent. There are, however, records of a *Clan Mac Mhic Uileim,* which claimed descent from an early chief of the Macleods, and during the sixteenth century the Robertsons of Pittagowan in Atholl went under the name of McWilliam.

MAITLAND

Tartan: *Maitland (only available with Chief's written authority)*

Motto: *Consilio et animis (Latin: By counsel and reasoning)*

Sir Richard of Maitland acquired the lands of Thirlestane, in the parish of Lauder, Berwickshire, through his wife, Avicia, in the thirteenth century in the reign of King Alexander II. Lethington, in Haddington, came into the family in about 1345. Sir Richard Maitland of Lethington (1496-1586), lawyer, judge (on his appointment as which, when he was now completely blind, he was

MCWHIRTER

MCWILLIAM

MAITLAND

MALCOLM

MALCOLM OF
POLTALLOCH

MALCOLM DRESS

made Lord Lethington), poet, and important collector of early Scots poetry, described as 'ane valiant, grave and worthy Knight', had two notable sons. The eldest, William Maitland of Lethington (*d.* 1573), known as 'Secretary Lethington' for his services to Mary, Queen of Scots, was given protection in Edinburgh Castle by its governor in the aftermath of her flight to England. After four months of siege and ten days solid bombardment by English artillery, the Governor only gave in when his men threatened to hang Maitland from the battlements. After the surrender, Maitland would, anyway, have been hanged by Regent Morton, had he not died in prison first.

The second son, John Maitland (1545-1595), judge and, from 1594, Secretary of State, was made Lord Thirlestane in 1590. His only son John (*d.* 1645), who purchased the baronies of Baghie and Bolton from his cousin, was made Earl of Lauderdale in 1624, and was President of Parliament 1644-5. His eldest son John (1616-82), Secretary of State on the Restoration of the Monarchy in 1660, was created Duke of Lauderdale in 1672, though that title became extinct on his death without a son, his brother Charles (1620-91) becoming 3rd Earl of Lauderdale. Charles, who acquired Halton through marriage, had been appointed General of the Mint in 1660, but in 1682, a week after succeeding to the earldom, he was sacked and later, with his son and others, fined £72,000 by the Court of Session for mismanagement.

The earls of Lauderdale are Hereditary Bearers of the National Flag of Scotland, an office which survives today.

MALCOLM (see also MacCALLUM)

Branches: *Malcolm of Balbedie, Malcolm of Poltalloch*

Tartans: *Malcolm, Malcolm (dress)*

Mottos: *Deus refugium nostrum (Latin: God is our refuge); In ardua petit (Latin: He takes on difficulties)*

The equivalent name in Gaelic is *Maol-Calum*, 'disciple of [St] Columba', and though the names Malcolm and MacCallum have been taken down the years to be the same, four kings of Scotland bore the name Malcolm, which has since become a common first name and surname in its own right.

John Malcolm of Balbedie, Lochore, and Innertiel was granted a charter of the Barony of Balbedie and Lochore in 1662. His three sons were John of Innertiel (*d.* 1729), who was made a baronet of Nova Scotia in 1665; Michael of Balbedie; and Alexander of Lochore, created Lord Lochore in 1688. Dugald MacCallum of Poltalloch, Argyll, who inherited his estate in 1779, seems to have been the first of his line to call himself Malcolm. He was succeeded by his cousin, Neil Malcolm (*d.* 1802). John Wingfield Malcolm (1833-1902) was made Lord Malcolm of Poltalloch in 1896.

TRIBE OF MAR

Tartan: *Tribe of Mar*

Motto: *Pans [pense] plus (French: Think more)*

Mar, stretching from the Braes of Mar in the west to Aberdeen, and from the Braes of Angus in the south to

THE CHIEF OF THE MATHESONS

the River Don, was one of the divisions of the ancient kingdom of the Picts, and it existed later as a geographical and political region under its mormaer long before Ruadri is recorded as its first earl in about 1120. The title is the oldest still existing in Scotland, and Mar is the premier Scottish earldom. Its present holder, the 31st since Ruadri, is Countess of Mar in her own right.

TRIBE OF MAR

MATHESON

MATHESON

Branches: *Matheson of Attadale, Matheson of Bennetsfield, Matheson of Little Scatwell, Matheson of Lochalsh. Matheson of Shiness*

Tartan: *Matheson, Matheson (hunting)*

Mottos: *Fac et spera (Latin: Do and hope); O'Chian (Gaelic: Of old)*

Slogan: *Achadh-da-thearnaidh (Gaelic: 'The Field of the Two Slopes')*

While there is an ancient record which names a Mathan as chief in 1263, and traditionally the clan occupied part of Lochalsh, the family seems to begin with Murdoch Buidhe, Constable of Eilean Donan Castle in 1570. From his eldest son, Roderick, descended the Mathesons of Bennetsfield, in the Black Isle district of Cromarty, and from the younger the Mathesons of Attadale. At the beginning of the nineteenth century, John Matheson of Attadale married Margaret, daughter of the head of the family of Matheson of Shiness, which had long been settled in Sutherland. Their son Alexander bought Lochalsh and was made a baronet in 1882. James Sutherland Matheson of Shiness purchased the island of Lewis in 1844, and was created a baronet in 1851.

MAXWELL

Branches: *Maxwell of Calderwood, Maxwell of Cardoness, Maxwell of Carruchan, Maxwell of Farnham, Maxwell of Monreith, Maxwell of Pollok*

Tartan: *Maxwell*

Mottos: *Reviresco (Latin: I flourish again); I bide ye fair*

Maxwell, or 'Maccus's Well', is a pool, or part, of the River Tweed by Kelso. Sir John Maxwell (*d.* 1241) was Chamberlain of Scotland, an office later held by his brother Aymer, from whose sons, Sir Herbert and Sir John, sprang many branches of the family.

Sir Herbert's descendant Herbert was made Lord Maxwell in about 1445, and from his second son comes Maxwell of Monreith, which became a baronetcy in 1681. The younger son of 4th Lord Maxwell became Lord Herries through his wife.

John (1553-1593), 6th Lord Maxwell, was briefly Earl of Morton after the incumbent of that title had been executed. He was killed while on an official mission to

MATHESON

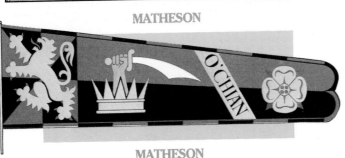

MATHESON

MAXWELL

put down the Johnstons, with whom his family had a long-standing feud. His son, 7th Lord, killed Sir James Johnston in 1608 in retaliation, for which he was executed in 1613, being succeeded by his brother Robert, who was made Earl of Nithsdale in about 1620.

William (*d.* 1744), 5th Earl, was sentenced to death for his part in the Rebellion of 1715. The day before his execution he was visited several times in the Tower of London by his wife, always accompanied by one or more female companions. The guards, totally confused by all these comings and goings, failed to notice that the figure who left with the Countess towards dusk was not female, but the Earl himself, dressed in female clothing.

The Maxwells, baronets of Cardoness, of Monreith, and of Springkell, and the barons of Farnham are all descended from Sir John, younger son of Aymer, as are the baronets of Pollok, whose seat was gifted to Glasgow in 1967 and in the grounds of which stands the Burrell Collection.

MELVILLE, EARL OF MELVILLE

MELVILLE

Tartan: *Melville*

Motto: *Denique coelum (Latin: Finally, the sky)*

Guillaume de Malleville came to England with William the Conqueror in 1066. Galfrid Melville was Sheriff of Edinburgh Castle in 1162. Sir John Melville of Raith was Captain of Dunbar Castle under King James V, but in 1548, in the infancy of Mary, Queen of Scots, he was found guilty of treason and was executed the same day. His third son, Sir Robert Melville of Murdocairnie (1527-1621), appointed Keeper of Linlithgow Palace by Mary in 1567, bought the lands of Monimail, Fife, in 1592. He was created Lord Melville of Monimail by King James VI in 1616.

GEORGE, 1ST EARL OF MELVILLE

George (1636-1707), 4th Lord, after showing himself to be a staunch royalist by his support of King Charles II, subsequently threw in his lot with the abortive rebellion against King James II (of England) by Charles II's illegitimate son, the Duke of Monmouth (1649-85). He escaped to Europe, where he attached himself to the court of William of Orange. He returned to Britain when William became King in 1689, and was rewarded with the earldom of Melville, becoming President of the Privy Council in 1696. In 1703 he successfully petitioned Parliament to order the public pathway through his estate at Monimail to be diverted. His son David (1660-1728), 2nd Earl of Melville, became also, through his mother's family, 3rd Earl of Leven.

MENZIES

Branches: *Menzies of Culdares, Menzies of Pitfoddels*

Tartans: *Menzies (old), Menzies (red and white), Menzies (black and white), Menzies (black and red), Menzies (hunting)*

Motto: *Vil God I zal (With God's will, I shall)*

Slogan: *Geal 'us dearg a suas (Gaelic: Up with the white and red)*

Menzies, Mengues, Meyners, or Mingies (which last is as the name is pronounced) appears in records of the twelfth century. Sir Robert of Meyners was Chamberlain of Scotland in 1251, and granted a charter of the lands of Culdares, in Glen Lyon, Perthshire, to the Moncreiffe family.

King Robert I (the Bruce) awarded vast stretches of territory to members of the clan for services rendered before, at, and after the Battle of Bannockburn in 1314.

Sir Robert de Mengues was granted the Barony of Menzies, Perthshire, in 1487, after his mansion house

had been destroyed by fire. The sixteenth-century tower house which replaced it, Castle Menzies, Weem, is now being restored and also includes the Clan Menzies museum. His descendant, Alexander Menzies of Castle Menzies, was made a baronet of Nova Scotia in 1665, and it was a distant relative of his, a Menzies of Culdares, who in 1738 brought back from the Tyrol in his suitcase seven larch saplings, which he planted on his estate and which became the ancestors of the Scottish larches.

The Pitfoddels branch was an ancient one. Thomas Menzies of Pitfoddels was Provost of Aberdeen in 1551, and 'a young Menzies of Pitfoddels' carried the royal standard, and died for it, in the last battle of the Marquis of Montrose, fought at Invercarron in 1650. The last of the line of Pitfoddels was John Menzies (1756-1843), who gave his house and estate of Blair for the foundation of the Catholic college of that name.

MIDDLETON

Tartan: *Middleton*

Motto: *Fortis in arduis (Latin: Strong in adversity)*

The lands of Middleton, Kincardineshire, were confirmed by charter to Malcolm in 1094 by King Duncan II.

Robert Middleton, who is said to have been killed in bed by the Marquis of Montrose in 1645 or stabbed by his soldiers as he sat in his chair, had ten children. The eldest, John Middleton of Caldhame (1608-73), was a senior officer of the Covenant against the royalists in 1645, and in 1646 personally granted Montrose the peace terms which enabled him to take ship for the

MENZIES OF
MENZIES

MENZIES HUNTING

MENZIES RED AND WHITE

MENZIES BLACK AND WHITE

MIDDLETON

Continent. Middleton subsequently changed sides, and as a major-general fought for King Charles II at the Battle of Worcester in 1651, and at the Restoration of the Monarchy in 1660 was created Earl of Middleton. In 1667 he was appointed Governor of Tangier, where he died of complications from a broken arm, sustained when he fell downstairs drunk.

The title was forfeited by the 2nd Earl (1650-1719) for his support of King James VII in exile. Robert's second son, Alexander (1610-86), Principal of King's College, Aberdeen, was succeeded in that post by his son George (1645-1726), whose wife Janet survived him and lived to be a hundred, having borne him eighteen children.

MILNE

Tartan: *Milne*

Motto: *Tam arte quam marte (Latin: As much by skill as by warfare); (Lord Milne) Efficiunt clarum studia (Latin: Studies make a thing clear)*

The name means 'at or near a corn-mill' and is found in Aberdeenshire documents in 1380.

John Milne of Urquhart, Morayshire, who was born in 1659, was the father of Harry Milne (*b*. 1695), 1st Laird of Chapelton, Forfar, which was acquired by the Milnes of Boyndie Milne, Banff, by the marriage of John Milne (*b*. 1772) to its heiress, whose brother is recorded as dying of laughter while on holiday in Lisbon.

Patrick Milne of Boyndie Milne, Notary Public of Banff, had to be forcibly restrained by the magistrates on one occasion from embarking on a duel, and his son James, in retaliation for an insult to his young wife, burned down the castle of Inchdrewer in 1713 and killed Lord Banff.

Field-Marshal George Milne (1866-1948), descended from George Milne of Rosehearty, Aberdeenshire, who died in 1832, was created Lord Milne in 1933.

MITCHELL

Tartan: *See Galbraith*

Motto: *In deo spes (Latin: There is hope in God)*

The name, which is Michael via the French form *Michel*, probably came to Scotland with the Normans. Sir Andrew Mitchell (1708-71), parliamentarian and diplomat, was born in Edinburgh. Admiral Sir Andrew Mitchell (1757-1806), commander-in-chief of the North American station 1802-5, was the second son of Charles Mitchell of Baldridge, Dunfermline. Major-General John Mitchell (1785-1859) was born in Stirlingshire. Sir Thomas Mitchell (1792-1855), Australian explorer, was the son of John Mitchell of Craigend, Stirlingshire. Harold Mitchell (1900-83), of Tulliallan, Fife, and Luscar, Alberta, descended from William Mitchell (1781-1854), who was co-founder of the Alloa Coal Co., and was created a baronet in 1945.

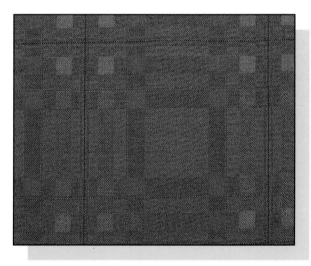

MOFFAT

MOFFAT

Tartan: *Moffat*

The name derives from Moffat, Dumfriesshire, and the first record of it is Nicholas de Mufet, Archdeacon of Teviotdale in 1245, who was elected Bishop of Glasgow in 1258 but was never confirmed in the post, partly because he refused to pay the sum of money demanded from him by the Pope.

In 1436 Robert de Moffat, treasurer of the church of Glasgow, bought a half-interest in three merchants' booths and two storage lofts in the main street, and rented a tenement in Gallowgate. A family of Moffetts in the Marches was listed as being 'unruly' in 1587. Robert Moffat (1795-1883), the missionary and father-in-law of David Livingstone (1813-73), was born in Ormiston, East Lothian.

Descendants of an original family of Moffats still have lands in Dumfriesshire.

MONCREIFFE OF   THAT ILK

MONCREIFFE

Branches: *Moncrieff of Brandiran, Moncreiffe of Easter Moncreiffe, Moncrieff of Kinmouth, Scott Moncrieff*

Tartan: *Moncreiffe*

Motto: *Sur esperance (French: In hope)*

Sir Mathew of Moncreiffe received a charter for his lands from King Alexander II in 1248, and another for lands in Perthshire from Sir Robert de Meyners (Menzies). The estate of Easter Moncreiffe was gifted to a younger son of the family in 1312.

A baronetcy was awarded to the family in 1626, but the lands of Moncreiffe were sold to a cousin, Thomas Moncreiffe, Clerk of the Exchequer, who was himself created a baronet in 1685. From the line of the former

baronetcy descended Sir James Moncreiff (1776-1851), the judge, made Lord Moncreiff in 1829, who as an advocate had defended Burke, the body-snatcher. His second son, James (1811-95), Lord Advocate and later Lord Justice Clerk, was made 1st Lord Moncreiff of Tullibole in 1874.

The line of the younger baronetcy returned to the older spelling of the name. Sir Iain Moncreiffe of that Ilk (1919-85), 11th Baronet, Albany Herald from 1961, succeeded to the title in 1957 when his cousin was killed in the fire which destroyed the family seat, built by the 1st Baronet. His elder son Merlin (*b.* 1948) succeeded to his mother's title of Earl of Erroll as well as to the baronetcy.

The branches of Brandiran, of Kinmouth, and of the Scott Moncrieffs, descended from a younger son of the 10th Laird of Moncreiffe.

MONCREIFFE

MONTGOMERIE MONTGOMERIE, EARL OF EGLINTON MONTGOMERIE GREEN

MONTGOMERIE, MONTGOMERY

Branches: *Montgomerie of Eglinton, Montgomerie of Laingshaw, Montgomerie of Skelmorlie, Montgomerie of Stanhope*

Tartans: *Montgomerie, Montgomerie (green)*

Motto: *Gardez bien (French: Keep a good look out)*

Montgomerie derives from French lands in Normandy, and Montgomeries came to England with William the Conqueror in 1066. Robert de Montgomerie, who died in about 1177, was granted the estate of Eaglesham, Renfrewshire. It was Sir John Montgomerie, 9th Laird of Eaglesham, who captured Sir Henry Percy (1364-1403), known as 'Hotspur', at the Battle of Otterburn in 1388, and built Polnoon Castle at Eaglesham with the ransom money. He married Elizabeth de Eglinton, through whom he acquired the baronies of Eglinton and Ardrossan in Ayrshire. Their grandson, Sir Alexander Montgomerie (*d.* 1470), member of King James I's privy council, was made 1st Lord Montgomerie. The Montgomeries of Skilmorlie descended from his younger son, and the Stanhope branch, which was granted a baronetcy in 1801, from his brother. Hugh (1460-1545), 3rd Lord Montgomerie, was created Earl of Eglinton in 1506, but had his house burned down in 1528 by the Cunninghams, who were also responsible for shooting the 4th Earl in 1586. The 4th Earl's sister Margaret married Robert Seton (*d.* 1603), 1st Earl of Winton, and the earldom of Eglinton devolved on their third son, Alexander (1588-1661), who took the name of Montgomerie. Alexander (1723-69), 10th Earl, public servant, was shot and killed by a poacher whom he had apprehended.

The title was inherited by his brother, General Archibald Montgomerie (1726-96), who raised the 77th Highland regiment of foot, which he commanded against the Cherokee Indians in 1758. Alexander Montgomerie (1545-98), a son of the Laird of Hessilhead Castle, Ayrshire, and a cousin of the Eglinton family, wrote a fine allegorical poem, *The Cherrie and the Slae*, a coarse but spirited satire, *The Flyting betwixt Montgomerie and Polwart*, and several delightful sonnets of love.

MORRISON

Branches: *Morrison of Bognie, Morrison of Islay, Morrison of Habost and Barras, Morrison of Pabbay, Morrison of Ruchdi*

Tartan: *Morrison (red), Morrison (blue and green)*

Motto: *Teaghlach Phabbay (Gaelic: The family Phabbay)*

Slogan: *Dun [Castle] Eisten*

It is said that the founder of Clan Morrison was Mores, an illegitimate son of the King of Norway, who arrived on the island of Lewis clinging to a piece of driftweed, Hugh

MORRISON RED

MOWAT

MOWBRAY

Morrison of Habost and Barras, whose stronghold was Dun Eisten, was Clan Chief in the sixteenth century, and held the hereditary office of brieve, or local judge.

An even older line was that of P(h)abbay, Harris, from which is descended the branch of Ruchdi, North Uist, which is the present chiefly branch and to which belonged William Morrison (1893-1961), 1st Viscount Dunrossil, Speaker of the House of Commons and Governor-General of Australia. John Morrison of Islay was created Lord Margadale in 1964.

The Morrisons of Bognie, Aberdeenshire, are the main family of that name in the northeast of Scotland. The Morrisons in Perth and Lennox, whose name derives from the Gaelic *Moiris*, are not connected with the clan.

MOWAT

Tartan: *Mowat*

The name is from the French *Mont Haut*, 'High Mount', and first appears in Scotland in its Latin form of Monte Alto with the arrival of Robert Montealbo from Wales in the reign of King David I. Michael de Montealbo was Sheriff of Inverness in 1234. Subsequently the family acquired lands in Angus, and there were Mowats in Ayrshire in the early fifteenth century, and around Edinburgh in the seventeenth century.

MOWBRAY

Tartan: *Mowbray*

Mottos: *Fortitudine (Latin: By courage); Let the deed show*

The origin of the name, which occurs in England also as Memory and Mulberry, is obscure, but it probably derives from the Barony of Mombray in France. A Robert de Moubray is recorded in the reign of King Malcolm IV.

The baronies of Barnbogle, Dalmeny, and Inverkeithing were acquired at the beginning of the thirteenth century by Philip de Mowbray, brother of William, ancestor of the dukes of Norfolk. Sir John Mowbray of Barnbogle (*d.* 1519) left an heiress, whose husband, Robert Burton, was ordered by Parliament to change his name to the 'old and honourable' one of Mowbray. Their grandson, Sir Robert Mowbray, was forced to part with all three baronies to the Earl of Haddington in 1615, 'through debts and other misfortunes'. Sir John had, however, given the estate of Cockairny, part of the Barony of Inverkeithing, to his uncle, William Mowbray, in 1511, and this remained in the family for several centuries.

MUIR OF ROWALLAN

MUIR

Tartan: *Muir*

Motto: *Durum patientia frango (Latin: By patience I break what is hard)*

The name means 'living by a moor or heath', and in 1291 Thomas de la More was executor of the will of Divorgilla, mother of King John (Balliol). The future King Robert II married Elizabeth, daughter of Sir Adam Mure of Rowallan, in 1346. Ten years later the marriage was challenged, possibly on the grounds of there being a degree of consanguinity between them, and a dispensation was sought from the Pope, which was granted in 1347, when the legitimacy of their children, including the future King Robert III, was formally accepted. Sir William Mure of Rowallan (*d.* 1616) married Elizabeth, sister of the poet Alexander Montgomerie (1545-98), but the male Rowallan line became extinct in 1700 on the death of their great-grandson.

MUIR

Alexander Muir Mackenzie (1764-1835), created a baronet in 1805, was of the line of Muirs of Cassencarie, and took his additional name on inheriting his uncle's estates in Perthshire. John Muir of Deanston (1828-1903), Provost of Glasgow, who was made a baronet in 1892, was the son of John Muir (1736-1851), a Glasgow merchant. Edwin Muir (1887-1959), poet and critic, was born in Deerness, Orkney, son of a farmer.

MUNRO

Branches: *Munro of Foulis, Munro of Opisdale*

Tartan: *Munro*

Motto: *Dread God*

Slogan: *Caisteal Fòlais 'n a theine (Gaelic: Castle Foulis ablaze)*

The main Munro territory is on the north shore of the Cromarty Firth. A Hugh Munro of Foulis is said to have died in 1126, and a charter to George Munro of Foulis is recorded as having been granted during the first half of the thirteenth century, but it has never been traced. Be that as it may, the present Clan Chief is accepted as 33rd Laird (or Baron) of Foulis. Robert Munro of Foulis (*d.*

1588), whose father died fighting the English at the Battle of Pinkie in 1547, had by his first wife, Margaret, Robert and Hector (*d.* 1603), each of whom was chief, and by his second wife, Katharine, who was later tried for and acquitted of witchcraft and attempted murder, a further son, George Munro of Opisdale. Hector was suceeded by his son Robert (*d.* 1633), known as the 'Black Baron', who served as a colonel both of horse and foot in the army of the King of Sweden and was killed in action. His brother Hector succeeded him as chief, and was created a baronet of Nova Scotia in 1634. With the 3rd Baronet, the title and the chiefship devolved on the Opisdale line. The clan, under its chief Sir Robert Munro, 5th Baronet (*d.* 1729), known as the 'Blind Baron', for he had been without sight from birth, sided with the Government in 1715, as it did again in 1745, under his son Sir Robert Munro (1684-1746), who was Lieut-Colonel of the Black Watch from 1740 until just before the Rebellion. Since 1935 the baronetcy and the chiefship,

with which goes the residence of Foulis Castle, have descended separately.

Neil Munro (1864-1930), born in Inveraray, Argyll, of a distant line of the family said to have descended from a survivor of the Battle of Flodden in 1513, was a distinguished journalist and novelist, who wrote, as 'Hugh Foulis', the 'Para Handy' tales about a Clyde 'puffer' and her crew. The novelist and distinctive short story writer 'Saki', Hector Hugh Munro (1870-1916), claimed pride in his Highland descent. He was killed in action in France in World War I, having refused to accept a commission.

MURRAY

Branches: *The numerous branches include the dukes of Atholl, the earls of Annandale, Dunmore, Dysart, Mansfield, and Tullibardine, and the lords Elibank*

Tartans: *Murray of Atholl, Murray of Tullibardine, Murray of Elibank*

Mottos: *Tout prêt (French: Absolutely ready): (Atholl) Furth fortune and fill the fetters*

The ultimate ancestor of all the Murrays is said to be Freskin, a Pict or possibly a Fleming, who was given charge of part of Moray by King David I in the twelfth century. His grandson William (d. 1226) called himself 'de Moravia', and from one of his sons descended the Murrays of Tullibardine, which was acquired by marriage in about 1280. Sir John Murray, 12th Laird, was created Earl of Tullibardine by King James VI in 1606.

By a marriage with the heiress of the Stewart earls of Atholl, the Murrays of Tullibardine became marquises and then, in 1703, dukes of Atholl. The eldest son of the 1st Duke, William (d. 1746), Marquis of Tullibardine, was not allowed, because of his Jacobite activities in 1715, to succeed to the dukedom, which went to his younger brother James (1690-1764). In 1736, on the death of his cousin, the Earl of Derby, James succeeded

MUNRO

to the sovereignty of the Isle of Man, which the family retained until 1765, when it was traded in to the Government in return for £70,000 and a life annuity of £2,000 each to the 3rd Duke and Duchess. It was the Marquis of Tullibardine who unfurled the royal standard to introduce Bonnie Prince Charlie to his troops at Glenfinnan in 1745, and his brother Lord George Murray (1694-1760) was one of the Prince's generals in the campaign, during which he laid siege to the family seat, Blair Castle, Perthshire, which was occupied by government troops.

The 10th Duke of Atholl (*b.* 1931) lives in the castle, part of which dates from 1269, and is Clan Chief, besides being the only British subject who has the right to maintain a private army, the Atholl Highlanders.

Also from the Tullibardine line came William Murray (1600-1651), adviser to and intriguer on behalf of royalty, made 1st Earl of Dysart in 1643; Lord Charles Murray (1661-1710), commander of the Scots Greys and Master of the Horse to Princess (later Queen) Anne, 1st Earl of Dunmore (1686); and William Murray (1705-93), Lord Chief Justice and parliamentarian, 1st Earl of Mansfield (1776), the family home of whose descendants is Scone Palace. From the southern Murrays of Cockpool descended John Murray (*d.* 1640), Keeper of the Privy Purse, created 1st Earl of Annandale in 1624, and from the Blackbarony branch Sir Gideon Murray (*d.* 1621), a judge of the Court of Session, 1st Lord Elibank (1613).

NAIRN(E)

Tartan: *Nairn*

Motto: *Usque conabor (Latin: I will try all the time)*

Nairn is the burgh in Moray, the first person of that name to be recorded being Adam de Narryn, chaplain of the altar of the Blessed Virgin at Inverness. Robert Nairne (*d.* 1652), of Mukkersy, Perthshire, President of the

MURRAY, EARL OF TULLIBARDINE

MURRAY

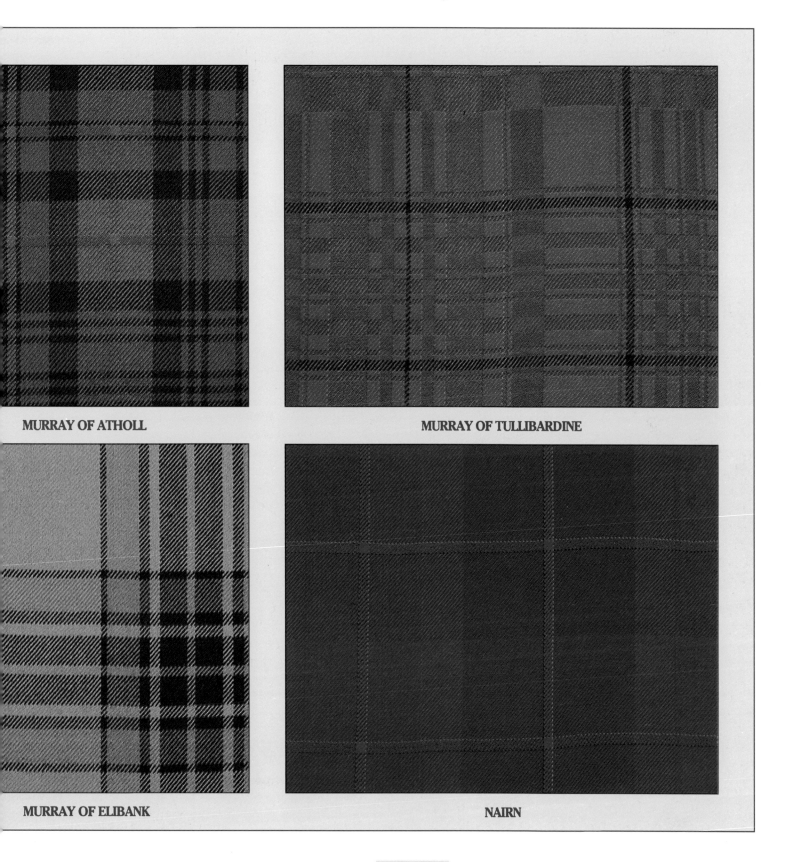

MURRAY OF ATHOLL

MURRAY OF TULLIBARDINE

MURRAY OF ELIBANK

NAIRN

Court of Session, was the father of Robert Nairne (*d.* 1683), who was imprisoned in the Tower of London for ten years during the Civil War for his support of the Crown, was appointed a judge at the Restoration of the Monarchy, and created Lord Nairne in 1681. He was succeeded in the title by his son-in-law, Lord William Murray (*d.* 1726), who was convicted of treason after the Rebellion of 1715 and condemned to death, but was reprieved and merely attainted. His eldest son John (*d.* 1770) was also attainted for his part during 1715, and was attainted again after the '45 Rebellion. The title was restored, however, to his grandson, William Nairne (1757-1830), who became 5th Lord Nairne and married Carolina Oliphant (1766-1845), the poet and Jacobite songstress.

Michael Nairn (1804-58), of Kirkcaldy, founded the Scottish linoleum industry. His eldest son, Michael Nairn (1838-1915), was created a baronet in 1904.

NAPIER, LORD NAPIER

NAPIER

Branch: *Napier of Merchiston*

Tartan: *Napier*

Motto: *Sans tache (French: Without stain)*

'Napery' is linen, and the naperer was in charge of the royal linen (hence the motto). John de Napier held lands in Dunbartonshire at the end of the thirteenth century. His descendant Alexander Napier, Provost of Edinburgh in 1437, made such a fortune as a wool-merchant that he was able to lend money to King James I, against the security of the lands of Merchiston, which were never redeemed in the confusion following the King's assassination. His son, Sir Alexander Napier (*d.* 1473), 2nd Laird of Merchiston, was Comptroller of the Royal Household, Vice-Admiral of Scotland, and a special

ambassador for King James III. John Napier (1550-1617), 8th Laird, invented logarithms and the first calculating-machine (known as 'Napier's Bones'), as well as an armoured tank and a submarine. His son, Sir Archibald Napier (1576-1645), devised a new form of manure, using salt, for which King James VI granted him a 21-year-patent in 1598, and became a judge of the Court of Session. He married an elder sister of the Marquis of Montrose and was created Lord Napier in 1627.

The title passed through a sister of the 3rd Lord to the family of the Scotts of Thirlestane. Sir Francis Napier (1819-98), 9th Lord Napier and 11th Baronet of Scott of Thirlestane (a Nova Scotia creation), statesman and Governor of Madras, was made 1st Lord Ettrick in the peerage of the United Kingdom in 1872.

Descendants of the Merchiston branch have been notable soldiers, including General Sir Charles Napier

NAPIER

(1782-1853), conqueror of Sind, and his brother General Sir William Napier (1785-1860), who wrote a history of the Peninsular War, in which he served, while their cousin, Admiral Sir Charles Napier (1786-1860), served and fought in many naval sectors, including north America, and commanded the Baltic Fleet in 1854.

NESBITT

OGILVY

NESBIT(T), NISBET(T)

Tartan: *Nesbitt*

Mottos: *I byd [endure] it*

The name, which is first recorded in the twelfth century, derives from the Barony of Nesbit, Berwickshire, and in 1633 Sir Robert Ker of Ancrum (1578-1654), Keeper of the Privy Purse, was created Earl of Ancrame and Lord Kerr of Nisbet, Langnewtoune, and Dolphinstoun. Sir John Nisbet of Dirleton (1609-87), Lord Advocate and persecutor of the Covenanters, was created Lord Dirleton in 1664.

James Nisbett, Dean of the Guild of Wrights 1726-38, was the ancestor of the Nisbetts of Cairnhill, whose name became More Nisbett during the time of the 7th Laird, who died in 1849.

OGILVY

Branches *Ogilvy of Airlie, Ogilvy of Dunlugus, Ogilvy of Findlater, Ogilvy of Inverquharity*

Tartan: *Ogilvy (old), Ogilvy (hunting), Ogilvy of Airlie*

Motto: *A fin (French: To the end)*

Gilbert, third son of Gillebride, Earl of Angus, was granted a charter of the Barony of Ogilvy in about 1172. His descendant, Sir Walter Ogilvy of Lintrathan (*d.* 1440), Lord High Treasurer of Scotland and second son of 'Good Sir Walter', who, with his brother and sixty of his clansmen was killed near Blairgowrie in 1392 while trying to combat an incursion led by a son of the Stewart Earl of Buchan, founded the line of Airlie. His grandson, Sir James, was created Lord Ogilvy of Airlie by King James IV in 1491. James (1593-1666), 8th Lord Airlie, was made Earl of Airlie by King Charles I in 1639. It was his castle, 'The Bonnie House of Airlie' in the ballad of that name, which was wrecked by the Marquis of Argyll and his Covenanters in 1640. In 1645, after the Battle of Philiphaugh, his son James (1615-1704), 2nd Earl, was captured and imprisoned for the second time for his support of the Marquis of Montrose. He was tried and

sentenced to death, but the day before his execution he changed places with his elder sister, who was visiting him, and escaped from St Andrews Castle wearing her clothes. David (1725-1803), Lord Ogilvy, son of the 4th Earl, joined Bonnie Prince Charlie at the head of a regiment of six hundred men of Angus, which protected the right of the line at the Battle of Culloden in 1746. Afterwards he escaped to France, and was later pardoned in the light of his youth at the time of the rebellion, though the earldom was not restored to the family until 1826. In 1963 Hon. (now Sir) Angus Ogilvy (*b.* 1928), second son of the 12th Earl of Airlie, married Princess Alexandra of Kent, first cousin of Her Majesty the Queen.

The Ogilvies of Inverquharity descended from a younger brother of Sir Walter of Lintrathan. From Sir Walter's younger son came the Ogilvies of Deskford and Findlater, the 7th Laird of which was created Lord Ogilvy of Deskford by King James VI in 1616, and his son Earl of Findlater by King Charles I in 1638. James Ogilvy (1664-1730), 4th Earl of Findlater, created also Earl of Seafield in 1701, was, as Lord Chancellor of Scotland, prominent in securing the union of the Scottish and English parliaments in 1707. From the same line descended the Ogilvies of Dunlugus, lords Banff. George Ogilvy of Barras, who died in about 1680, was Governor of Dunnottar Castle in 1652, when it was besieged and then bombarded by Cromwell's troops, who were trying to get at the crown jewels and Regalia of Scotland, which were being held there. For his courageous defence of them, and his ingenuity in spiriting them away into safe keeping, he was created a baronet of Nova Scotia in 1660.

OLIPHANT

Tartan: *Oliphant (also known as Oliphant and Melville)*

Motto: *A tout pourvoir (French: To provide for everything)*

Whether or not the name derives from elephant, signifying strength, David de Olifard, of a Norman family settled in Northamptonshire, rescued King David I at the siege of Winchester Castle in 1141, for which he was rewarded with a small portion of land in Scotland. King Malcolm IV was more generous, and granted him Bothwell in Lanarkshire, and King William I (the Lion) added Arbuthnott in the Mearns to the family possessions. Sir Laurence Oliphant of Aberdalgie, who died in about 1500, was made Lord Oliphant, and became a Member of Parliament, statesman, ambassador, and Keeper of Edinburgh Castle. His grandson died at the Battle of Flodden in 1513, and his great-grandson, 3rd Lord Oliphant (*d.* 1586), was taken prisoner by the English at the Battle of Solway Moss in 1542. The 4th Lord, who died in 1593, was a firm supporter of Mary, Queen of Scots. His eldest son Laurence was expelled from the country for his part in 1582 in the Ruthven Raid, a conspiracy to secure the person of the young King James VI. The ship in which he sailed was never seen

OGILVY OF AIRLIE

OGILVY,
EARL OF AIRLIE

OGILVY HUNTING

again, and he was reported either to have been hanged from the mast by Dutch pirates or sold into Turkish slavery.

The Oliphants were confirmed Jacobites. The 9th Lord (*d.* 1728) fought at the Battle of Killiecrankie in 1689 and was afterwards imprisoned. He supported the cause again in 1715, as did his distant cousin, Laurence Oliphant of Gask (1691-1767), the estate in Perthshire having been in the family since the time of the 3rd Lord, but not confirmed by charter until 1625. Gask and his eldest son Laurence (1724-1792) played most active roles in the campaign of 1745, after which they escaped to Sweden, and from there to France. They were allowed to return in 1763, but neither ever recognised the House of Hanover. The younger Laurence was father of Carolina Oliphant (1766-1845), named after Bonnie Prince Charlie. Best known as a Jacobite songstress, in which capacity she wrote *Charlie is My Darling*, *Will Ye No' Come Back Again*, and *The Hundred Pipers an A'*, she also wrote other notable poems, including *Caller Herrin'* and the romantic *The Land o' the Leal*. She married her cousin, Major William Nairne, who in 1824 was restored by King George IV to his hereditary title of Lord Nairne, which had been forfeited. Baroness Nairne, as she is usually known, continued to write, but always anonymously and often as 'Mrs Bogan of Bogan', only agreeing just before her death that her poems could be attributed to her.

OLIVER

Tartan: *Oliver*

The name probably derives from the French *olivier*, 'maker or seller of olive oil', and it became popular and common through the influence of the Norse name Olaf. It is first recorded in Scotland in the twelfth century. Olivers exercised considerable influence in the Borders.

POLLOCK

Tartan: *Pollock*

Peter, son of Fulbert, was granted the lands of Upper Pollock, Renfrewshire, in the latter part of the twelfth century, and later gave the church to Paisley Monastery. He also owned lands in Moray. Other people of the name of Pollock are recorded in Lanarkshire and Forfarshire in the thirteenth century, and in Glasgow in the fifteenth century. The main line of the family is believed to have disappeared at the end of the seventeenth century.

PORTEOUS

PORTEOUS

Tartan: *Porteous*

The origin of the name is obscure, but it was entrenched in Peebleshire and Fife in the fifteenth century. John Porteous, Captain of the Edinburgh City Guard, ordered his men to fire on a mob which was demonstrating at the execution of a smuggler in 1736, killing several people. He was convicted of murder and sentenced to death, but reprieved. He was then seized from prison by a body of men, who hanged him from the pole outside a dyer's shop, into which they had broken to procure a length of rope for the purpose.

Dr William Porteous (1735-1812), Minister of the Wynd Church, Glasgow, was so orthodox in his views that he rigorously opposed the use of the organ in church, but was also rational and brave enough to preach a sermon on 'Toleration' in November 1778, at the height of the mob violence which followed the repeal of acts penalising Roman Catholics, and which was condoned by other churchmen and most of the Scottish synods.

RAMSAY, EARL OF DALHOUSIE

RAMSAY

Branches: *Ramsay of Balmain, Ramsay of Bamff, Ramsay of Dalhousie*

Tartans: *Ramsay, Ramsay (hunting, blue)*

Motto: *Ora et labora (Latin: Pray and work)*

Simon de Ramsay, of Anglo-Norman descent, lived in Lothian in the twelfth century. William Ramsay of Dalhousie swore homage to King Edward I of England in 1296 but then joined the forces of King Robert I (the Bruce). His son, Sir Alexander Ramsay (*d.* 1342), was an even greater thorn in the English side, raising the siege of Dunbar Castle in 1342 by running in provisions by boat, and capturing Roxburgh Castle in 1342, for which he was made Governor of the castle and Sheriff of Teviotdale by King David II. Unfortunately William Douglas (1300-53), Knight of Liddesdale, who had held both posts earlier, was so incensed that he kidnapped Ramsay and starved him to death in Hermitage Castle.

From a younger son of one of Sir Alexander's descendants came the Ramsays of Cockpen and of Whitehill. The eldest son was the ancestor of George, who was made Lord Ramsay of Melrose in 1618, which he changed to Dalhousie the following year, his son being created Earl of Dalhousie in 1633. George (1770-1838), 9th Earl, Governor of Canada, Nova Scotia, and New Brunswick 1819-28, was made Lord Dalhousie in the peerage of the United Kingdom in 1815. His son James Brown-Ramsay (1812-60), 10th Earl, was appointed Governor-General of India at the age of 34, and performed wonders in the fields of imperial expansion, material progress, and administration until forced by ill-health to return home in 1856. He was created Marquis of Dalhousie in 1849, but the title died with him, the earldom of Dalhousie in the Scottish peerage devolving on his cousin Fox Maule (1801-74), 2nd Lord Panmure.

RAMSAY

RANKINE

RATTRAY

Allan Ramsay (1684-1758), master wig maker, founder of the first British circulating library, poet, and dramatist, was descended from the Ramsays of Cockpen. His son Allan (1713-84) was royal portrait painter to King George III. The Ramsays of Bamff are descended from Neis de Ramsay, physician to King Alexander II, who received a charter for the estate in 1232. The family was granted a Nova Scotia baronetcy in 1666. Sir Alexander Burnett succeeded his uncle in 1808, when he changed his name to Ramsay and acquired the new baronetcy of Balmain.

RANKINE

Tartan: *Rankine*

The name may have come into being through the addition of the diminutive *-kin* to an existing form. People called by it held minor landholdings in Ayrshire in the sixteenth century. It is also recorded as a first name.

RATTRAY

Tartan: *Rattray*

Motto: *Super sidera votum (Latin: A desire beyond the stars)*

The name comes from the Barony of Rattray, Perthshire, whose first laird was Alan of Rattray at the beginning of the thirteenth century. John Rattray, 11th Laird, was knighted by King James IV in 1488, and died at the Battle of Flodden in 1513, unwittingly bequeathing a damaging controversy to his family. His eldest son John had died

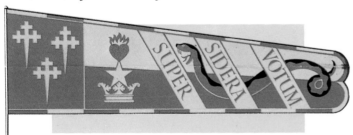

before his father, leaving two small daughters. Thus the second son, Patrick, inherited Rattray, but was intimidated into giving it up to John Stewart (*d.* 1521), 2nd Earl of Atholl, who, seeing Patrick's elder niece as a suitable match for his son, also took control of both

little girls. Patrick retired for safety to his other estate at Craighall, two miles away, but was murdered there by Atholl men in 1533 while seeking sanctuary in his own chapel. Rattray was not restored to the family until 1648, when the new Barony of Craighall-Rattray was created, in the time of Patrick Rattray (*d.* 1677), 18th Laird of Rattray and Chief of the Rattrays.

ROBERTSON

Branches: *The main line is that of Robertson of Struan, the Clan Chief being known as Struan-Robertson. Of many branches, most of which stem from Atholl and other parts of Perthshire, the oldest is Robertson of Lude, which came to the clan by a marriage between the 1st Chief and a daughter of the Thane of Glentilt*

Tartans: *Robertson (red), Robertson (hunting)*

Motto: *Virtutis gloria merces (Latin: The reward of valour is glory)*

Slogan: *Garg'n uair dhuisgear (Gaelic: Fierce when roused)*

Duncan 'the Stout', founder and 1st Chief of Clan Donnachaidh, was descended from the ancient earls of Atholl and through them from Crinan, Abbot of Dunkeld, who was also father of King Duncan I. Duncan 'the Stout' led his clan at the Battle of Bannockburn in 1314, on the way to which the tip of the battle standard is said mysteriously to have acquired, during the night, the piece of rock crystal which has been the clan's talisman ever since. Robert 'the Grizzled', 4th Chief, from whom the clan took its name of Robertson, hunted down and captured in a lonely Atholl glen the murderers of King James I, and handed them over to a grisly justice. When King James II came of age, he rewarded Robert by creating his lands in Atholl the Barony of Struan.

Alexander Robertson (1670-1749), 13th Chief, known as the 'Poet Chief', was studying for the Church at St

the first cannon was fired by Lady Robertson of Lude, who had acted as hostess the previous year when Bonnie Prince Charlie had visited the castle. There is a Clan Donnachaidh Museum at Bruar, four miles from Blair Atholl.

ROLLO

Tartan: *Rollo*

Motto: *La fortune passe partout (French: Fortune is the key)*

John Rollo (*d.* 1390), secretary to the Earl of Strathearn, a son of King Robert II, was granted by the King a charter of the lands of Duncrub, Strathern, in 1381. In 1572 David Rattray of Craighall (*d.* 1586) killed two men in a fight with some Rollos, but was relieved of responsibility on payment of a fine of 500 merks. Sir Andrew Rollo of Duncrub (1577-1659) was created Lord Rollo in 1651.

ROLLO

ALEXANDER ROBERTSON OF STRUAN, 13TH CHIEF

ROSE

Andrews University when he suddenly became chief on the deaths of his father and elder brother. In 1689 he left university to take up arms for Viscount Dundee, against the wishes of his formidable mother, who wrote round to the clan branches: 'He is going to Badenoch just now; for Christ's sake come in all haste and stop him, for he will not be advised by me.' They delayed him only long enough to catch up with him with their men. Alexander was 'out' in 1715, too, and again in 1745. Having personally led the clan at the Battle of Prestonpans, he was persuaded to return home, which he did in style in the captured coach of the defeated general, though he had to be carried, carriage and all, the last part of the way, the road not being suitable for wheels.

In March 1746, when Lord George Murray besieged Blair Castle, which was occupied by Hanoverian troops,

ROSE

Tartans: *Rose (dress), Rose (hunting)*

Motto: *Constant and true*

Hugh Rose of Geddes, Invernessshire, whose ancestor may have come to England after the Norman Conquest with Bishop Odo of Bayeux, witnessed the charter of foundation of Beauly Priory in 1219. His son, Hugh, acquired by marriage the lands of Kilravock, Nairn, on

ROBERTSON HUNTING

ROLLO

ROSE

which another Hugh Rose, 7th Laird of Kilravock, built the old castle tower in 1460. Both lands and castle are still in the family.

Though the clan supported the Government in 1689, 1715, and 1745, the 16th Laird was of sufficiently diplomatic disposition to agree to entertain Bonnie Prince Charlie at the castle just before the Battle of Culloden in 1746.

Field-Marshal Hugh Rose (1801-85) volunteered for service during the Indian Mutiny, and between 1857 and 1860, when he succeeded Sir Colin Campbell (1792-1863) as commander-in-chief, won numerous battles and recaptured many forts and several towns. He was made Lord Strathnairn in 1866.

ROSE OF KILRAVOCK

ROSS

Branches: *Ross of Balnagown, Ross of Pitcalnie, Ross of Shandwick*

Tartans: *Ross, Ross (hunting)*

Motto: *Spem successus alit (Latin: Success nourishes hope)*

Ross means 'promontory', and the first of the ancient earls of Ross was Ferquhard Macintaggart, who was rewarded with the title by King Alexander II in 1215. Hugh, younger son of the 4th Earl, died in about 1374, having received the lands of Balnagown from his eldest brother William (*d.* 1372), 5th Earl of Ross, whom he succeeded as Clan Chief, the earldom passing to William's daughter, Euphemia, and ultimately to the lords of the Isles. The chiefship remained with the Balnagown branch until the death of the 13th Laird in 1711, when the estate was settled on the Rosses of Hawkhead, represented by William (1656-1738), 12th

ROSS

Lord Ross and descendant of Sir John Ross of Hawkhead, one of the three Scottish champions chosen to joust against three French knights before King James II in 1449. This family, however, could not legitimately claim any connection with the original earls of Ross, and the direct line continued through the Rosses of Pitcalnie, descended from a younger son of the 10th Laird of Balnagown, who re-established the right to the chiefship in 1903. In 1936 it passed to the family of Ross of Shandwick, Nigg, descended from a younger son of the 4th Laird of Balnagown, whose most notable member is Sir Ronald Ross (1857-1931), discoverer of the cause of malaria.

RUSSELL

Tartan: *See Galbraith*

The name is probably descriptive, meaning 'red', and

ROSS HUNTING

thus appears in different areas of the country as far apart as Aberdeenshire and Berwickshire at an early date. Jerome Russell, an 18-year-old friar from Dumfries, was burned at the stake outside Glasgow Cathedral in 1539 for questioning the teaching of the Catholic clergy.

RUTHVEN, EARL OF GOWRIE

RUTHVEN

Branch: *Ruthven of Freeland*

Tartan: *Ruthven*

Motto: *Deid schaw (Deeds show)*

The ruins of Ruthven Barracks, Perthshire, built after the 1715 Rebellion and blown up after the Battle of Culloden in 1746 by disappointed Jacobite troops, stand in the unfriendly lands granted to the family in about 1298. Sir William Ruthven was made Lord Ruthven in 1487. Patrick (1520-66), 3rd Lord Ruthven, rose from his

sickbed to lead the murderers of David Rizzio, favourite of Mary, Queen of Scots, into her private chamber in 1566. He died soon afterwards. His son William (1541-84), 4th Lord, was appointed the Queen's jailor at Lochleven Castle the following year. He was so obviously attracted to her that he was soon removed from his post, but not before he had been instrumental in obtaining her formal abdication from the throne, for which, and for other services, he was made Earl of Gowrie in 1581. In 1582 he lured the young King James VI to his castle and kept him there for a year, while he and his fellow conspirators governed the country in his name. He was finally executed in 1584 for attempting to seize Stirling Castle.

John (1578-1600), 3rd Earl, and his brother were killed in their house in Perth in a mysterious mix-up known as the 'Gowrie Conspiracy', involving an alleged attempt to assassinate the King. Whatever actually

RUTHVEN

happened, the earldom was abolished by Parliament, and the very name of Ruthven was proscribed until 1641. Thomas Ruthven of Freeland, descended from the youngest son of the 2nd Lord Ruthven, was created Lord Ruthven in 1651. His descendant through the female line, Walter, 8th Lord Ruthven of Freeland, was created 1st Lord Ruthven in the peerage of the United Kingdom in 1919. His son, Alexander Hore-Ruthven (1872-1955), Governor-General of Australia 1936-44, was made 1st Earl of Gowrie of the new creation in 1945.

SCOTT, DUKE OF BUCCLEUCH

SCOTT

Branches: *Scott of Balweary, from which Scott of Ancrum; Scott of Buccleuch, from which Scott of Synton, from which Scott of Harden, from which Scott of Polwarth*

Tartans: *Scott, Scott (hunting), Sir Walter Scott (check)*

SCOTT

SCOTT HUNTING

Motto: *Amo (Latin: I love)*

Slogan: *A Bellendaine ('To Bellendean', the meeting place of the clan, near the head of Borthwick Water, Roxburghshire)*

Uchtredus filius Scotus, 'Uchtred, son of the Scot', witnessed charters between 1107 and 1128. From his two sons descended the Scotts of Balweary (Fife) and the Scotts of Buccleuch (Selkirk). Michael Scott of Balweary (1175-1234), known throughout Europe as 'The Wizard' for his study of magic, was also a mathematician and physician. Sir Michael Scott of Balweary, probably his direct descendant, was in 1286 sent to fetch home Margaret, 'Maid of Norway', heir to the throne, after the death of her grandfather, King Alexander III.

Sir Walter Scott of Buccleuch (1565-1611), Keeper of Liddesdale, was created Lord Scott in 1606, and his son Walter was made Earl of Buccleuch in 1619. Anne, Countess of Buccleuch, to whom the earldom and the chiefship of the clan passed after the deaths of her father, 2nd Earl, in 1651 and subsequently of her elder sister, married James, Duke of Monmouth (1649-1685), illegitimate son of King Charles II, in 1673, when they were made Duke and Duchess of Buccleuch. Even though Monmouth was beheaded for rebelling against

his uncle, King James II (of England), the dukedom was unaffected, and Henry (1746-1812), 3rd Duke, became also Duke of Queensberry in 1810, through his grandfather's marriage into that line.

Walter Scott of Harden (*d.* 1629) was a notorious cattle-rustler, of whom it is said that when the last beast of a particular haul had been eaten, his wife would serve him a dish on which was a pair of clean spurs, indicating that the larder should be replenished. His first wife was Mary, 'Flower of Yarrow', and from them descended the Hepburne-Scotts, lords Polwarth, and Sir Walter Scott (1771-1832), 1st Laird of Abbotsford, poet and novelist, historian and folklorist, and instigator of much of the modern Highland and tartan image. The baronetcy which he was given by King George IV in 1820 became extinct on the death of his son, Walter, in 1847, but the direct line of descent continued through his daughter Sophia (*d.* 1837), wife of John Gibson Lockhart (1794-1854), biographer of Sir Walter. Their daughter Charlotte married James Hope, who assumed the name Hope-Scott when she succeeded to Abbotsford House on the death of her brother in 1853. Their daughter, Mary Hope-Scott, heiress to Abbotsford, married in 1874 Joseph Maxwell, third son of Lord Herries, who took the name of Maxwell-Scott.

SCRYMGEOUR, EARL OF DUNDEE

SCRYMGEOUR

Branches *Scrymgeour of Dudhope, Scrymgeour of Glassary*

Tartan: *Scrymgeour*

Motto: *Dissipate (disperse, put to flight)*

Alexander Schyrmeschur was in 1298 confirmed as Royal Standard Bearer, a hereditary office first held by Sir Alexander Carron (nicknamed 'Skirmisher') in the reign of King Alexander I and still held by the family's representative today. He was also made Constable of Dundee, near which he was granted lands. The lands of Glassary, Argyll, came to the family in the fourteenth century by a marriage with the heiress.

John Scrymgeour (*d.* 1643) was created Viscount Dudhope in 1641. John (*d.* 1668), 3rd Viscount, was made Earl of Dundee in 1660 for his loyal and active support of King Charles II. His son and heir, John Scrymgeour (*d.*

1698) was deprived of the titles and his estates on the advice and through the intrigues of John Maitland (1616-82), 1st Duke of Lauderdale, who gave Dudhope Castle to his brother. On the brother's conviction and fine for mismanaging the affairs of the Mint, the castle was forfeited in 1683 and given by King Charles II to Viscount Dundee, who was a distant relative of the Scrymgeour family and was very keen to have it as his seat.

The titles were restored in 1953 to Henry Scrymgeour-Wedderburn (1902-83), who became 11th Earl of Dundee and also Viscount Dudhope, and was created Lord Glassary in 1954.

SELLARS, SILLARS

Tartan: *Sellars*

The name probably means 'saddler', or else 'cellarer', the person in charge of a cellar or storeroom, and a Colin Sellar owned some land in Aberdeen in 1281. A family called Sellars followed the trade of blacksmith in Botriphnie, Banff, for four hundred years. The form Sillars may have a different derivation, referring to a silversmith.

SETON

Branches: *Seton of Abercorn, Seton of Meldrum, Seton of Pitmedden*

Tartan: *Seton*

Motto: *Hazard yet forward*

Seton means 'sea town', and probably referred originally to Tranent, a few miles east of Edinburgh, where Alexander Seton held lands in about 1150. Sir Christopher Seton (1278-1306) married the sister of King Robert I (the Bruce), for which, and his firm support of his brother-in-law, he was captured and hanged by the English. Sir Alexander Seton, who was probably his brother, was Governor of Berwick from 1327 to 1333, when it was surrendered to the English, but only after they had hanged his son, Thomas, who had been given as a hostage. His heiress, Margaret, married Alan of Winton in about 1347, and from them descended the lords Seton.

SCRYMGEOUR

George (1530-85), 5th Lord Seton, brother of Mary Seton, one of the 'Four Maries' who were the attendants of Mary, Queen of Scots, from childhood, gave the greatest support to his queen after the murders of David Rizzio in 1566 and her husband, Lord Darnley, in 1567, and aided her escape from Lochleven Castle in 1568. His second son, Robert (*d.* 1607), 6th Lord, was created Earl of Winton by her son, King James VI, in 1600. His fourth son, Sir Alexander Seton (1555-1622), Prior of Pluscardine, Lord President of the Court of Session, and then Chancellor of Scotland, was made Earl of Dunfermline in 1606. The 4th Earl of Dunfermline forfeited the title for his support of Viscount Dundee on the field of battle in 1689, as did the 5th Earl of Winton after the Rebellion of 1715. Sir Bruce Seton of Abercorn was made a baronet of Nova Scotia in 1663. Sir Alexander Seton of Pitmedden (1639-1719), descended from the Setons of Meldrum, became Lord Pitmedden on his appointment as a judge in 1677, and was created a baronet of Nova Scotia in 1684.

SETON, EARL OF WINTON

SHAW OF TORDARROCH

Tartans: *Shaw of Tordarroch (hunting), Shaw of Tordarroch (red), Shaw*

Motto: *Fide et fortitudine (Latin: By faithfulness and fortitude)*

The Shaws were one of the three most important of the 'Nine tribes of Clan Mackintosh' which formed the basis of Clan Chattan. Shaw *Mór*, great-grandson of Angus, 6th Chief of Clan Mackintosh, was granted the lands of Rothiemurcus, to which his grandson, Alasdair, eventually succeeded. Alasdair's brother, Adam of Tordarroch, Strathnairn, who flourished in the early part of the fifteenth century, founded the branch of that name, which now holds the chiefship of Clan Shaw.

SINCLAIR

Branches: *Sinclair of Dunbeath, Sinclair of Herdmanston, Sinclair of Rosslyn, Sinclair of Ulbster*

Tartans: *Sinclair, Sinclair (hunting)*

Motto: *Commit thy work to God*

Sir William St Clair, or Sinclair, of Norman descent, was

SINCLAIR

SETON

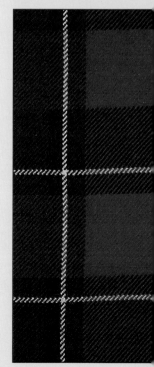

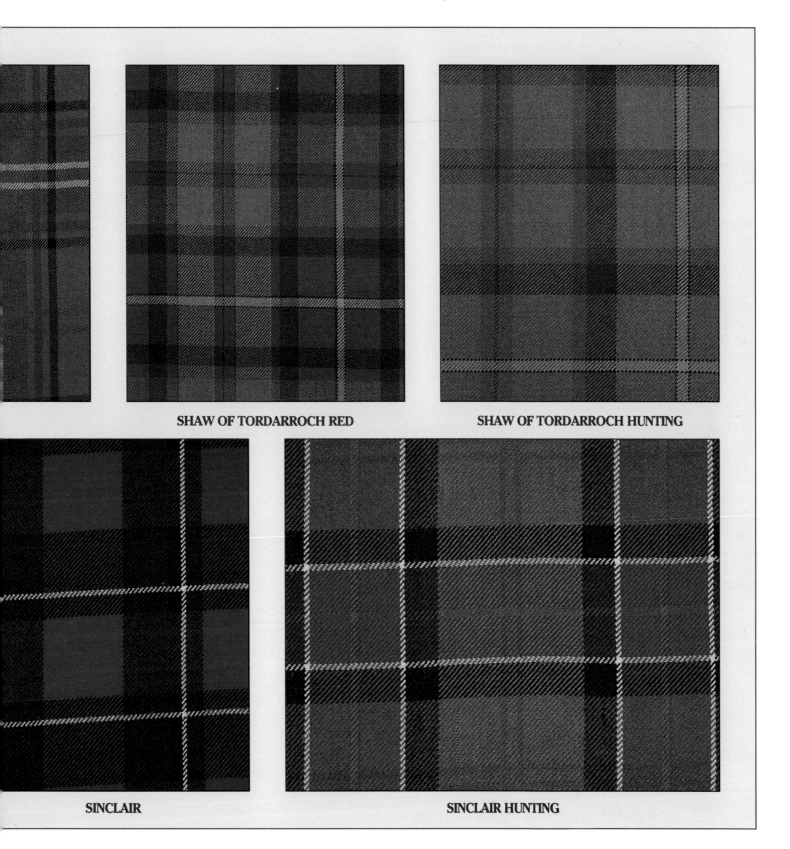

SHAW OF TORDARROCH RED

SHAW OF TORDARROCH HUNTING

SINCLAIR

SINCLAIR HUNTING

SINCLAIR, EARL OF CAITHNESS

French bishop called him 'the most indefatigable man in Britain'. John Sinclair (1860-1925), of the Dunbeath branch, Secretary for Scotland 1905-1909 and Governor of Madras 1912-19, was created Baron Pentland in 1909.

SKENE

one of the most powerful men in Scotland at the time of King Alexander III. Sheriff of Edinburgh, Linlithgow, and Haddington in about 1263, he became guardian of the heir to the throne and Governor of Edinburgh Castle, where the King's treasury was. In 1279 he was granted the Barony of Rosslyn, to the south of Edinburgh. His grandson, Sir William Sinclair, died in Spain in 1330 defending the heart of King Robert I (the Bruce) on its way to burial in the Holy Land. Sir William's grandson, Henry (*d.* 1400), became through his mother's inheritance recognised as Earl (or Prince) of Orkney under the King of Norway, in which capacity he conquered the Faroe Islands and discovered Greenland.

William Sinclair (1404-80), 3rd and last Earl of Orkney, was created Earl of Caithness by King James III, and resigned his rights to Orkney when it became part of the kingdom of Scotland. He settled the earldom of Caithness on William, eldest son of his second marriage, who was killed at the Battle of Flodden in 1513, and Rosslyn on the younger son of that marriage. The Sinclairs of Rosslyn, Hereditary Grand Master Masons of Scotland, inherited the earldom of Rosslyn, first granted to Alexander Wedderburn (1733-1805), Lord Chancellor, through his nephew, General Sir James St Clair Erskine (1762-1837).

The lords Sinclair descended from 'William the Waster', eldest son of the 1st Earl of Caithness by his first wife, the title passing to the Sinclairs of Herdmanston in 1677.

The earldom of Caithness, with which goes the chiefship of the clan, may only be inherited by a male, and has passed through several branches and families as a line failed. The Sinclairs of Ulbster descended from an illegitimate son of the 4th Earl of Caithness. John Sinclair of Ulbster (1754-1835), politician, agriculturalist, and compiler of 21 substantial volumes of *The Statistical Account of Scotland*, was created a baronet in 1786. A

SKENE

Branches: *Skene of Curriehill, Skene of Hallyards, Skene of Rubislaw*

Tartan: *Skene*

Motto: *Virtutis regia merces (Latin: Regality is the reward of virtue)*

It is said that in the eleventh century a younger son of the chief of Clan Donnachaidh (Robertson) saved his king by killing a wolf with his *sgian* (dagger), for which he was rewarded with the lands of Skene, Aberdeenshire. The estate (including Loch Skene), which was made into a barony by King Robert I (the Bruce) as a reward for its holder, passed to the earls of Fife by inheritance when the original family line failed in 1827. John Skene of Curriehill (1543-1617), Currie being a village on the River Leith by Edinburgh, was created Lord Curriehill on his appointment as a judge of the Court of Session in

SKENE OF   THAT ILK

1594. His eldest son, Sir James Skene (*d.* 1633), President of the Court of Session, was created a baronet of Nova Scotia in 1630, while his second son, who died in 1633, was John Skene of Hallyards, Fife, who became Lord Clerk Register. It was one of the Skenes of Hallyards who founded Skeneborough on Lake Champlain in North America.

A notable member of the Skenes of Rubislaw, Aberdeenshire, was Dr William Forbes Skene (1809-92), Historiographer Royal for Scotland and author of *Celtic Scotland*

SMITH

Tartan: *Smith*

Motto: *(Jordanhill) Macte (Latin: Do honour)*

Smith means 'worker in iron', and the name first occurs in southeast Scotland in the thirteenth century. Adam Smith (1723-90), the political economist, was born in Kirkcaldy, though his father came from Aberdeen. James Smith (1789-1850), inventor of the thorough drainage system of agriculture, was born in Glasgow of parents from Galloway. William Robertson Smith (1846-94), scholar and theologian, was born in Keig, Aberdeenshire. Sydney Goodsir Smith (1915-75), foremost of the second wave of poets of the Scottish Renaissance, was born in New Zealand. Iain Crichton Smith (*b.* 1928), poet and novelist, who writes also in Gaelic, was born in the island of Lewis.

The most notable family of the name emerged in the Barony of Mugdock, in the parish of Strathblane, Stirlingshire, where for four hundred years its members were hereditary tenants of Craigend and armourers, latterly to the Grahams of Montrose. In 1660 Robert Smith bought Craigend and became its first laird, the property remaining in the family until the death of the

7th Laird. A younger brother of the 3rd Laird was John Smith of Finnieston (1724-1814), who in 1751 founded the Glasgow firm of John Smith and Son, the second-oldest bookshop in the United Kingdom, and probably in the English-speaking world, still trading under its original name. He was followed in the business by his son, John Smith, Younger (1753-1833), and his grandson, John Smith, Youngest, of Crutherland (1784-1849). The line of the descendants of John Smith, Younger, expired in 1974.

SMITH

The younger son of the 2nd Laird of Craigend, and thus nephew of Smith of Finnieston, was Archibald Smith (*d.* 1821), West India merchant, who purchased the estate of Jordanhill, Glasgow, and married Isobel Ewing, who died in 1855 at the age of a hundred. Their eldest son James (1782-1867), known as 'Smith of Jordanhill', was a famous geologist and notable writer, who like his son Archibald (1813-72), lawyer and mathematician, was a Fellow of the Royal Society. Descendants of that line include James Parker Smith (1854-1929), 4th Laird of Jordanhill, Member of Parliament and Privy Councillor, and Constance Babington Smith (*b.* 1912), biographer and war historian, while others are today to be found in the USA and in Australia.

SNODGRASS

Tartan: *Snodgrass*

The name derives from ancient lands in the parish of Irvine, Ayrshire, known as Snodgrasse or Snodgers, which were rented out in plots. Both forms are recorded in Ayrshire and in Glasgow between the thirteenth and sixteenth centuries.

SOMERVILLE, LORD   SOMERVILLE

SOMERVILLE

Tartan: *Somerville*

Motto: *Fear God in life*

The name is of Norman origin. A John, or William, de Somerville is said to have been granted lands in Roxburghshire for killing 'ane hydeous monster in the forme of a worme' by pushing an ingenious fiery contraption down its throat, but the first recorded appearance of the name in Scotland is that of William de Somerville in 1124. His probable descendant, Thomas de Somerville of Linton and Carnwath (1370-1444), was the father of William (*d*. 1456), who was created Lord Somerville in 1445. Hugh (1547-97), 6th Lord, built the original house of Drum, in the Edinburgh parish of Liberton. It was pulled down and rebuilt by James (1698-1765), 12th Lord, who in 1724 had married a rich English widow and thereby restored the family fortunes, to which was added in 1742 the estate of Aston Somerville in Gloucestershire, long the seat of the English family of Somerville.

The title became dormant in 1870 on the death at the age of 32 of the 18th Lord, sometime 4th mate of an Australian packet ship, who was buried at Aston Somerville.

SNODGRASS

SOMERVILLE

SPENS

SPENS

Tartan: *Spens*

Motto: *Si deus quis contra (Latin: If God is present, who is against?)*

The name, which is the same as Spence, means custodian, or dispenser, of the larder, and the main Scottish family claims descent from one of the ancient earls of Fife. Henry de Spens of Lathallan, Fife, died in 1300, and the lands were made into a barony in 1430.

From a younger son of James Spens (*d.* 1437), 2nd Laird, descended the French family of Spens d'Estignols de Lassere.

Craigsanquhar, Fife, which belonged to the family from 1385 to 1524, was bought back in 1792 by Dr Nathaniel Spens (1728-1815), second son of the 15th Laird of Lathallan, who was President of the Royal College of Surgeons, Edinburgh 1794-6. His descendant, Sir Patrick Spens (1885-1973), was created 1st Lord Spens of Blairsanquhar, Fife, in 1959.

STEVENSON

STEVENSON

Tartan: *Stevenson*

The name means 'son of Steven' and is first recorded in Scotland in 1388. The famous family of lighthouse engineers, Robert Stevenson (1772-1850) and his sons

Alan (1807-1865), David (1815-86), and Thomas (1818-87), father of Robert Louis Stevenson (1850-94), novelist, short story writer, and poet, came of a family which originally farmed land in the parish of Neilston, Renfrewshire.

EARL OF   GALLOWAY

STEWART

Branches: *See below*

Tartans: *Stewart (old), Stewart (dress), Stewart (hunting); Stewart (Royal), Stewart (Victoria), Stewart (Prince Charles Edward), Stewart of Fingask; Stewart of Appin (red), Stewart of Appin (hunting); Stewart of Atholl; Stewart of Bute; Stewart of Galloway*

Mottos: *Nobilis est ira leonis (Latin: Noble is the wrath of a lion); (Appin) Quhidder will zie (Whither will ye); (Earls of Galloway) Virescit vulnere virtus (Latin: Courage gains strength from a wound)*

The line of Stewart monarchs of Scotland, and then of Great Britain, which lasted from 1371 to 1714, descended

STEWART (VICTORIA)

STEWART OF BUTE

STEWART OF ATHOLL

PRINCE CHARLES EDWARD STEWART

STEWART OLD

STEWART OF APPIN

STUART,
MARQUIS OF BUTE

STEWART OF APPIN

STEWART

from Marjorie, daughter of King Robert I (the Bruce), and her husband Walter, 6th High Steward (or Stewart) of Scotland, who at the age of 21 had commanded the centre of the Scottish army at the Battle of Bannockburn in 1314. His ancestor, and 1st High Steward, which was a hereditary office from 1157, was Walter Fitz Alan, the younger son of the Sheriff of Shropshire, who had come to England from Brittany. Alexander, 4th High Steward, had several sons, of whom the second, Sir John Stewart of Bonkyl (or Buncle or Bonkhill, meaning 'the church at the foot of the hill'), Berwickshire, was the ancestor of numerous notable branches of the name, including the earls of Galloway, the Stewart earls of Atholl, and the Stewarts of Appin. From one of King Robert II's illegitimate sons descended the marquises of Bute, and from illegitimate sons of his legitimate fourth son, Alexander (1343-1405), Earl of Buchan, 'Wolf of Badenoch', many families of the name of Stewart in Aberdeenshire, Atholl, Banffshire, and Moray. The ancestor of the Stewarts of Balquhidder was the Duke of Albany (1340-1420), third son of Robert II.

The powerful and influential Clan Stewart of Appin, Argyll, was founded by Dougal Stewart, who after the murder of his father, John Stewart of Lorn, in 1463, was only able to salvage from his inheritance the district of Appin. The clan joined the Marquis of Montrose in time for the Battle of Inverlochy in January 1645, and fought with him at Auldearn and Kilsyth, though the Stewarts of Balquhidder joined the opposition in 1646 to plunder the lands of royalist supporters. The Appin Stewarts turned out in force to fight for Viscount Dundee in 1689, under their chief's son, and again at the Battle of Sheriffmuir in 1715, when they were in that part of the line which buckled under the onslaught of the cavalry of the Duke of Argyll. They fought through the campaign of 1745-6 under Charles Stewart of Ardshiel, who was a member of the Prince's council of war, and lost a hundred of their men at the Battle of Culloden.

If the tartan known as Prince Charles Edward really was, as it is claimed, worn by Bonnie Prince Charlie and his followers in 1745, then this would be the earliest form in which the Royal Stewart tartan appeared. In which case, of almost as early an origin would be the sett of the Stewart of Fingask tartan, which is said to derive from a cloak left by him at Fingask Castle near Perth in 1746. The Royal Stewart tartan is not a clan tartan, but the property of the Royal Family.

STURROCK

Tartan: *Sturrock*

The name originated in Angus, where it is said to have meant a farmer or sheep farmer, and is first recorded in 1448.

SUTHERLAND

Branch: *Sutherland of Forse*

Tartan: *Sutherland*

Motto: *Sans peur (French: Without fear)*

Sutherland, that part of the country immediately to the south of Caithness, is Norse *Sudrland*, or Southland. Here gathered the survivors of the Celtic tribes of the region after the Norse invasions in the eleventh century.

In about 1235 William, a descendant of Freskin, who was ancestor also of the Murrays, was created Earl of Sutherland. The Sutherlands were staunch patriots and doughty fighters, but the original family and the earldom fell into the hands of the Gordons when in 1514, on the death of the 9th Earl, his sister succeeded to the title and married Adam Gordon, second son of the 2nd Earl of Huntly. John Gordon (1526-67), 11th Earl of Sutherland, and his wife were poisoned at supper by a female cousin in the course of a family feud, though he was able to warn his heir, who had arrived late from

SUTHERLAND, EARL OF SUTHERLAND

hunting, that there was something wrong with the meal.

In 1601 the Gordons obtained a royal ruling that if the sole heir to the earldom was ever female, it should pass instead to the Gordons of Huntly. This was challenged on the death of the 17th Earl, who left an only daughter, Elizabeth, and in 1771 justice prevailed and the House of Lords awarded the earldom to her. Subsequently she married George Granville Leveson-Gower (1758-1833) who, just before his death, was raised to a dukedom, for which he chose the title of Duke of Sutherland.

On the death of the 5th Duke in 1962, the earldom and the chiefship of the Clan were vested in the daughter of the second son of the 4th Duke, who as Countess of Sutherland is the 22nd to hold the title. The Sutherlands of Forse, who also had an interest in the legal case in 1771, first held the estate of that name in 1408.

STURROCK

SUTHERLAND

TAYLOR

TAYLOR

Tartan: *Taylor*

The number of references to the name in early records from the thirteenth century reflects the significance of the craft of tailoring, from which it derives. The Latin version is *cissor*, and people of the name of Cissor or Scissor are recorded in the fourteenth and fifteenth centuries.

TENNANT

Tartan: *Tennant*

Motto: *Deus dabit vela (Latin: God will give protection)*

The name is first recorded in 1309. John Tennant of Glenconner (1726-1810), whose ancestors were tenant farmers near Ayr in the fifteenth century, was a friend of the poet Robert Burns (1759-96), who wrote a verse epistle to his son, in which several other members of the family are referred to. His great-grandson Charles Tennant (1823-1906) was created a baronet in 1885. His eldest son, Sir Edward Tennant (1859-1920), Lord Lieutenant of Peebles 1908-20, was made 1st Lord Glenconner in 1911.

TENNANT

A family by the name of Tennent was established as farmers and private brewers at Easter Common, Glasgow, in 1556. A descendant built the Saracen's Head Inn, whose comforts, and coal fire, Dr Johnson and James Boswell enjoyed in 1773, while three years later John and Robert Tennent founded the public brewery which still bears their names.

Dumfriesshire and were tenant farmers on the Buccleuch estates in 1679. His ancestor Archibald Thomson (*b.* 1749), Master Mason, emigrated to Canada in 1773. William Thomson (1824-1907), scientist and inventor, son of the Professor of Mathematics at Glasgow University, was born in Belfast, but his family believed that they were descended from Covenanters in Ayr who had found refuge in Ulster in the seventeenth century. He was Professor of Natural Philosophy at Glasgow University for 53 years, and was created Lord Kelvin of Netherhall, Largs, in 1892.

THOMSON DRESS

THOM(P)SON

Tartans: *Thomson (dress), Thomson (hunting)*

Mottos: *(Corstorphine) Veritas praevalebit (Latin: Truth will prevail); (Glendarroch) Deus providebit (Latin: God will provide); (Fleet) Never a backward step*

'Son of Thomas' is a common appellation throughout Scotland, and there were Thomsons of Glenshee who were a branch of Clan Chattan. There is a Thomson sept of Clan Campbell, and also one of MacThomas. Derick Thomson (*b.* 1921), born in Stornoway on the island of Lewis, has been Professor of Celtic at Glasgow University since 1963, and is a distinguished modern poet both in English and, as Ruaraidh MacThómais, in Gaelic. Alexander Thomson (1460-1513), said to have been the grandson of a bastard son of the 11th Earl of Mar, grandson of King Robert II, was born in Corstorphine, near Edinburgh, and died at the Battle of Flodden. His descendants are described as being 'of Corstorphine'. Frederick Thomson (1875-1935), Solicitor-General for Scotland 1923-4, who was created a baronet in 1929, was the grandson of a native of Linlithgow. He was succeeded by his son, Sir Douglas Thomson (1905-72), of Glendarroch, Midlothian. Roy Thomson (1894-1976), the newspaper baron, who was created Lord Thomson of Fleet, of Northbridge, in the City of Edinburgh, in 1964, was born in Canada. His family originated in

TURNBULL OF   BEDRULE

TURNBULL

Tartan: *Turnbull (dress), Turnbull (hunting)*

Motto: *I saved the King*

It is said that a man named Rule or Roull saved the life of Robert I (the Bruce) from a wild bull by holding on to its horns and wrestling it to the ground. For this he was rewarded with the lands of Bedrule, Teviotdale, and he took the name of Turnbull. The Turnbulls became a fierce, and troublesome, Border clan, but men of their name also followed more useful and intellectual pursuits. William Turnbull was Bishop of Glasgow 1448-54, having been Archdeacon of St Andrews and Lord Privy Seal. William Turnbull (1729-76) was a notable physician. Thomas Turnbull (1824-1908) was an architect in San Francisco and then in New Zealand.

URQUHART

Branches: *Urquhart of Craigston, Urquhart of Meldrum*

Tartans: *Urquhart, Urquhart (old)*

TURNBULL HUNTING

TURNBULL DRESS

URQUHART OLD

URQUHART OF   URQUHART

Motto: *Meane weil [well], speak weil, and doe weil*

The district of Urquhart is in Cromarty, and Adam Urchard was appointed hereditary Sheriff of Cromarty in about 1350. The branch of Craigfintry was founded by a younger son of the 7th Sheriff, that line continuing through the Urquharts of Craigston, who built Craigston Castle, Banffshire, still the seat of the Urquhart family, between 1604 and 1607.

Sir Thomas Urquhart of Cromarty (1611-60), eccentric, prose writer, and brilliant translator of the idiosyncratic, bawdy works of the French writer Rabelais (1494-1553), published in 1652 a genealogical work which traced his family back to the Creation and to Adam, from whom he calculated that he was 143rd in direct descent. A confirmed royalist, he lost his estates and his manuscripts after the Battle of Worcester in 1651, and died in Europe, it is said from a fit of laughing at the news of the Restoration of King Charles II. After his brother's death, representation of the family passed to the Urquharts of Craigston, and in 1741 to the Urquharts of Meldrum, descended from a younger son of John Urquhart of Craigston (known as 'Tutor of Cromarty'), who married the heiress of Meldrum, Aberdeenshire, at the beginning of the seventeenth century. The chiefship was dormant from 1898 to 1958, when it was revived and vested in an American Urquhart whose ancestor, a descendant of the Cromarty line, went to America in the eighteenth century.

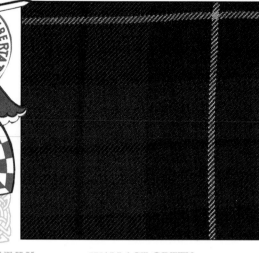

WALLACE   WALLACE OF THAT ILK   WALLACE GREEN

WALLACE

Branches: *Wallace of Cairnhill, Wallace of Cessnock, Wallace of Craigie, Wallace of Elderslie, Wallace of Kelly, Wallace of Riccarton*

Tartans: *Wallace, Wallace (green), Wallace (blue)*

Motto: *Pro libertate (Latin: For freedom)*

Wallensis, in Latin, meant a Briton of Strathclyde, which was a separate kingdom until 1018. In about 1170 Richard Wallensis obtained the lands of Riccarton (Richard's Town), in Ayrshire. His grandson, Adam, had two sons, of whom the younger was Sir Malcom Wallace of Elderslie, Renfrewshire, father of Sir William Wallace (1274-1305), the national hero. Sir William was not only a patriot and fearsome warrior, but a great leader, who established a chain of military command much like that in the army today, and who defeated the English at the Battle of Stirling Bridge in 1297, pushing them for a time out of Scotland altogether. He was finally betrayed, captured, and taken in chains to London. There, in Westminster Hall, he was tried for treason, which he could hardly be regarded as having committed, in that he had not signed the oath of allegiance to King Edward I in 1296, and after the abdication of King John (Balliol)

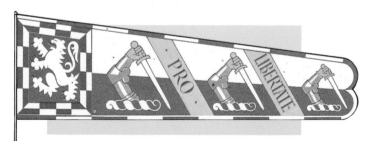

he had been properly appointed by acclamation Guardian of Scotland, charged with protecting his country against the invader. Nevertheless he was convicted, and sentenced to be hanged, drawn and quartered.

Sir John Wallace of Riccarton, whose ancestor was Sir Malcolm Wallace's elder brother, married the heiress of Craigie, and the branches of Wallace of Cairnhill, Cessnock, and Kelly were founded by their descendants.

WALLACE BLUE

SIR WILLIAM WALLACE

WATSON

Tartan: *Watson*

Watson, 'son of Walter', first occurs as a name in Edinburgh in 1392. Robert Watson (1746-1838), who was born in Elgin, claimed to have fought on the American side in the War of Independence of 1775-8. After his return to Britain he led a lively life, avoiding arrest by escaping to France, from where he moved to Rome, always hoping that his money-making schemes, which included the purchase for £22. 10s of two cartloads of Jacobite archives, would bring him riches rather than notoriety. He finally strangled himself in a London tavern. By contrast, George Watson (1767-1837), who was born on his father's estate in Berwickshire, was a distinguished portrait painter who became first President of the Royal Scottish Academy.

WEIR

Tartan: *Weir (also Hope-Vere)*

Motto: *Vero nihil verius (Latin: Nothing is more true than the truth)*

The name derives from the Norman place-name Vere. Ralph de Ver, from whom the Weirs of Blackwood,

WATSON

WEIR OF BLACKWOOD

WEIR

Lanarkshire, claim descent, was captured, with King William I (the Lion), in 1174 while besieging the castle of Alnwick in Northumberland. Others of the name held lands in Lesmahagow, Lanarkshire, in the fifteenth century.

Major Thomas Weir (1599-1670), born at Kirkton House, Carluke, was burned at the stake in Edinburgh for incest, adultery, bestiality, and witchcraft, his sister being hanged the next day for her part in some of his activities. Subsequently, his ghost was said to have been seen galloping down the High Street on a headless black horse.

William Weir (1877-1950), engineer, industrialist, and statesman, who was descended from an illegitimate daughter of the poet Robert Burns (1759-96), was created 1st Viscount Weir in 1918. Andrew Weir (1865-1955), shipowner, born in Kirkcaldy, was made 1st Lord Inverforth in 1919.

WEMYSS

Branches: *See below*

Tartan: *Wemyss*

Motto: *Je pense (French: I think)*

A younger son of the line of the MacDuff earls of Fife obtained the lands of Wemyss, Fife, in about 1160. By the beginning of the seventeenth century many branches of the family had been generated, including those of Reres, Kilmany, Wintbank, Caskyberry, and Pitkennie. Sir John Wemyss of Wemyss (1586-1649) was granted a baronetcy of Nova Scotia by King Charles I in 1625, with 16,000 acres of territory there to be called New Wemyss. He was, however, slow to pay up the required 3,000 merks. The King wrote urging him to do so, assuring him that the baronetcy was simply 'a stepp to a further title'. He was duly created Lord Wemyss of

WEMYSS

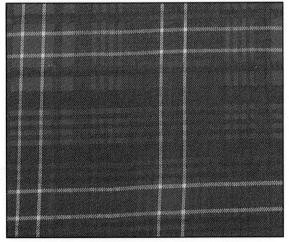

WILSON

WOTHERSPOON

Wemyss in 1628, and Earl of Wemyss in 1633. James (1699-1756), 5th Earl, made a romantic marriage with Janet (*d.* 1778), daughter of Francis Charteris of Amisfield (1675-1732), a notorious gambler and profligate. Their eldest son, Lord Elcho (1721-87), was commander of Bonnie Prince Charlie's troop of life guards in 1745-6, after which he was attainted. Their second son, Francis (1723-1808), who at the age of 13 had only just been rescued in time from a re-enaction by younger members of the family of the Porteous mob riot of 1736, in which he was playing the part of the hanged man, assumed the title of Earl of Wemyss on his brother's death. He had already, on the death of his grandfather, succeeded to the Amisfield estates and taken the name of Charteris. The chiefship of the family, however, together with Wemyss Castle, built in the fifteenth century, passed to the third son, James Wemyss of Wemyss (1726-1803), in whose descendant they are vested today.

WILSON

Tartan: *Wilson*

Motto: *Semper vigilans (Latin: Ever watchful)*

The name means 'son of Will' and is first recorded in Scotland at the beginning of the fifteenth century. James Wilson, whose father was from Eastforth, Lanark, bought the lands of Hinschelwood and Cleugh, Carnwath, in 1655. His descendant John Wilson (1809-89), of Airdrie, was created a baronet in 1906. David Wilson (1805-98), of Carbeth, who was descended from a family which lived in Berwickshire in the seventeenth century, was made a baronet in 1920. Another notable family is that of Wilson of Ashmore, Perthshire, whose ancestor was James Wilson (1829-1905), solicitor, of Falkirk. Wilsons of Bannockburn were pioneers in the industrialisation of tartan weaving and in the marketing of clan and district tartans.

WOTHERSPOON

Tartan: *Wotherspoon*

The derivation and meaning of this pleasing name are obscure. A Roger Wythisspon is recorded in Renfrewshire in the thirteenth century, and a Widderspune was the King's fowler in 1496.

**Immaculately worn kilt of the Hay tartan, cut to exactly
the right length. Note the *sgian dubh* in the stocking.**

Scotland and Her Tartans

Wearing the Tartan

Those who cannot claim any connection with a particular clan or sept which has its own tartan, but who still wish to enjoy the distinction and participate in a broader kinship by wearing a Scottish tartan need not despair.

Tartans for General Wear

There are four genuine tartans which may be worn by anyone, of which the most appropriate is usually that of the Black Watch.

The Jacobite tartan has quite a respectable genealogy in that the design was known in the early

The Black Watch tartan, part of the uniform of the 42nd Regiment.

years of the eighteenth century and may have been displayed by Lowlanders as a protest against the Act of Union in 1707, whereby the Scottish and English parliaments were amalgamated and henceforth only sat in London, of course! It may have got its name from the suggestion that the tartan was worn by a Jacobite supporter during the Rebellion of 1715, though present-day wearers of it are not expected to express or even to have Jacobite sympathies.

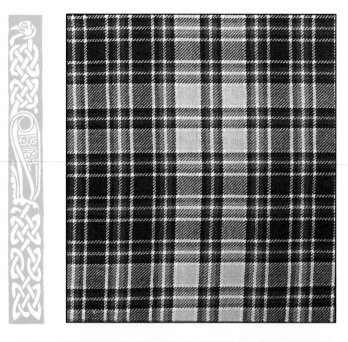

The Caledonia tartan is as authentic as many clan tartans in that it was originally No 155 in Wilson and Son's pattern book, being a variation of No 43, also called Caledonia, which ended up as the Macpherson tartan.

The Hunting Stewart tartan also first saw the light of day in Wilsons' pattern book but, in spite of its name and its being often worn by members of the present royal family, it seems always to have been in general use. Under no circumstances, however, should the Royal Stewart tartan be worn. This was the one with which

Caledonia

King George IV was decked in 1822, but it is not a clan tartan, rather one which has become exclusive to the royal family, and is also worn by the pipers of the Scots Guards. Those, incidentally, who are baffled by the distinction between the spelling of Stewart and Stuart may take comfort from the knowledge that there are sound historical and linguistic justifications for both. Stewart is the older, and is the same as Steward; Walter the Steward (the sixth to hold that title, originally granted by King David I) being the husband of Marjorie, daughter of King Robert I (the Bruce), from whom the Stewart dynasty descended. The form Stuart came about because there is no 'w' in the French alphabet and so no way of spelling the name in French in its original form. Thus Mary, Queen of Scots, who was of course

Top: Jacobite. Above: Hunting Stewart.

A parade of pipers in full dress at the
Braemar Gathering.

Mary Stewart by birth, took on the alternative form when she spent her childhood and first marriage in France, and kept it when she returned to Britain as Queen of Scotland. Curiously enough, she was to become a Stuart twice over, as her second husband was Henry Stuart, Lord Darnley, son of Matthew Stewart, Earl of Lennox, who had become a naturalised Frenchman in 1537, when he adopted the spelling Stuart.

District Tartans

The original concept of the district tartan, which may quite reasonably be worn by anyone with the appropriate residential or birth qualification, is older than the clan

tartan. For Martin Martin, who visited the Highlands to study 'the habits and costume' of the inhabitants, wrote in his *Description of the Western Isles of Scotland* (1703): 'Every Isle differs from each other in their fancy of making Plaids as to the stripes in breadth and colours. The humour is as different through the mainland of the Highlands, in so far as they who have seen those places are able at the first view of a man's Plaid, to guess the place of his residence.' This may mean no more than that certain patterns, and colours, were commonest in particular regions, as indeed one might expect to be the case, but it has nevertheless often been interpreted as a justification of the ancient origin of district tartans.

The extrovert firm of Wilson and Son, in a laudable attempt to increase the range, as well as the market, certainly did make an effort to research patterns which

had a genuine local affiliation. They also, however, gave the names of districts, towns, and cities to a number of tartans of their own design, though at least these can be said to date from the beginning of the nineteenth century, as do many of the earliest clan tartans themselves. Other district tartans are more recent in origin.

Among accepted district setts are Aberdeen, Crieff, Dundee, Galloway (both green and hunting), Glasgow, Huntly, Lennox, Lochaber, Nithsdale, Paisley, Stirling

Above: sporran for evening wear. Facing page: 1868 Mackenzie of Seaforth tartan (left), and McNeill of Colonsay (right).

and Bannockburn (designed in 1825 for the local Caledonian Society), Strathearn, and Tweedside (both red and hunting). Each of the provinces and territories of Canada, with the understandable exception of Quebec, has its own district tartan, of which that of Nova Scotia was in 1956 the earliest to be registered with the Lord Lyon Court.

Special Tartans

Of all the associations of people and callings which have their own tartan, the earliest is undoubtedly the Scottish Presbyterian Church. The Reformed Kirk banned its ministers from wearing tartan while taking service, insisting that proper clerical garb was 'of grave colour, black, russet, sad grey, sad brown'. From this injunction developed

the Clerical tartan, in a straightforward sett of blue and black, with overlines of green or white or light blue.

Tartan is a 'living fabric' and is now being adopted by numerous bodies and organisations all over the world as a mark of corporate or kindred identity. The vogue for altering the colours of established designs and renaming them, however, debases the fabric and is also unnecessary, as tartan is capable of infinite variety while still being in good taste.

Forms of Highland Dress

The kilt is essentially male attire. The usual form in which women wear their appropriate tartan is as a skirt, short during the day and long for evening wear, or as a sash worn diagonally across the breast over a plain dress for more formal occasions. There are various protocols surrounding the shoulder on which the sash is pinned, and the disposition of its loose ends.

For ordinary daytime wear the kilt looks best if it is worn with a tweed jacket and a tie which matches the jacket rather than the kilt, but it is perfectly acceptable to wear a sweater without a jacket. A sporran, the original purpose of which was to hold one's valuables (including the daily ration of oatmeal) in the absence of pockets, plain knitted stockings held up with elastic garters with flashes protruding from the turn-overs, the *sgian dubh* in the stocking of the right leg (unless you are left-handed!), and brogues complete the outfit satisfactorily. In the evening, a dark jacket and plain tie can be worn, though care should be taken to ensure that in cut and length the jacket suits the form of the kilt. A hat or cap is not obligatory out of doors, but if headgear is worn it should be a bonnet (Balmoral style). The badge will be that of the chief of the clan, encircled by a depiction in metal of a buckled strap with the chief's motto engraved on it, indicating that the wearer is a follower of that chief. Only the chief and his or her heir may wear the crest within a plain circlet. Any Scot, however, may wear the saltire, or cross of St Andrew.

Formal evening wear is more elaborate. Shoes are light, with buckles. Stockings are checked or patterned to match the kilt. The kilt may be in the clan's dress tartan, and the sporran is silver-mounted. The jacket, of a plain velvet or evening-dress cloth or tartan, has silver buttons, and may be worn over a black waistcoat. Either a bow tie or a jabot may be worn, whichever is more suited to the cut and style of the jacket.

Correct outdoor wear: Highland bonnet complete with clansman's badge.

Tracing Your Scottish Ancestry

Kilts are the proper wear for competitors at the
Braemar Gathering.

Per head of population, the Scots must be the most widely distributed nation in the world, and also one of the most successful in so many walks of life, and fields of activity and learning.

Of all Scottish successes, in regions as far apart as North America, Africa, India, Australia and New Zealand, one of the most oustanding must be the story of how Upper and Lower Canada (Ontario and Quebec) were united and ultimately merged into one whole Dominion of Canada, with ready communication between the east and west coasts. Four of the principal architects of the overall operation were not just of Scottish origin, but

were actually of Scottish birth. Sir John A. Macdonald was born in Glasgow in 1815, son of a Sutherland crofter who had been evicted from his home and who emigrated with his family to Kingston, Ontario, in 1820. As Prime Minister of Ontario, Macdonald organised in 1867 the establishment of the Dominion, and was its first Prime Minister. He saw that to enlarge the Dominion to include British Columbia on the western seaboard and the thousand miles or so of prairies, lakes, and mountains

succeeded in transporting, in ten days in the middle of winter, three thousand troops halfway across the country to put down an Indian revolt, in spite of there still being four vast gaps in the line. The railway was completed in 1875, by which time Manitoba and Prince Edward Island, as well as British Columbia, had joined the Dominion.

While the Scottish race has been formed from an amalgam of Scots, Picts, Vikings, Britons, Angles, and Normans, with later Irish, Jewish, and now Asian accretions, and in spite of the traditional Highland/Lowland, Edinburgh/Glasgow cultural divides, there remains a strong sense of corporate identity. Those whose families have long settled in, and so often enriched, the newer nations of the world are loathe to sever their ancestral links.

That the clan spirit survives outside Scotland as well as within it is clearly demonstrated by the number of clan societies in active operation, many with branches in the United States of America and Canada. It is particularly because Scotland is geographically so small that centralised sources of family records are readily accessible and usually agreeably indexed. *Scottish Family Histories* (National Library of Scotland, 1986), for instance, lists not only published works and unpublished manuscripts but also where they can be seen or even borrowed. While national government and Church of Scotland archives are mainly housed in the Scottish Record Office in Edinburgh, the development of regional and district archives offers wider and often more specialist sources of information to supplement what is held centrally. There is a National Register of Archives for Scotland, maintained by the Scottish Record Office, which lists the contents and whereabouts of a vast amount of valuable and rare material, whether it is in private or public hands.

Available at the Scottish Record Office for the serious researcher or the family historian is a splendid range of material which includes the record of every birth, marriage, and death since 1 January 1855; parish records for the period before 1855; the census returns for the years 1841, 1851, 1861, 1871, 1881 and 1891 (census information can normally only be publicly scrutinised when a hundred years have elapsed); every recorded will from the sixteenth century onwards, often with an inventory of effects; and other legal deeds and records. Provided you can supply enough details for the

in between, would require the building of the world's longest and most expensive railway. It would need to be 2500 miles long, and be constructed across some of the most rugged terrain in the world, much of it unexplored, let alone unmapped. A proposal was forthcoming from Sandford Fleming, who was born in Kirkcaldy, Fife, and who became the railway's first engineer-in-chief. To survey possible routes, he and a small party of engineers and other stalwarts (including a Scottish Presbyterian minister called George Grant) travelled over five thousand miles in 103 days, using whatever transport they could find, but often slogging it out on foot. The company that built the railway was formed for the purpose by Donald A. Smith, born in Forres, Morayshire, and his cousin, George Stephen, from Dufftown in the same county. Several times they faced personal ruin as costs increased and the debts mounted up. The scheme was finally saved at the last minute when the company

document you want to be identified, the staff will find it for you and supply a copy, wherever you are.

In exactly the same way as children learn history best when they are going backwards in time from today (Where was your father born? Where did your mother's parents meet? Where did *their* parents come from?), so family genealogy properly begins in the present, with as much information as possible from written and oral sources being sifted for those clues which will illuminate earlier generations. If you live away from Scotland, once you have all the relevant information that there is to find from your relatives who are around you or living elsewhere, then you may well be in a position to begin the long-distance search, using resources in Scotland. Full names, dates, places of birth and residence are most helpful and in many cases essential. Equally

helpful can be the names of schools and universities which your ancestors may have attended, and the trades that they practised. There are freelance experts in Scotland who specialise in family research, besides the clan and genealogical societies, and the Scots Ancestry Research Society (3 Albany Street, Edinburgh EH1 3PY).

The fascinating thing about family research is that where it is fruitful it almost always results in the recreation of pieces of the past from historical facts which have never been put together before. Sometimes these fragments form a longer history covering several generations or even provide a fresh and personal insight into a period or historical event. The disposition and organisation of records in Scotland give the researcher every chance to succeed.

'…wild solitudes, lengthen'd and deep,
where the sheep's bleat or that rare sound,
the harsh scream of an eagle,
serves only to intensify the silence following after.'

Scotland and Her Tartans

Index

Scotland and Her Tartans

Picture Credits

The Clan Tartan Centre: 85 (bottom right), 125 (top left and top right), 137 (bottom), 147, 148/9 (top left), 154, 158 (bottom left and top right), 183 (left), 202 (right), 212 (top right and bottom right)

Highland Folk Museum: 35 (top)

Highlands and Islands Development Board: 8, 9, 10 (top), 33

National Galleries of Scotland: 12, 14, 15, 16, 17, 19, 20, 23, 24, 27, 31, 40, 67 (top), 69 (right), 70, 72 (top left), 79 (top left), 96 (left), 99 (left), 100 (left), 102 (right), 106 (right), 144 (top), 155 (bottom), 159 (top), 161, 166, 171, 188, 207 (top)

Claude Poulet/Colour Library Books: 4, 6, 10 (bottom), 32, 35 (bottom), 44, 210, 213, 216, 217, 218, 219

The Royal Collection, St. James's Palace: 22, 28-29, 39

Windsor Castle, Royal Library ©1991 Her Majesty The Queen: 38, 43, 45, 215

Scottish Tourist Board: Cover photograph, 13, 18

Neil Sutherland/Colour Library Books: 3, 36, 37, 41, 42, 56-66, 67 (bottom), 68, 69 (left), 71, 72 (bottom left), 73, 74-78, 79 (bottom left and right), 80–82, 84, 85 (left and top right), 86-95, 96 (right), 97, 98, 99 (right), 100 (right), 101, 102 (left), 103, 104, 105, 106 (left), 107-124, 125 (bottom), 126, 128-136, 137 (top left and top right), 138-143, 144 (bottom), 145, 146, 148/9 (bottom), 149, 150-153, 155 (top left and top right), 156, 157, 158 (top left and bottom right), 159 (bottom), 160, 162-165, 167-170, 172-182, 183 (right), 184-186, 189-201, 202 (left), 203-206, 207 (bottom), 208, 209, 211, 212 (left), 214